Douglas Johnson

RENDERING THE WORD IN THEOLOGICAL HERMENEUTICS

This book proposes an original typology for grasping the differences between diverse types of biblical interpretation, fashioned in a triangle around a major theological and philosophical lacuna: the relation between divine and human action. Despite their purported concern for reading God's word, most modern and postmodern approaches to biblical interpretation do not seriously consider the role of divine agency as having a real influence in and on the process of reading Scripture. Mark Bowald seeks to correct and clarify this deficiency by demonstrating the inevitable role that divine agency plays in contemporary proposals in relation to human agency enacted in the composition of the biblical text and the reader. This book presents an important contribution to the emerging field of theological hermeneutics.

Bowald discusses in depth the hermeneutics of George Lindbeck, Hans Frei, Kevin Vanhoozer, Francis Watson, Stephen Fowl, David Kelsey, Werner Jeanrond, Karl Barth, James K.A. Smith, and Nicholas Wolterstorff.

To Dora Lee
Sine qua non

Rendering the Word in Theological Hermeneutics

Mapping Divine and Human Agency

MARK ALAN BOWALD
Redeemer University College, Canada

ASHGATE

Published by
Ashgate Publishing Limited
Gower House
Croft Road
Aldershot
Hampshire GU11 3HR
England

Ashgate Publishing Company
Suite 420
101 Cherry Street
Burlington, VT 05401-4405
USA

Ashgate website: http://www.ashgate.com

British Library Cataloguing in Publication Data
Bowald, Mark Alan
  Rendering the word in theological hermeneutics : mapping divine and human agency
  1. Bible – Hermeneutics 2. Bible – Criticism, interpretation, etc. – History
  I. Title
  220.6'01

Library of Congress Cataloging in Publication Data
Bowald, Mark Alan.
  Rendering the Word in theological hermeneutics : mapping divine and human agency / Mark Alan Bowald.
     p. cm.
  Includes bibliographical references.
  ISBN 978-0-7546-5877-1 (hardcover : alk. paper) 1. Bible–Hermeneutics. 2.
Hermeneutics–Religious aspects–Christianity. 3. Providence and government of God–Christianity. I. Title.

  BS476.B587 2007
  220.601–dc22

2007004392

ISBN 978-0-7546-5877-1

.Printed and bound in Great Britain by TJ International, Padstow, Cornwall.

Contents

List of Figures

Preface

Recent years have witnessed a dramatic increase in the interest in theological interpretation of Scripture.[1] This has been indicated in three ways: first, new historical works invested in recovering an appreciation for methods of reading the Bible in pre-modern settings, particularly in the Church fathers; second, in the gradual emergence of the field of hermeneutics as a legitimate free standing arena of inquiry; and, third, in the growing interest in reaching across and rethinking well-established dividing lines among theological disciplines in order to better understand the act of reading Scripture. These interdisciplinary movements seek to overcome weaknesses in the contemporary perception of the event of reading the Bible.

It is assumed in what follows that this trend is good and necessary: that the reading of Christian Scripture is undertaken properly by diversely gifted members of self-consciously Christian communities, both ecclesiastical and scholarly. Further, that this reading is always a response to the free and gracious speech action of God. As old scholarly dividing lines are erased and new ones are drawn it behooves us to be self critical about the assumptions that shape and guide our understanding of the very act of hearing God's Word in the reading of Scripture. Here we contribute to this movement by taking a careful look at one aspect of this discussion: the relationship between divine and human agency. In place of the ideal objectivity of the singular unaffected reader advocated by the Enlightenment the picture that will emerge and recommend itself is, rather, for readers who are aware of their theological and social location and the matrix of agencies (*both* human and divine) that shape their reading. This is undertaken with the goal that we (re)learn to embrace these in

---

[1]   The annual meetings of the *Society of Biblical Literature* now include thirteen (and counting) sections and groups that are devoted to both narrow and broad considerations of theological hermeneutics. There are also several important new and ongoing projects that have drawn significant interest: the *Scripture and Hermeneutics Series* (Craig Bartholomew, General Editor) published by Paternoster and Zondervan is now in its seventh year of annual conferences and is annually publishing the papers from them; both Eerdmans and Baker Academic Press have begun publishing commentary series that are written by theologians. A few (among many, many more) other noteworthy recent publications that reinforce the significance of this movement include: *The Dictionary for Theological Interpretation of Scripture*, edited by Kevin Vanhoozer (SPCK and Baker Academic Press, 2005);   *The Rule of Faith: Scripture, Canon and Creed in a Critical Age* (Harrisburg: Morehouse, 1998), edited by Ephraim Radner and George Sumner; *Theology and Scriptural Imagination* (Oxford: Blackwell, 1998), edited by L. Gregory Jones and James J. Buckley; *Reclaiming the Bible for the Church* (Grand Rapids: Eerdmans, 1995), edited by Carl Braaten and Robert Jenson; *Theological Exegesis: Essays in Honor of Brevard S. Childs* (Grand Rapids: Eerdmans, 1999), edited by Christopher Seitz and Kathryn Greene-McCreight; Richard S. Briggs, *Words in Action: Speech Act Theory and Biblical Interpretation* (New York: Continuum T and T Clark, 2001). See also Timothy Ward, *Word and Supplement: Speech Acts, Biblical Texts, and the Sufficiency of Scripture* (Oxford: Oxford University Press, 2002).

their complexity and proceed to critically and constructively read the Bible with a sense of encountering God's gracious rhetorical Word. The word "render" in the title evokes the diversity of these influences. So: "rendering" the text of Scripture can be an act of grace or judgment; of respectful deference or of dismissive violence; and is most often some admixture of both. It also evokes the complexity of the relationship between agents. So "rendering" the work of another person becomes a way of imaging the relationship between the divine author and human authors and readers of God's Word.

We will examine how the idealist Enlightenment epistemological tradition continues to exert influence over how the act of reading of the Bible is construed in such a manner that inhibits a fuller awareness of divine agency in reading Scripture. This is shown in the continuing bias *against* the influence of other agents (human or divine) on a supposedly objective, morally and spiritually self-sufficient reader. The developments in postmodern epistemology and hermeneutics have contributed to partially correct this idealism by demonstrating the intersubjectivity of all interpretation. However, while the full spectrum of the influences of *human* agency is more fully acknowledged, there nevertheless remains a bias against the influence of *divine* agency.

Further: the very notion of removing oneself from the influence of divine agency is untenable: the idea of setting ourselves up as agents *outside* the milieu of God's activity quickly fails to give us any purchase on how it is that we attend to the *viva vox Dei* and neglects the appropriate and helpful ways that God's faithful and corrective leading accompanies and underwrites our communal and tradition-laden locations and influences these at every point and turn. Nevertheless, there remains an influential contingent of Enlightenment epistemological ideals that descry these influences and continue to distort our understanding of the act of reading the Bible.

An initial goal of this work is to survey a range of contemporary proposals; to both demonstrate the continuing bias of this idealism as well as show how each representative approach assumes a constructive theological stance regarding the relationship of the mixture of human and divine agencies. The ultimate goal is to lay bare in a more comprehensive manner the basic dynamics of the reading of Scripture that underwrite any and all hermeneutical proposals. It asserts that any conscientious hermeneutical theory of reading the Bible must account for both dynamics: between the text and readers *and* between the divine and human agents. Also there is proffered a shared framework within which members of disparate fields can meet and find a common parlance to negotiate the similarities and differences that characterize their work: differences that are more clearly defined and, therefore, more easily negotiated (although not resolved) when their theological character is revealed. In this way, this project contributes a modicum of clarity to the emerging interdisciplinary movement that recognizes the value of reaching across the stale and rigid theological divides. The goal: new ways of joining together to listen to God's gracious Word and reading and responding together in faith are obtained and encouraged.

Acknowledgments

The individual graces expressed to this author in the process of writing this book were profound and humbling. First and foremost: thanks to John Webster, for his patience, encouragement and sure handed guidance and Dora Lee for extraordinary things too precious to name in print.

Appreciations also to a group who variously shared coffee, comradery, conversation, and valuable verbal and written responses along the way: Frederick Bauerschmidt, Joe Mangina, Iain Nicol, Jim Olthuis, Jim Reimer, Fr. George Schner S. J. (requiescat in pace), Dan Treier, Kevin Vanhoozer, and Nick Wolterstorff.

Also to a circle of friends, family and colleagues who also contributed support and help both personal and professional during this project: Craig Bartholomew, Kurt Berends, Benjamin and Linda Bowald, Jim Buckley, Brian Cooper, The Dead Theologian Society, David Demson, Fr. Adelmo Dunghe S. J., The Grables, Gene Haas, Carl B. Hoch jr. (requiescat in pace), Chris Holmes, Anna Laansma (requiescat in pace), Jon Laansma, Very Rev. Jean-Marc Laporte S. J., George Lindbeck, Sarah Lloyd, Merv Mercer, Gene and Mary Lynne Peterson, The "other" Petersons, The Phillips, The Richards, George Sumner, Allen Sundsmo, Brian Walsh, Jeff Wilcox, many friends from our time at Wycliffe College and at St. Paul's on Bloor St., and the Zelenkas.

Finally, for profound ministrations, depths to which they will never be aware, loving thanks to my three muses: Anna, Edward and Meredith.

Chapter 1

The Eclipsing and Usurping of Divine Agency in Enlightenment Epistemology and their Influence on Scriptural Hermeneutics

The typology we will present in the next chapter is designed to bring greater clarity to the full character of divine and human agencies involved in reading Scripture. This suggestion implies the *need* for clarity. This chapter will describe this need. It will be argued that certain developments in Enlightenment epistemology contributed to create an obscurity in the perception of the ideal act of discerning knowledge, of which reading books, including Scripture, has been treated as a subset.

The epistemological development we are concerned with involves the nature of the agency of the knowing person, particularly in the limitation of the investigation of knowledge to immanent spheres and actions. This resulted in the ideal situation being envisioned as that in which both the knower and the object are immediately and immanently present to each other. Further, that the action of the *knower* is, ideally, performed independent of the influence of other agents. The *object* is, likewise, limited to that which can be perceived via instruments of immanent human perception.

With respect to the reading of Scripture, both the moratorium on the influence of another agent on the knower and the limit of the object to that which can be perceived by human perception effectively combine to restrict any appropriate or constructive role for God's activity. In the wake of these limitations the task of interpreting Scripture came to be defined in terms of two arenas of agency, both competing with one another. These are the "text" and the "reader(s)." The tension between text and reader(s), as such, limits the range of activity responsible for determining the "meaning." As these epistemological limits gained purchase the result is that both the "text" and the "reader(s)" of Scripture are increasingly defined strictly by immanent parameters. The "text" reflects this in that it is perceived initially or primarily as being a container possessing the literary production or action of deceased and "distanciated" human beings. The reader(s) reflected these limits insofar as it is the perception that they should be "objective" and, as far as possible, set aside any prior judgments or be influenced by other agents.

The obscurity produced here is that these developments combine to exclude God's agency from the picture, with the result that the ideal post-Enlightenment reading of Scripture arises against what is effectively a deistic or atheistic horizon or "worldview." Against this it is asserted that it is a highly specious notion for the agency comprising the reading of Scripture to be defined initially, primarily or exclusively in these terms. Limiting the fields of agency to human agency in the text and human agency in the reading of Holy Scripture is an imposing reductionism.

To the contrary: properly construed, the activity of reading Scripture must also give an accounting of the concurrent *divine* agency that accompanies the "text" and the reader. In fact, the horizon of divine agency that frames the horizon of the interpreter is more fundamental and directive in how they negotiate hermeneutical problems than whatever they may hold regarding human agency. The approaches we will survey in Chapters 3 through 5 will demonstrate how the interaction of divine and human agency is formative and ingredient to any and all proposals for reading Scripture, and how it shapes subsequent decisions made about "texts" and "readers," "reading communities," "contexts," and so on. The time is right and ripe in biblical and theological hermeneutics for approaching the task intentionally focusing on divine agency, as the most revealing manner to both expose and redress the obscurity created in the course of following modernity's epistemological strictures.

Having said this, the concern with agency *per se* is by no means absent from contemporary debates on hermeneutics. A survey of recent work quickly reveals that notions of agency associated with the act of the reader or reading community, as well as the human agency ingredient in the text, are used with great frequency and force. We hear and read about what the text "does," "says," or "effects" and as the corollary issue how the "reader" or "community" "reads" or "uses" the text. The problem with these is that their discussion attributes agency with clumsiness and offhandedness; obscuring the relationship of divine and human agency. So: when one makes an assertion about what the "text says" or "how the church uses" the Bible one is, at the same time, making an assertion (or a denial) about the relative presence (or absence) and pattern of divine action. "What Scripture says" or "how the community reads" is, then, awkward and shorthand language for a constellation of theological assertions which orbit around divine agency.

And here is the rub. Even as notions of divine agency accompany and underwrite these proposals the residual influence of the dominant epistemological tradition tells us that it is preferable to minimize, remove ourselves from, or ignore the dynamic influence of another agent or influence (including God) on our investigations. Thus with respect to reading Scripture, caught between modernity and postmodernity, we live under a cloud of tension between the assumptions we continue to believe in, use and cannot escape from, accompanied by a nagging sense that we should not have them. Understanding and resolving this tension is necessary if we are to make any substantial progress in the debates over biblical hermeneutics.

This investigation follows in the long and fashionable tradition of attempting to describe "what went wrong." That which I argue has gone wrong is the perception of how the Bible is ideally read and interpreted in its function as the speech action of God in the salvific[1] economy and milieu of God's active and personal willing, self-

---

[1] I would include here, without distinction, encompassing issues which revolve around justification and sanctification. On this point see the creative proposal of Telford Work, *Living and Active: Scripture in the Economy of Salvation* (Grand Rapids, 2002) and John Webster, *Holy Scripture* (Cambridge, 2003).

revealing, and self-interpreting.[2] I will not seek to narrate the process which resulted in the immanentization of the hermeneutics of Scripture. That history has been well plumbed.[3]

To assist us in clarifying this errant aspect of the hermeneutical problem we will initially look to the work of Immanuel Kant and briefly discuss aspects of his epistemological framework and its implications for metaphysical knowledge, knowledge about God, and for reading Scripture. In doing so I am not setting Kant up as either the primary or sole cause of the problems. Other representatives could have just as easily been selected. Kant's thought is a convenient point of entry for several reasons. His writings are a definitive expression of a great variance of streams of thought which preceded him and are acknowledged as a uniquely powerful influence in those who followed. He is of particular importance for our purposes in that he stands at a key crossroads for Empiricist and Rationalist (as well as Phenomenological) traditions. The influence of these on theological and biblical studies is profound and unquestioned. Further, the influence of the Enlightenment on Western theology and narrating how these had this detrimental effect on the Church, theology and interpretation of the Bible, continue to be a well worn path of discussion.[4] The reader is, therefore, more likely to be familiar with the basic terms with which we will be engaging. Finally, Kant is selected because of the way

---

[2] I am now working on projects related to this point. One utilizes ancient rhetorical theory to provide a framework to see theological hermeneutics as "divine rhetoric." The other is a dogmatic account of the Church's reading of Scripture by way of the Doctrine of the "Heavenly Session of Christ."

[3] One compelling example would be the arguments and discussion in the 16th and 17th centuries leading up to and culminating in the work of Baruch Spinoza. Important new light has been shed on this period by J. Samuel Preus, *Spinoza and the Irrelevance of Biblical Authority* (Cambridge, 2002). Also see Christopher Norris, *Spinoza and the Origins of Modern Critical Theory* (Oxford, 1991). Also A. K. M. Adam, *Making Sense of New Testament Theology,* (Macon, 1995). Other accounts include Hans-Joachim Kraus, *Die Biblische Theologie: Ihre Geschichte und Problematik* (Neukirchen-Vluyn, 1970); Werner Georg Kümmel, *The New Testament: The History of the Investigation of Its Problems* (Nashville, 1972); Klaus Scholder, *The Birth of Modern Critical Theology* (London, 1990); Roy A. Harrisville and Walter Sundberg, *The Bible in Modern Culture: Theology and Historical-Critical Method from Spinoza to Käseman* 2nd ed. (Grand Rapids, 2002); Robert M. Grant and David Tracy, *A Short History of the Interpretation of the Bible,* 2nd ed. (Philadelphia, 1984). Also highly relevant is Isaak Dorner, *History of Protestant Theology Particularly in Germany* (Edinburgh, 1871).

[4] Michael Buckley, *At the Origins of Modern Atheism* (New Haven, 1987); Hans Frei, *The Eclipse of Biblical Narrative* (New Haven, 1974); Philip Clayton, *The Problem of God in Modern Thought* (Grand Rapids, 2000); Jeffrey Stout, *The Flight From Authority* (South Bend, 1981); John Milbank, *Theology and Social Theory* (Oxford, 1990) and *The Word Made Strange* (Oxford, 1997); C. D. Cashdollar, *The Transformation of Theology: Positivism and Protestant Thought in Britain and America* (Princeton, 1989). The ultimate genesis of the epistemological influences I discuss is not at issue here. Whether Descartes (Stout, Harrisville and Sundberg, Scholder et al.) bears greater responsibility, or whether the roots go back to the Medieval Disputations (John Milbank) or the influence of Bacon is a debatable point which does not ultimately affect the argument put forth here. This work *does* hinge on whether the

in which he discusses the ideal knowing moment. His discussion is precise, and helpful in providing a vocabulary from which we will draw to illuminate our own analysis.[5]

Finally, there may be certain readers who, because of the somewhat technical nature of the discussion that follows immediately in this next session, might benefit by skipping to the summary below, and returning to this section later.

Kant's Proscriptions to Reason's Activity: Defining the Ideal Knowing Act

We begin by looking to some relevant passages in Kant's corpus to see how he imposes immanent limits on both the knowing agent as well as the object in the epistemological action of creating or building knowledge. We will pay particular attention to his own qualitative judgments regarding the influence of other agents in the act of knowing and especially to comments he makes regarding the relationship of God's agency to human agency.

In his *Critique of Pure Reason* he makes an important distinction between "having an opinion," "believing," and "knowing."[6] This results in a hierarchy. "Having an opinion" is at the bottom from the standpoint of pure reason because it is "objectively and subjectively insufficient." It is insufficient in both of these ways insofar as there is no *a priori* or *a posteriori* way of validating it. "Beliefs" are higher on the ladder because they are subjectively sufficient (*a priori*) but are still objectively insufficient (*a posteriori*). The object of beliefs is beyond the pale of the senses of pure reason to discern rightly or wrongly, yet, the very structure of reason (the categories) gives necessary rise to the belief. "Knowledge" proper, is highest on the ladder and is superior to both beliefs and opinions in that it is both objectively and subjectively sufficient.

Notions about God, Kant says, can be no more than "beliefs" in that they proceed from a subjective *a priori* awareness of a "purposive unity" that is rooted both in the world and in one's moral nature yet are lacking in any possible objective demonstration.[7] Thus the belief in God is implicitly of a lesser quality than knowledge but greater than opinion. Beliefs about God solely originate from subjective grounds. Here, then, are two restrictions on the nature and origin of our notions of God which are imposed as a result: firstly, they are objectively insufficient as the perception of God by human beings is impossible; and secondly, that they then exclusively arise from the subjective ground of the structure of the knower's inherent awareness of the meaningful structure of the world which comports with the categories of experience.

---

account offered by Kant is representative of Enlightenment ideals, broadly speaking, and that those ideals have been implicitly or otherwise accepted as normative by biblical theologians.

   [5] See Gordon Michalson jr., *Kant and the Problem of God* (Oxford, 1999). Also Philip Clayton, *The Problem of God in Modern Thought* (Grand Rapids: Eerdmans, 2000), Chapters 5 and 6.

   [6] Kant, *Critique of Pure Reason* (Cambridge, 1997), pp. 684 ff. German edition A 820/B 848 ff.

   [7] Kant, *Critique of Pure Reason*, p. 688-89, A 826/B 854.

Having sketched out Kant's taxonomy of knowledge with respect to *potential* knowledge, we now go on to look at limitations he imposes on the very process by which one would then go ahead and attempt to obtain knowledge, and particularly, knowledge of God. In the appendix to *Prolegomena to Any Future Metaphysics* Kant iterates the need for a thorough examination and critique of any metaphysical investigation undertaken by any person in seeking knowledge. He makes an initial distinction breaking the act of investigation down into two moments: he writes,

> If the course of events is taken as it actually runs and not as it should run, then there are two kinds of judgments: a judgment that *precedes* the investigation…and then a different judgment that *comes after* the investigation, in which the reader is able to set aside for a while the consequences of the critical investigation…and first tests the ground from which these consequences may have been derived.[8]

He delineates two moments where judgments come into play; judgments which *precede* the investigation and judgments which *come after* the investigation. He suggests that the presence of both of these is characteristic of the way things often run but "not as it should run." He continues, discussing "antecedent" judgments— those that *precede* the investigation:

> If what ordinary metaphysics presents were undeniably certain (like geometry, for instance), the first way of judging would be valid … But if it is not the case that metaphysics has a supply of incontestably certain (synthetic) propositions, and it is perhaps the case that a good number of them …are, in their consequences, in conflict even among themselves, and that overall there is not to be found in metaphysics any secure criterion whatsoever of the truth of properly metaphysical (synthetic) propositions: then the antecedent kind of judging cannot be allowed, but rather the investigation of the principles of the *Critique* must precede all judgment of its worth or unworth.[9]

Here Kant denies any appropriate role for antecedent judgments in the investigation of metaphysical knowledge. When applied to the investigation of beliefs about God as potential knowledge we see this as another restriction over and above the limitation to subjective grounds as "beliefs" noted at the outset. So: if a person wanted to investigate the possibility of metaphysical knowledge of God (or God's activity) on Kant's terms, they would be required to set aside any antecedent judgments *about* God.

Kant describes this in *What Does It Mean to Orient Oneself in Thinking?* He returns to the subject of antecedent judgments and their relationship to the investigation of "supersensible objects" and explores the implications of these limitations of antecedent judgments for the investigation of beliefs about God as potential knowledge.

> A pure rational faith is therefore the signpost or compass by means of which the speculative thinker orients himself in his rational excursions into the field of supersensible objects … and it is this rational faith which must also be taken as the ground of every other faith, and

---

[8] Immanuel Kant, *Prolegomena to Any Future Metaphysics* (Cambridge, 1997), p. 126.
[9] Kant, *Prolegomena*, pp. 126-7.

even of every revelation …The concept of God and even the conviction of his existence can be met with only in reason, and *it cannot first come to us either through inspiration (Eingebung) or through tidings communicated to us (erteilte Nachricht)*, however great the authority behind them.[10]

Kant again affirms the necessity to remove the influence of antecedent judgments, in this case as they relate to our investigation of God's revelation. He also makes another important distinction when he describes antecedent judgments as being comprised of two varieties, *both* of which need to be guarded against in the investigation of pure reason. For our purposes we will call these "operational" and "notional" judgments.

The first, operational, variety is "inspiration" which is offered as the translation of *Eingebung*. The word connotes a kind of influencing action of one person on another. The verb form *eingeben* can also be translated as "putting forward," "administering to," "suggest" or "put into his or her head." The word is used elsewhere by Kant in contexts where he is also considering the question of God's revelation (*Offenbarung*), but it has a more precise meaning than "revelation" in that it connotes the influence of another personal agent in the process of the individual obtaining or making knowledge. His discussion of revelation takes up this issue and, again, proscribes the agency of the knower in such a way that any antecedent influence should be, as far as possible, set aside or nullified, including the influence of God: "inspiration." Here, as in contexts where Kant discusses revelation he focuses primarily on questions involving the influence, assistance, or help of God but is not as critically interested in the question of the form or content of *notional* beliefs we may acquire or inherit from others. There is a reason for this: throughout his corpus *operational* judgments that assert any sort of assistance from God are considered a diminishment and a hindrance to the ethical powers fully resident within each and every person whereas *notional* judgments about God as a creating or judging agent are permitted insofar as they serve to pragmatically frame the moral action of the individual.

This relates specifically in the quote above to the other type of antecedent judgments that need to be restricted: notional judgments as "tidings communicated to us." These can be thought of as ideas which are given or delivered to us; bits of knowledge we can possess and manipulate. Alternate English words which can be used to translate this German term *Nachricht* are "news," "message" or "report." A simplistic way to describe the difference between these two types of antecedent judgments would be that the former, operational variety is like the influence of another person pushing or pulling us in a particular direction, directing of our attention. The latter, notional type of judgments, are like pieces of paper with bits of information written on them composed by others to which we might refer in our investigations.

---

[10]   Immanuel Kant, "What Does It Mean to Orient Oneself in Thinking?," in *Religion and Rational Theology* (New York, 1996), pp. 14-5. Emphasis mine. From the *Gesammelte Schriften*, V. 8: p. 142. The last sentence in German reads *"Der Begriff von Gott, und selbst die Überzeugung von seinem Dasein, kann nur allein in der Vernunft angetroffen werden, von ihr allein ausgehen und weder durch Eingebung, noch durch eine erteilte Nachricht von noch so großer Auctorität zuerst in uns kommen."*

Kant goes on to describe the origins of both of these types of antecedent judgments and how they both violate the freedom of reason and rational faith in that they do not allow rational faith to have the "right to speak first" and therefore attack the "freedom to think."[11] This freedom is preserved by eliminating these influences from three sources of compulsion: "civil compulsion" which is the influence and control of civil institutions; "compulsion over conscience" which is the influence of religious institutions; and finally any other law or influence other than "those which [Reason] gives itself."[12] The indictment of these three realms has an exhaustive quality with respect to any sort of antecedent judgment that originates within a traditional or communal purview: political, sociological or religious.

The net result of these limitations on the investigation of knowledge is that the agency of the knower must begin unaffected by others and that the object of investigation should only be supplied by the immanent senses and measured by the subjective ground present within the individual. This circumscribes the knowing investigation to purely immanent actions and spheres initiated and maintained exclusively by the knower.

Summarizing up to this point: there are two limitations in Kant's epistemology that have important implications for knowledge of God. First, the quality of any potential knowing of God can never attain pure or true knowledge insofar as our human faculties are insufficient to supply us with the requisite experience. The most we can attain is "faith" which is of a lesser quality than "knowledge." Second, Kant places a strict quarantine on two types of influence that would hinder or taint the process; both the influence of other agents and the impact of opinions and prior judgments.

Kant continues this discussion in *What Does it Mean to Orient Oneself in Thinking?*, extending his critical evaluation to *subsequent* judgments. It is fortuitous for our purposes that he chooses to discuss the possibility of a subsequent judgment about God. He writes:

> [I]n order to judge whether what appears to me, what works internally or externally on my feelings, is God, I would have to hold it up to my rational concept of God and test it accordingly...even if nothing in what [I] discovered immediately contradicted that concept, nevertheless this appearance, intuition, immediate revelation, or whatever else one wants to call such a presentation, never proves the existence of a being whose concept...demands that it be of infinite magnitude...but no experience or intuition at all can be adequate to that concept, hence none can unambiguously prove the existence of such a being. Thus no one can first be convinced of the existence of a highest being though any intuition; rational faith must come first, and then certain appearances of disclosures could at most provide the occasion for investigating whether we are warranted in taking what speaks or presents itself to us to be a Deity, and thus serve to confirm that faith according to these findings.[13]

---

[11] Kant, "What does it Mean to Orient Oneself in Thinking?", p. 15.
[12] Kant, "What does it Mean to Orient Oneself in Thinking?", pp. 16-7.
[13] Kant, "What does it Mean to Orient Oneself in Thinking?", pp. 16-7.

Kant does not, here, decisively shut the door on the possibility of God's *existence*, nor does he deny that God could attempt to give us an experience or expression of God's own being. However, these are irrelevant in that there are epistemological gaps and limits that humans cannot transcend. We lack both infinite categories of knowing as well as the sensory possibility of having an infinite experience. Therefore the possibility of human beings either actually having an experience of something supersensible, or of having reliable knowledge of a transcendent being which can translate into a subsequent judgment of the investigation of reason, are both impossible.[14] Thus the terms for the investigation of potential knowledge of God is, again, limited to immanent spheres for both kinds of judgments; those that precede the investigation and those which result or follow.

Contemporary epistemological traditions tend to proceed by critiquing and limiting the moment of experience and the investigation of reason in similar ways. Antecedent judgments are heavily scrutinized; their influence is deemed to be an impediment to a purer kind of investigation; a fly in the ointment of reason; a pinch of unwanted leaven. They are to be set aside, or, if this is not possible, the imposition of their influence is to be strictly controlled and eradicated as far as is possible. The immanent moment of experience or investigation is thus left unfettered in order to better perceive and/or appropriate the truth in the perceiving moment. Subsequent judgments are then carefully measured in light of the "ground" of immanent experience and/or by the categories from and by which the investigation proceeded.

This is the general layout for how Kant constructed the ideal knowing activity of the human being in the pursuit of knowledge and how he imposes limits on that action which restrict it to immanent spheres. We now go on to tease out further the nature of those restrictions with respect to how they become an unnatural impediment to theological undertakings and especially to the reading of Scripture.

---

[14] This is a common claim. He also makes it in Book 3 of "Religion within the Limits of Mere Reason" in *Religion and Rational Theology*, pp. 129-171 see esp. 122-5, and also periodically in the section "The Conflict of the Philosophy Faculty with the Theology Faculty" in "The Conflict of the Faculties," pp. 247-93. A.K.M Adam notes that Gabler had an ongoing dispute with Kant over the nature of biblical interpretation. J. P. Gabler, who is counted as one of the founding fathers of modern biblical criticism, took exception that Kant, in "Religion within the Limits," allowed interpretations that defied or surpassed the literal sense of the text if those interpretations encouraged true morality. See Adam, *Making Sense of New Testament Theology* (Macon: Mercer University Press, 1995), pp. 56-9. Important for our purposes is the point that Gabler, who is often cited as a father of modern biblical criticism, felt that Kant *was not being strict enough* in the limitation and criticism of subsequent judgments arising from the study of the Bible. The degree to which this attitude continues in the course of modern biblical studies, as exemplified in Wrede and Stendahl et al., is indicative of a commitment to the criticism of judgments which is even more epistemologically exacting than Kant. See Adam, *Making Sense*, pp. 62-86 and chapter 3 for more recent interpreters. An important recent expression of the criticism of judgments and the commitment to modern historical methods to do the critiquing is Van Harvey, *The Historian and the Believer* (Philadelphia, 1966).

Further Defining Kant's Critique of Antecedent Judgments with Special Attention to the Relationship of Human and Divine Agency

> Reason must regard itself as the author of its principles independently of alien influences; consequently, as practical reason of the will of a rational being it must be regarded of itself as free, that is, the will of such a being cannot be a will of his own except under the idea of freedom, and such a will must, in a practical respect, be attributed to every rational being.[15]

Kant's underlying concern in limiting the influence of judgments in the gaining of knowledge is rooted in his idea of freedom. Any assistance or influence from others undermines our absolute responsibility as free agents to act morally. If we indeed received help from God in any tangible sense we would be relieved of our responsibilities as independent accountable moral agents and our motivation for improving ourselves and society would be deflated. His fear is not without justification. So, he suggests that judgments of others are to be set aside so as not to bias the free thinking of the knowing subject. This includes any prior judgments pertaining to God, especially operational antecedent judgments that claim knowledge that comes *from* God or of some claim of assistance *by* God. He writes,

> [N]o one can *first* be convinced of the existence of a highest being through any intuition; rational faith must come first, and then certain appearances or disclosures could at most provide the occasion for investigating whether we are warranted in taking what speaks or presents itself to us to be a Deity, and thus serve to confirm that faith according to these findings.[16]

One problem we encounter in considering the relationship of operational and notional antecedent judgments is that they are, to some degree, constitutive to one another. Their interwoven relationship and their immediate proximity to the investigative action of reason must be taken into account whenever the question of epistemological method arises. Kant would agree. We disagree, however, that, with respect to theology and particularly the reading of Scripture, it is either within our capacity to remove ourselves from either of these influences, particularly that of the prior action and influence of God, nor is it appropriate to set this setting aside as ideal and the alternative as morally deficient. Further, we could ask, even if we could set them aside, whether it would be advantageous to do so, *especially* from the prior and concurrent action of the Triune God as Creator, Redeemer and Sustainer. Would not the abstraction of any of the activities of our lives, including the use of our reason, from the first and third of these divine actions and influences entail the negation or cessation of our existence? Wouldn't removing ourselves from the sphere of the second negate our salvation and acquire judgment: truly, then, *obtaining* our slavery instead of our freedom?

---

[15]　Immanuel Kant, "Groundwork of the Metaphysics of Morals," in *Practical Philosophy* (Cambridge, 1996), p. 96.

[16]　Kant, "What Does it Mean to Orient Oneself in Thinking?", p. 15.

Setting these questions aside, we continue to look at Kant's writing, first summarizing that the results of Kant's exacting limitation on any and all *antecedent* judgments is that the *direction* (both in the sense of agency and orientation) of reason's investigation is viewed as being wholly and exclusively originating with, and the responsibility of, the knowing subject. The agency, activity, and impetus for the application of categories from the mind of the knowing subject to the perceived object originates and is, ideally, under complete control of the subject(s).[17] The immanent criticism of *subsequent* judgments also imposes strict limits on the object of the investigation in a manner that reinforces this view.

These immanent limitations are applied in writings where he considers the question of religion and morality. For example, in *Religion within the Bounds of Mere Reason* there is a telling occasion for Kant to comment on the possibility of God's *Eingebung*. In the General Observation section for Part Three "The Victory of the Good Principle over the Evil Principle, and the Founding of a Kingdom of God on Earth" he clarifies what he sees as the proper way to view the "mystery of faith" which lies at the heart of personal religion. He suggests that there are two options; belief is either "divinely prompted" (*göttlich eingegebenen*) or is a "pure rational faith." (*reinen Vernunftglauben*). He recommends that "unless impelled by the most extreme need to accept the first kind, we shall make it a maxim to abide by the second."[18] The way to the mysteries of rational faith, then, is through the idea of freedom. And freedom implies the removal of alien influences or judgments.

The idea and ideal of freedom is also the one true route to the mysteries of faith because, on the one hand, freedom is an attribute which is *not* a mystery because it is potentially revealed to every person in the "determinability of their will" and thus *can* be publicly shared knowledge. On the other hand, the *ground* of freedom *is* a mystery, and *cannot* be communicated publicly. This combination makes the idea of freedom the one available avenue for understanding the mysteries of pure rational faith and its accompanying ethical benefit.

In the context of this freedom the person becomes aware that there resides within him or herself "the idea of the highest good." Kant goes on to indicate three things about God that can be deduced from the idea of the highest good: first, the idea that God is, as a holy Legislator, the omnipotent creator of heaven and earth; second, the

---

[17]   The plural indicator here accounts for the recent arguments of those like Jürgen Habermas, who accept the Kantian epistemological features but relocate their operation from the individual to the community.

[18]   He continues; "Feelings are not knowledge (*Gefühle sind nicht Erkenntnisse*) and so do not indicate [the presence of] a mystery; and since the latter is related to reason, yet cannot be shared universally, each individual will have to search for it (if ever there is such a thing) solely in his own reason." Immanuel Kant *Religion within the Bounds of Mere Reason*, 6:137 in the German collected works edition, pp163-4 in *Religion and Rational Theology* Allen W. Wood and George di Giovanni (eds), The Cambridge Edition of the Works of Immanuel Kant (Cambridge: Cambridge University Press, 1996). This indicates two of the key places where Friedrich Schleiermacher would issue his challenge; in the positive role of *Gefühl* and in the relocating of the individual's experience as dependent on the collective within the religious community. On this second point see Schleiermacher's important and neglected *Christmas Eve: Dialogue on the Incarnation* (Richmond, John Knox Press 1967).

idea that God is the benevolent Ruler and Preserver of the human race; and third, the idea that God is a righteous Judge and the Administrator of His own laws. We are warned not to take these three things as anything other than as a representation (*Vorstellung*) of a practical idea because to do so stretches human concepts beyond their abilities. [19] This warning is one with which Kant repeatedly hounds his reader.

Kant, in this moral cautioning, assumes an additional distinction between ideas (or judgments) as actually having some relationship to the way things are, and ideas as simply claims which have an indeterminate or nonexistent relationship to the things to which they seem to refer. The way this consistently works in Kant's writing is that he frequently allows for purely notional judgments about God as long as he can see them as somehow enabling people to spur themselves on to pursue the highest good. Yet he always makes it very clear that these judgments should not be seen as actually somehow capturing or referring to any true detail of what God may or may not actually be like, denying them any operational truck. Kant is concerned about walking the fine line between allowing the unenlightened masses to have their dogmatic pacifiers and crutches, and keeping them from drawing conclusions that could potentially lead them to absolve themselves of the moral and civic responsibilities they themselves should shoulder.

One result of this distinction between the purely functional aspect of an idea as being separable from whatever relationship it may or may not have to things-in-themselves is that this reinforces a bias in his writing towards being more amenable to judgments of the notional type over operational types (the *idea* that God created the world over the claim that God did, in fact create and does sustain the world).

Notional judgments have to do with the nature and essence of things which (to some degree) can be discussed in relative abstraction from their operation. Thus, on the one hand, the notional idea of God as creator of the earth has greater potential pragmatic value in encouraging people to pursue the greatest good. This is so, for one, in that the moment of the action of creation stands at a safe distance and serves as a kind of backdrop from the present moment of moral decision and therefore has a more acceptable risk level relative to the potential danger of someone thinking that this is truly the way God is or acts. On the other hand, any idea that implies that God actively and personally sustains me possesses much greater immediate risk in that one could then conclude that they are inadequate in and of themselves to face the demands of the immediate moral task. Kant, then, believes that there is a much greater moral danger in the influence of the operational judgment that God sustains creation and creatures than the notional judgment that God is the Creator of the world in undermining morality.

Furthermore, all three of the "beliefs" about God that Kant allows in the *Critique of Practical Judgment* lend themselves efficiently to observe this danger and to preserve the immanent limitations of reason, thus maintaining the independent self-sufficient moral agent. Considered from the standpoint of God's activity none of these considered on their own need necessarily impose themselves on the immanent sphere of the agency of the individual. God as Creator and as Future Judge are both logically resigned to a distant unknown past and future, respectively. Likewise, the

---

[19] Kant, *Religion and Rational Theology*, pp. 165 ff.

image of God as "preserver" of the human race need not imply anything more than a kind of deistic oversight; a guarding and maintaining of the clock tower. Even these three beliefs about God that Kant promotes, then, continue to reinforce the clear and exact immanent prescriptions Kant imposes to keep clear the space for the independent self-sufficient moral agent.[20]

Returning to another point in Kant's discussion above, we recall that the "mysteries of pure rational faith" are the grounds from which these ideas about God actually proceed. Of these grounds, he writes, "God has revealed nothing to us, nor can he reveal anything, for we would not understand it."[21] In the text at this point there is a footnote which gives us another excellent example of what *Eingebung* indicates and how exacting is Kant's denial of its possibility.

> Now we can with right require of every mystery proposed for belief that we understand what is meant by it. And this does not happen just because we understand one by one the words by which the mystery is enunciated, i.e. by attaching a meaning to each separately, but because, when combined together in one concept, the words still allow a meaning and do not, on the contrary, thereby escape all thought.—*It is unthinkable that God could make this cognition come to us through inspiration, (Eingebung) if we for our part do not fail earnestly to wish for it, for such cognition could simply not take hold in us, since the nature of our understanding is incapable of it.*[22]

It is significant to note that Kant felt compelled here to discuss an interpretive question about the nature of language. He notes the difficulty, yet necessity, of moving from the meanings of individual words to how words indicate a developed meaning as they are collected under concepts. Consistent with our reading, he thought it more important to issue a strong warning about considering God an agent assisting us than to warn us about the influence that notional claims supplied to us in tradition may inveigh. This emphasis, then, remains firmly in place as he moves from the critique of pure to practical reason.[23] Thus practical reason can, and must, avail itself of these minimal notional ideas about God, but must refrain from ever making operational judgments about God's present activity in the world.

The tendency to distinguish between the functional and the referential nature of judgments (and focus on the prior) also shows itself in the section called "The Philosophy Faculty versus the Theological Faculty" in *The Conflict of the Faculties*. There Kant suggests that the heart of the conflict between the faculties is that they have a strong difference of opinion over the nature of the influence (*Einfluß*) of God, or of some supernatural spirit. Kant continues to deny the appropriateness of influences as this undermines our moral freedom and our corresponding responsibilities. However, he cautiously suggests that he would allow, in certain situations, for the

---

[20] It is no coincidence that modern theologians and hermeneuticians are drawn to the doctrines of creation and eschatology to underwrite their proposals. We shall see this trend emerge in our survey in later chapters.

[21] Kant, *Religion and Rational Theology*, p. 169.

[22] Ibid. Emphasis mine

[23] See Michalson jr., Gordon E., *Kant and the Problem of God* (Oxford: Blackwell, 1999), chapter 2.

idea of such influence, if it serves to motivate individuals in the improvement of their moral disposition.

This discussion indicates the difficulty in attempting to maintain a strict distinction between notional and operational judgments. For example, keeping straight the difference between the notional judgment that God is an assisting God and the operational judgment that God does, and is, in fact, assisting us can make our heads swim a bit, and rightfully so. Insofar as we are limited and immanent beings who, by necessity, employ language to engage our world and each other, at some point the distinction cannot be maintained and requires that we recognize that whenever we "talk about God" the congruous relationship of the functional and the referential (and ethical) will at some point be inextricable and unavoidable.[24] Rather, it is when the natural relationship between the functional and referential aspects are strained or severed, as it is in both cases in Kant, that the crises in modern theology and biblical studies find their roots and sustenance. Modern views of the freedom of reason compelled theologians and biblical scholars to take up a variety of positions relative to these in how they perceived the ideal investigation in their particular field. Among them there is one relatively consistent feature: It became the *status quo* that antecedent operational judgments should be resisted as a subjective imposition on the investigation of the "objective" individual. Thus an essentially deistic hermeneutical framework becomes the default setting.

Clearing the Modern Ground: The Eclipse of God's Agency

If the picture painted above is accurate then it is of obvious value to pursue the question of how these developments affected theological and biblical investigations. There is a fairly wide consensus that something like the terms we have laid out were also gradually and variously adopted and employed as the standard for biblical studies.[25] One implication of their adoption will receive a greater level of attention: the limitation to strictly immanent spheres of agency and investigation became the *status quo* in the self-perception of the task of reading Scripture; the limiting and removal of the influence of antecedent judgments, particularly those related to the agency of God Himself, in the act of reading the Bible became accepted norms both *de jure* and *de facto*.

Insofar as this is the case there are two tendencies that emerge. First, the theological scholar, as the knowing subject, perceives his or her task to be one in which the prior influence of other agents (or traditions) should be strictly controlled and if possible,

---

[24] See the fine discussion in David Bentley Hart, *The Beauty of the Infinite* (Grand Rapids, 2003), pp. 300-18.

[25] Adam, *Making Sense*, p. 109. See Craig Bartholomew *Reading Ecclesiastes* (Rome, 1998), Chapter 1. See bibliography for other relevant works by Bartholomew. He describes in *Reading* that DeWette, the oft proclaimed father of modern biblical criticism, was deeply influenced by a lecture he heard Kant give and that he himself saw his work as an effort to implement the basic features of Kantian thought. On this point also see John W. Rogerson, *W. M. L. de Wette: Founder of Modern Biblical Criticism* (Sheffield, 1992).

eliminated. "Objectivity" is the watchword.[26] In biblical studies this manifests itself in the perception that studies which set aside tangible theological frameworks are superlative to those which do not. In debates biblical scholars invariably point to any hint of the presence of theological interests that may remain in the writing of their opponents as if this is a point of weakness.

Second, the object of study for the biblical scholar is limited to those things which are immediately available to immanent categories and experience. The intense scrutiny of "events" under the general rubric and guidance of "history" is evidence of this. Increasing preoccupation with finding the exact text is another. The well known passions with which certain Protestant denominations have rallied around the King James Version as well as the exaggerated efforts of the Jesus Seminar are both examples of these tendencies fully working themselves out.

The net result of both of these for theology as well as the reading of Scripture is that the task in either case is ideally viewed as presiding strictly and wholly under the agency of human knowing subject(s) and is limited to attending to immediately available immanent objects of study. In both cases the investigation proceeds in relative abstraction not only from the perceived contaminating influence of other human agents but also from God's immediate and/or mediate agency and presence in, with, and under, both the objects of study and the activity of the reader(s). For example, modern theologians increasingly turned their initial, primary or exclusive attention to anthropological issues, whether individually, or collectively, or to some immanent dynamic at work in relation to human phenomena. The other option which stood alongside like a younger brother, or better, as a lower caste cousin to this was, and is, to look to nature, and natural occurring phenomena for the raw material for theology.[27] For biblical studies the turn was to the sorting out of historical questions, taking their cue from sociological and historical categories and methodologies.

In both cases there is a tendency to abstract the fields of study from any consideration of God and God's activity in, with, and under the object of study or with the knowing subject in the study. Talk of God's activity is, in these scenarios, ideally, only a *result* of the investigation.[28] Accompanying these developments there gradually grew a consensus that accepted the superiority of the kind of investigation

---

[26] Of course this is a Modern definition of "objectivity"; a term which underwent severe transformations from the early Medieval period forward. See S. Bordo, *The Flight to Objectivity: Essays on Cartesianism and Culture* (Syracuse, 1987); E. Cassirer, "The Subject-Object Problem in the Philosophy of the Renaissance" in *The Individual and the Cosmos in Renaissance Philosophy* (New York, 1963); Daston, L., "Objectivity and the Escape from Perspective" *Social Studies of Science* V. 22 (1992), 597-618; T. Nagel, *The View from Nowhere* (Oxford, 1986); J. R. Solomon, *Objectivity in the Making: Francis Bacon and the Politics of Inquiry* (Baltimore, 1998); M. Bowald, "Objectivity" in *The Dictionary for the Theological Interpretation of the Bible* (Grand Rapids, 2005).

[27] An excellent account of the relationship of the development of natural science to Protestant notions of reading Scripture is found in Harrison, *The Bible, Protestantism and the Rise of Natural Science* (Cambridge: Cambridge University Press, 1998).

[28] See the interesting and highly relevant account in Preus, *Spinoza and the Irrelevance of Biblical Authority* (Cambridge: Cambridge University Press, 2001).

which exercised careful and exacting controls on *all* antecedent judgments which indicate any prior influence of another agent. Thus those who sought to challenge the results of other scholars *perceived* the only arena for challenge to be that of *subsequent* judgments.

Once these boundaries settled the terms for disagreement were set as well. Biblical scholars of a conservative stripe argue against the more radical conclusions of their opponents in terms of the textual and historical evidence suggesting that a fuller and more objective accounting of the evidence at hand leads one to a different conclusion. In this they nevertheless continued to accept the moratorium on antecedent judgments. The investment in historical critical methods, underwritten by the immanent epistemological preferences and limitations of the Enlightenment, was unanimous across the theological and denominational spectrum at this point.

Furthermore, biblical scholars tended to issue their challenging criticisms not only with respect to subsequent judgments, but to *notional* subsequent judgments. This is a more subtle point. I have in mind here the occasions when biblical scholars discuss the conclusions of their work. Often they talk *about* God as if describing the features of a painting. Their discussion tends toward description and yet the implications are disregarded as to whatever this description might suggest in terms of God as a personal and active agent, and how the admission of this shape of agency would transform the self perception of the very act of reading Scripture which they themselves are undertaking. Thus the self-perceived activity of the theologian, as well as the self-perception of the task of reading Scripture received increasing abstraction from their prior (and proper) location within the milieu of gracious divine agency and presence. This occurred in concert with the developments William Placher has helpfully narrated as the "domestication of transcendence."[29]

Louis Dupre eloquently characterizes the results of these trends and their implications and results for religious traditions in Western culture:

> The unity of the integrated culture on which Western metaphysics once rested became fragmented into isolated spheres: nature, the meaning-giving mind, the inscrutable God. The transcendent component gradually withdrew from culture. That process now appears to have become completed. It is, of course, not the case that contemporary culture *denies* the existence of God or of the divine. But transcendence plays no vital role in the integration of our culture. The fragmentation …has not halted at the ultimate principles. Once the human subject became solely responsible for the constitution of meaning and value, tradition lost its former authority. Each group, if not each individual, eventually felt free to advance a cultural synthesis of its own, ransacking the tradition for spare parts. Freedom was restricted only by the right of others to be equally free. Symbolic universes became sovereign realms, beholden only to self-made rules.[30]

---

[29] William Placher, *The Domestication of Transcendence* (Louisville, 1996).

[30] Louis Dupre, *Metaphysics and Culture* (Milwaukee, 1994), pp. 44 and 48. Also George Schner writes, "This fundamental shift occasions the move to illogical discourse within Christianity itself … it involves the effort to preside both over the identity of God and over our own facticity. Thus, what has accompanied our particularly modern conception of the deep and persuasive factors accounting for human inventiveness … has been a loss of a sense of the transcendent, of the sacred." Schner, "Waiting for Godot," *Toronto Journal of*

The loss of tradition's authority is one of the additional features of the impact of the developments we have been tracing.[31] Going beyond Dupre's suggestion, it is only when tradition is relativized and abstracted with respect to its prior perceived location within the milieu of God's gracious action that the possibility of denying or misconstruing the nature of its authoritative role in relation to the reading of Scripture becomes a live option.

The inclination of the enlightenment epistemological tradition that has concerned us here is the eclipse of God's agency in the perception of the task of reading Scripture. This development has, at its foundation, an overt theological dilemma. If it is true that one can remove oneself, even "for the sake of argument" from the milieu of God's gracious activity, then God is not the God attested to in Christian Scripture and the tasks of a particular Christian reading of the Bible or theology quickly become moot. On the other hand, if one cannot remove oneself from the sphere of divine assistance and influence then the Enlightenment valuation of detached objectivity is flawed and the self-perception of the reader of Scripture and the theologian need to be redefined accordingly. This is an unavoidable, clear cut and significant either / or to negotiate.

It presently still tends to be the case that scholars (and many ordained and laypersons) still idealize the reading of Scripture from *within* the limits and strictures of the epistemological tradition of the Enlightenment. In the wake of the eclipse of divine agency that this inaugurates comes a usurping of that action by the only other arena of agency available in the immanent sphere to replace or supplement it: human agency.

The Hermeneutic Reversal: The Usurping of God's Agency

Once God's antecedent agency is set aside as an improper imposition on Scripture's reading there is a vacuum formed from the traditional or pre-critical perception of the task. Formerly, it was God's supervenance and guidance which accompanied and administered the reading. Once God's instructive role is diminished, denied or lost there arises a need to account for whom or what is controlling or animating the act of reading Scripture. In God's absence humans are the only agents left to take up the responsibility for this action. Michalson identifies this as the logical outcome of Kant's epistemology:

> The transfer of transcendence to the immanent human domain is itself an activity implicitly structuring Kant's thinking, as it is structuring reason itself. Indeed, the aspects of the principle of immanence identifiable in the details of the moral argument and in Kant's aggressive theory of autonomy are considerably reinforced here by the virtual personification of reason. In assuming the very characteristics of divine agency, reason

---

Theology, 17/1, 2001, p. 42. See also William Placher, *The Domestication of Transcendence* for a compatible reading of history which supports this conclusion.

[31] A story narrated eloquently by Jeffrey Stout in *The Flight from Authority* (South Bend: The University of Notre Dame Press, 1981).

becomes providential in both its restless quest for the satisfaction of its aim and the definition of the aim itself. In light of the effects of the other aspects of the principle of immanence, this personification of reason occurs against the backdrop of the increasingly faceless nature of God, for now God has less and less to do.[32]

This shift has been described by others as a sort of "reversal". George Schner, a Jesuit who studied under Louis Dupre and Hans Frei at Yale, has aptly described the results of these shifts of thinking about theology in the course of the Enlightenment in contrast to the assumptions of the prior Christian tradition in these terms:

> The Great Tradition has generally presumed that the order of reality is reflected in the order of possibilities ... because Jesus was raised from the dead, others can come to know this act of God and to live according to it, and ultimately the whole of reality will manifest its effects. This order of happenings leads to an order of discussion: first, of the identity of Jesus and the nature of such an event in history; second, of the relation of the believer as observer and participant—in general a matter of Jesus' calling, commissioning, and upholding his disciples;[33] and third, of the implications of the resurrection of Jesus for the ultimate transformation of the whole universe ... For many scholars, not to mention believers, the order is presently reversed. There is a force or power for transformation (whether developmentally progressive or serendipitous) within the universe; individuals can come to know and be empowered by that force; Jesus can be construed as someone who also participated in, was effected by, or functions as a symbol of this same force.[34]

The direction of the theological logic which orients the relationships of God, Christ, human and creation is important for our purposes. The prior Christian tradition understood the shaping, direction and *telos* of knowledge to flow from the actions of God in Christ in, with, and under events in time and space to the elect people of God, to all humanity and to the cosmos. This is the theological logic that flows from the very shape of our basic ecumenical creeds. The modern situation perceives this relationship as reversed; there is a latent power in the cosmos that awaits our knowing action to animate it, organize it, give it meaning and make it effectual. We reason our way *to* God, not *from* God. Schner implicates Kant and the role of the same two key regulative principles in Kant's epistemology detailed above, which have contributed to this reordering:

> The first [implication] concerns how the meaning of things is arrived at: it is produced by the careful (i.e. logical) application of the structuring activities of the mind, *not by either a receptive intellectual perception of things or an inspiration independent of the senses*. The tendency among humans not to function in this way leads to the second...all knowledge not formed in this fashion is naïve ....[35].

---

[32] Michalson, *Problem*, p. 23.

[33] Schner's endnote here refers to David Demson, *Hans Frei and Karl Barth: Different Ways of Reading Scripture* (Grand Rapids, 1997).

[34] George Schner, "Waiting for Godot: Scripture, Tradition and Church at Century's End", *Toronto Journal of Theology* 17, no. 1 (Summer 2001),p. 39.

[35] George Schner, "Waiting for Godot," p. 39. Emphasis mine

For Kant, as for the majority of post-Enlightenment thinkers, meaning does not in any way *come to us* nor should it be *given* to us. It is neither received nor inspired. We saw this in the survey of his work above and his critique of antecedent judgments. The act of meaning making is initiated, maintained, and substantiated by us. *We go to it and/or make it.*[36] It is an action that originates within us and is initiated by us using the raw material of experience and shaped by the immanent categories of human understanding. The validity of any sort of prior action in the production of meaning by things themselves or by another agent is, from this view, naïve or morally suspect. Michalson again:

> Instead of moving from the reality of God to judgments about human freedom, the argument must account for God and the divine will *subsequent* to our apodictic certainty of the reality of human freedom. Kant's position never really modifies the important reversals that are at stake in this ordering of thought.[37]

The net results of this reversal are that the modern enlightened path to meaning is one which humans perceive themselves to travel alone. We approach nature; we examine rocks; we measure and explore the universe. In fact, we tend to view ourselves as being *ideally*, and even *preferably* unaccompanied, unaffected, and unaided in this activity.[38] "Henceforth the entire burden of conveying meaning falls upon the person who must find his way in an opaque and dark world."[39] At best, this is methodological Deism. At worst, there is a transfer of attributes and actions that rightfully belong to God, to humans.[40]

Hans Frei, in his seminal book *The Eclipse of Biblical Narrative,* also discusses a kind of "reversal" which preceded and anticipated Schner's. Frei's reversal also brings us nearer to the primary point of our study in that he is describing the impact of the same influences on the reading and interpretation of Scripture. He writes,

> Originally, the current reader would submit their world to the one impressed on them by the reading of the biblical story. This story was one history, one world, the one true real world, comprised of a literal-realistic reading, which included, but did not distinguish, reference to the events that they portrayed. These two aspects were gathered into the figural reading that gave the whole its unity. This figural reading contained all of these aspects without distinction. The figural reading impressed itself on the reader in a fashion which dictated that the reader interpret their own life and world in terms of the biblical

---

[36] So Michalson, *Problem,* Chapter 1.

[37] Michalson, *Problem,* p. 22. Emphasis mine.

[38] See William Placher, *The Domestication of Transcendence: How Modern Thinking About God Went Wrong* (Louisville: Westminster John Knox, 1996).

[39] Dupre, *Metaphysics,* p. 48.

[40] Michalson writes, "…the transfer of transcendence to the immanent human domain is itself an activity implicitly structuring Kant's thinking, as it is structuring reason itself. Indeed, the aspects of the principle of immanence identifiable in the details of the moral argument and in Kant's aggressive theory of autonomy are considerably reinforced here by the virtual personification of reason. *In assuming the very characteristics of divine agency, reason becomes providential* in both its restless quest for the satisfaction of its aim and the definition of the aim itself." Michalson, *Problem,* p. 23. Emphasis mine.

world. The figural reading is the link between the text and us. In the original direction the figural reading is determined by the literal-realistic reading. Once the direction is reversed the figural reading loses this determination and seems, to the modern reader, to be directed by the individual interpreter. Conservative readers sensed this and, assuming there was no other option, quickly eschewed figural reading as subjective and dangerous. Liberal readers also viewed it as subjective but did not dismiss it as dangerous, but as foolish, as an unnecessary distraction.[41]

Frei identifies the reversal from the former to the present way of reading in terms which have been aptly summed by George Lindbeck as from "the text absorbing the world" to "the world absorbing the text."[42] Schner's comments are instructive at this point in that the key difference between Schner's reversal and Frei's is that the latter's occurs primarily *within* the Kantian limitations on antecedent judgments we discussed above, particularly as they relate to *operational* antecedent judgments, whereas Schner's reversal carries within it a challenge to the validity of those limitations on antecedent judgments, especially as they relate to God's agency and action on the knowing subject(s). Schner's characterization of the reversal is, then, the more exacting comment on modernity for our purposes.[43]

Summary

The purpose of this book and typology is to challenge a misleading legacy of Enlightenment epistemology. That legacy insists that the prior influence of another agent on the reasoning act of the person is an act that impinges on the freedom of the individual and corrupts the knowing process. This produced a bias against "confessional" readings of Scripture and instills "neutral" and "objective" readings of Scripture with greater authority. Neutrality is, however, both unattainable and, in the end, impeding, for discerning the full character of the dynamic of human and divine agency that comprise all aspects involved in the reading of Scripture. To continue to see antecedent judgments about God's action as something to set aside is effectively to remove something that constitutes our very lives; dislocating this key activity that constitutes and sustains our spiritual life from the active milieu of the transformative power of the Holy Spirit in the administration of Christ's Heavenly Session. The attempt to remove ourselves from the divine agency in, with and under this text as an instrument of God's gracious judgment, salvation, guidance and comfort is, from this perspective, an act of denial or resistance; even defiance.

Chapters 3, 4 and 5 survey how recent contemporary hermeneutical proposals on the reading of Scripture tend to be prone to these problems and neglect these fundamental issues in that they still (to various degrees) accept the limiting terms of the Enlightenment for reading. In this they tacitly or explicitly assume judgments

---

[41] Hans Frei, *The Eclipse of Biblical Narrative*, pp. 6-7; see full discussion pp. 5-12.
[42] George Lindbeck, *The Nature of Doctrine* (Philadelphia, 1984), p. 118.
[43] David Kolb, in *The Critique of Pure Modernity* (Chicago, 1986), p. 11 describes the reversal between the relationship of "substantive rationality" and "formal rationality."

against both types of antecedent judgments, especially *operational* antecedent judgments.[44] They also share a tendency to accept the Enlightenment's terms for the criticism of *subsequent* judgments by initially limiting the object of the investigation to that for which we have categories and can experience. As we survey these proposals we will also carefully exegete the manner in which the representatives we have selected all, nevertheless, manifest antecedent judgments particularly with respect to the role and relationship of human and divine action in the reading of Scripture.

Regardless of whether or how exacting the theologian or biblical scholar is in his or her handling of antecedent judgments, it is still broadly assumed that greater degrees of "objectivity" have greater value as scholarship. This may not be true *de jure* insofar as many biblical theologians would, when asked, wish to acknowledge the location of their work within the milieu of divine action. Nevertheless, the neglect of the accounting of this divine action in biblical scholarship still tends to be *de facto* prevalent in the way scholars actually proceed in their tasks. The acknowledgment of God's active presence as an actual influence within their methodology, in their consideration of the admixture of authorial agency in the composition of the text or its reading, normally only occurs as a notional judgment and is typically not relational or operational in the self-perception of the practitioner. Thus one question that will be more compelling in this study will be how the reader of Scripture acknowledges, appropriates, and indicates divine action in, with and under the form and content in the host of exegetical, hermeneutical, and theological questions to which he or she attends.

For example: one common area of contention where we can observe these tensions is in the question of the role of tradition in biblical studies. Specifically, the role and function of canonicity is fraught with these problems. Many biblical scholars will accept the authority of the canonical corpus as possessing a unique or unquestioned authoritative quality and yet, at the same time, see the process and influence of the theological judgments of the first four ecumenical councils and creeds as either an unnecessary hindrance or irrelevant. In making such a distinction, the net effect is to make a positive judgment about God's activity in, with and under the historical process of the church's recognition and acceptance of God's gift of the canon, while at the same time making a relative and simultaneous negative judgment about the nature of God's activity in the same course of events which culminated in the councils and the creeds. The intimate interconnectedness of these issues historically and theologically forces the acknowledgment that this is a very difficult and awkward position to justify and maintain.

Another reason why focusing on operational antecedent theological judgments will be more telling involves a recent softening of attitudes towards notional antecedent judgments. This is a result of the postmodern criticisms of the idea of neutrality in methods.[45] The recognition that we necessarily bring assumptions to our task is once again becoming an accepted term for theological debates. At the same time the moratorium on any constructive role for *operational* antecedent judgments

---

[44]   See Louis Dupre, *Metaphysics*, pp. 6-11, 38-40.
[45]   See Roy A. Clouser, *The Myth of Religious Neutrality* (South Bend, 1991).

is still by and large in place. In other words: it is becoming more acceptable for theologians to express themselves overtly out of a confessional framework, as long as those frameworks do not assert that the beliefs they hold to divine agency have any purchase with God's true nature or activity.

Therefore, greater attention to the relationship of divine and human agency that is indicated in the hermeneutical proposals that follow will produce a better barometric measure of the present atmospheric pressure that the Enlightenment epistemological limitations still exert. Attention to these will allow us to be able to discern with greater clarity the degree to which proposals and enactments of reading Scripture continue to operate within the reversals named by Frei and Schner.

There is a familiar way that the results of this bias against antecedent operational judgments in modern perceptions of reading Scripture can be named: that God's action is, for "practical purposes," limited to a deistic framework.[46] The possibility of God's revealing particular knowledge or of guiding us to any knowledge through God's own ongoing, personal, and present action is more strictly controlled and denied whereas notional ideas that project God as creator, ruler or judge is allowed as long as we remain agnostic about its referential status.

The possibility and even necessity of separating and isolating the functional and representational aspects of language about God also remains as one of the basic modern features of debates in theology and biblical studies. These distinctions tend to be employed on behalf of more radically oriented reform efforts from within and without the Christian church. It will not be a central concern of this work to discuss this phenomenon. However, it is increasingly clear that this claim, not only of the *necessity* of separation of the functional and referential aspects of language, but even of the *possibility* of such a separation, is a myth which, in an ironic reversal of Kant's intentions, tends to just as easily underwrite the very same self-serving and self-justifying morality that he sought to resist.

Again, it tends to be the case that modern theologians, if they challenge the epistemological critique of judgments, primarily do so only regarding the limits imposed on subsequent judgments and secondarily to the limits of antecedent judgments but typically only in terms of notional judgments. If this is true, then the net result is methodological Deism. In other words, if one still accepts the limits of *operational* antecedent judgments, either *de jure* or *de facto*, one begins the study of theology assuming no prior influencing action of God on the investigative action of the person(s) doing the investigation. Once this stance is assumed the best or the most one can arrive at in one's resulting investigation is that God may exist, and may purportedly have this or that feature. However, the *subsequent* affirmation of God's prior and on-going personal activity in the world is not a conclusion which can be consistently made.[47] If one attempts to make a claim that God's creating, sustaining

---

[46] So Michalson, *Problem*, chapter 2. See also Vanhoozer, *First Theology* (Downer's Grove, 2002), p. 128.

[47] This is one of the chief arguments of Michalson, *Problem*. So, he concludes, even though one can attempt to utilize Kant in the name of some kind of accommodating theology, the most consistent position relative to Kant's philosophy is atheism. An alternate reading of Kant is found in the work of Allen W. Wood who argues that, in the end, for Kant belief in

and redeeming activity in any way has a prior shaping influence on the stance and direction of the person engaged in the investigation, then the original epistemological stance of the knowing subject, in setting aside judgments pertaining to antecedent influences, is negated, thus voiding the terms under which the investigation initially defines its own validity.

One could respond that something exactly like this occurs in the conversion of an individual to the Christian faith and that therefore the move is not impossible. Hans Frei, as Karl Barth and St. Paul, before him was appropriately agnostic on the mechanisms of conversion.[48] Yet this case helpfully illustrates the point. Certainly conversion occurs; individuals move from positions of unbelief or denial of God's existence or activity to positions of acceptance. However, the corollary to this as a way to argue for the legitimacy of the modern criticism of antecedent judgments in reading Scripture would be like asking the Christian, each time he or she enters into a reading, to reverse or eschew themselves of their conversion.

The net result of this is that the modern ideal for reading Scripture places immense responsibility on every new act of reading. Every time a pastor, scholar or layperson reads their Bible, a host of decisions must again be sorted out and evidences weighed; whether this passage indicates that Christ is God, whether God is one, two or three "persons," etc. The impracticality of asking the individual to do what the collective Christian tradition could itself do, and only awkwardly at best, over the course of many centuries each and every time they read their Bible is absurd. Yet this is essentially the burden that the Enlightenment criticism of antecedent judgments places on the responsible reader of Scripture. Is it any wonder that doctrines like the Trinity and the divinity of Christ have become, in many circles, awkward and impractical notions?

In this study I will push these observations even further in the construction of the typology. I have made suggestions along this line above but it bears repeating and emphasizing here. For Christian theology, and even more resoundingly for the Christian reading of Scripture it is effectively *impossible* for anyone, including biblical scholars, to assume an investigative posture like the one Kant recommends towards operational antecedent judgments. If God exists, and if God is the God whose actions are faithfully indicated in the Christian Scripture and Creeds, then it is impossible *not* to assume a stance of judgments or, better, orientation, toward the prior action this God has taken in time and space, preeminently in Jesus Christ. There is no third alternative position (or location or realm) in the listening attentiveness to God's Word between acknowledging God's present unique and personal speech action and denying it. To attempt some kind of neutrality is to attempt to set oneself outside of the sphere of God's presence and prior action, which is operationally a denial or removal. If one could remove oneself from the field of God's action, then this is not

---

God is necessary. See among others *Kant's Moral Religion* (Ithaca, 1970) and *Kant's Rational Theology* (Ithaca, 1978). My reading falls in between Michalson and Wood (but closer to Wood) in that I see a strong agnosticism, or some mix of agnosticism and Deism, is the most consistent outcome of Kant's work and maintaining any substantial Theism is awkward at best.

48   Hans Frei, *The Identity of Jesus Christ* (Philadelphia, 1975).

the God of the Christian tradition and the question of the particularity of a Christian reading of Scripture is moot. Thus, if one wishes to take with any seriousness the legitimacy of the Christian God the only real alternatives in the stance one assumes in reading the Bible are cooperation or resistance.[49]

For Christians, reasoning in faith implies that the exacting limits enlightenment epistemology places on both antecedent and subsequent judgments stand together or fall together. They are challenged together, or they cannot be challenged at all. Further, the primary point where they are best challenged is with respect to the appropriate and constructive role that operational antecedent judgments play in reading Scripture.

My comments toward the Enlightenment epistemological trends could be construed as predominantly negative. To clarify: I am sympathetic, with some reservations, of Charles Taylor's perspective, for example, on the relative but substantial value for modernity to the Christian faith,[50] and with Karl Barth who continued to affirm a relative value to historical criticism of the Bible and who described the value of philosophy as the *advocatus hominis et mundi*.[51] Nevertheless, I am convinced that the reading and interpretation of Scripture are, in their initial epistemological and hermeneutical posture, *sui generis*. We do not read Scripture, as the adage goes, "like any other book." In this book alone we may gather to hear the *viva vox Dei*. This is an utterly exceptional activity because God's action is uniquely present in, with, and under this text in a way that it is not for any and all others. Other texts, even the most "inspiring", are the written speech actions of human beings, thus the categorical limits of antecedent and subsequent judgments have greater relevance for their reading. Human authors (if they are deceased or not in direct communication with us) are not personally present to us as we read. They are incapable of giving us additional guidance in the way we should read them. They were not personally involved (beyond their lifetime) in the formation of the tradition of reading their books that stands between them and us. Beyond these simple distinctions, human speech actions are definitively limited in comparison to God's. To some degree, then, these epistemological ideals are more useful for writings other than Scripture. Finally, they continue to maintain their greatest usefulness in areas of so-called hard or pure sciences, although the degree of objectivity one can attain in these fields has also been challenged and has assumed a much more (appropriately) humble bearing as a result.

We can now proceed in the next chapter to outline and develop the triangle typology by which we will measure and map recent proposals for reading Scripture. Using it we will attend to the adequacy (and inadequacy) to which they account for the stance they necessarily assume toward the relationship of divine and human agency in their hermeneutical proposals.

---

[49] "Our ultimate question in this existential situation of dependent freedom is not whether we will choose in accordance with reason or by faith, but whether we will choose with reasoning faithlessness or reasoning faith." H. Richard Niebuhr, *Christ and Culture* (New York, 1951), p. 251.

[50] Charles Taylor, *A Catholic Modernity?*, pp. 13-38.

[51] Karl Barth: "Philosophy and Theology" in *The Way of Theology in Karl Barth Essays and Comments* (Allison Park, 1986), p. 94.

Chapter 2

A Triangle Typology: Mapping Divine and Human Agency in Contemporary Theological Hermeneutics

Kant's exacting proscription against the prior influence of other agents as a foundational value of the Enlightenment continues to enjoy prominence in both modern and postmodern epistemologies. Viewing the ideal act of investigation as an action that is free from any prior influence or control also continues to underwrite methodologies in contemporary theological work, including biblical studies.[1]

The problem is that in theological enterprises the very idea of removing oneself from the prior influence of God's agency is, at *best*, awkward. To what location could one go where one is free from the effects of God's prior and accompanying action of creation and sustenance? What perspective could one ever assume that has not already received benefit from God's grace and detriment from God's judgment? Thus, when doing theology and especially when reading Scripture, it is an ingredient feature of our bearing to assume something like what Kant describes as operational antecedent judgments pertaining to the shape and nature of God's agency.[2]

In this chapter we will construct a typology that seeks to both illuminate and redress this deficiency. It has three types with each occupying the corner of a triangle. Representative approaches for each type will be discussed in each of the subsequent three chapters. Our typology stands indebted to other attempts to describe or typify methodological options and choices within theological activities. I have in mind here works like H. Richard Niebuhr's *Christ and Culture*,[3] David Kelsey's *The Use of Scripture in Recent Theology*,[4] George Lindbeck's *The Nature of Doctrine*,[5] Ingolf Dalferth's *Philosophy and Theology*,[6] Hans Frei's *Types of Christian Theology*,[7]

---

[1] "Biblical criticism is church thinking adapted to Enlightenment and post-Enlightenment modes." Hans Frei, *Theology and Narrative* (Oxford, 1993), p. 156.

[2] My thinking on this point and in many aspects of this book has benefited greatly from interaction with the writings of Charles Taylor, particularly *Philosophical Arguments* (Cambridge, 1995), *Sources of the Self* (Cambridge, 1989), *Philosophical Papers I* (Cambridge, 1985) and *A Catholic Modernity?* (Oxford, 1999).

[3] H. Richard Niebuhr, *Christ and Culture* (New York, 1951).

[4] David Kelsey, *The Use of Scripture in Recent Theology* (Philadelphia, 1975), reprinted as *Proving Doctrine* (Harrisburg, 1999).

[5] George Lindbeck, *The Nature of Doctrine.* (Philadelphia, 1984).

[6] Ingolf Dalferth, *Theology and Philosophy* (Cambridge, 1988).

[7] Hans Frei, *Types of Christian Theology* (Yale, 1992).

George Schner's article "Metaphors for Theology"[8] and James Buckley's "Beyond the Hermeneutical Deadlock." [9] There is a familial relationship for most of these works in their relationship to the so-called postliberal school of theology. Niebuhr, with the possible exception of Karl Barth, was the most important figure in the theological development of Hans Frei. Lindbeck's thinking evolved in a fraternally constructive relationship with Frei's. Buckley and Schner were students of both Frei and Lindbeck. Our triangle typology was born in conversation with this group and is constructively indebted to them. At the end of this chapter we will show this indebtedness.

The Triangle: Coordinating Divine and Human Action

The typologies above all share a common feature in that they assume a linear arrangement. Linear typologies have limitations in that they can only identify a particular approach with respect to the negotiation of two issues represented as the two points that anchor each end of the line. The linear typology is also hampered from accounting for the uniqueness of an individual's thought as it evolves and becomes more nuanced depending on the particularity of the question or situation. Our typology seeks to make an advance upon linear typologies by creating a two dimensional typological space in the shape of a triangle. Whereas linear typologies coordinate their types with respect to two issues, the two dimensional space of a triangle allows us to coordinate individual approaches to reading Scripture with respect to four. Simply put: the higher up or down in the triangle a proposal for reading is located is indicative of the emphasis that approach takes within the relationship of divine and human agency. Likewise, the location to the left or to the right within the triangle is determined by the greater place the proposal gives to the "text" or "reader" respectively. We clarify this below.

We begin by setting up two horizontal parallel planes. The top plane metaphorically represents the origin of all the various activities of God. The creation of the world, the sustaining of life, the gracious action of redemption in all of the events of the life of Christ, as well as God's presence and ongoing action in the life of the Church and the events in the world are all examples of things included in this plane as the field of God's general and particular providential action. The bottom plane represents human activity: it encompasses all the various reflective and expressive actions of human

---

[8] George Schner, "Metaphors for Theology" in *Theology after Liberalism,* edited by John Webster and George Schner (Oxford, 2000), pp. 3-51.

[9] James J. Buckley, "Beyond the Hermeneutical Deadlock" in *Theology after Liberalism*, pp. 188-204. Other typological studies that could be fruitfully compared include Mark G. Brett, "Four or Five Things to Do with Texts: A Taxonomy of Interpretive Interests" in *The Bible in Three Dimensions* (Sheffield, 1990), and Kevin J. Vanhoozer, "Christ and Concept: Doing Theology and the 'Ministry' of Theology" in *Doing Theology in Today's World* (Grand Rapids, 1991), pp. 99-145. These two typologies are strongly informed by Hans Frei's *Types of Theology*. Also relevant is Alvin Plantinga, "Two (or More) Kinds of Scripture Scholarship" in *Theology and Scriptural Imagination*, pp. 81-116, and John Goldingay, *Models for Scripture* (Grand Rapids, 1994), and *Models for Interpretation of Scripture* (Grand Rapids, 1995).

culture. This includes speaking and writing, art and technology, science, politics and religion. In between these two planes there are many coincidental activities which have an obvious relationship to both the plane of God's action and the plane of human action. For example, the history of the church is a history of the interaction, both in terms of cooperation and resistance, between God and human beings as God's elect people.

Now we add two vertical planes, one on the left and one on the right, which represent the tension between the text and the reader in scriptural hermeneutics. As we discussed, in our contemporary context the hermeneutical problem of reading the Bible is normally cast in terms of this tension between the "text" (in which I include all aspects related to the "author") and the "reader." For example, Werner Jeanrond defines the relevant hermeneutical issues to be between the dialectic relationship between "text and reading" or "text production" and "text reception."[10] Another recent commentator remarks:

> Over the past two hundred years of biblical interpretation the basic background theories have multiplied, so that we now have author-centered models, text-centered models, and reader- or audience-centered models of interpretation. The focal point has changed over the years from the genesis of a text to the text in its literary integrity and more recently to the reception of the text. Numerous biblical scholars attempt to be eclectic, but usually work with or two specific methods.[11]

He is describing a variety of positions in the tension on the axis in the typology between text and reader. As a byproduct of the influences we discussed in Chapter 1 methodological questions related to the "text" and the "reader(s)" in modern theological hermeneutics tend to be reduced to issues related only to the *human* agency in each. For example, the role of the "text" is normally thought of in terms of the "intention" or "composition" of the human authors, the literary and grammatical shape of the text, and/or the actions of redactors, editors, canonizers and so on. Likewise, the evaluation of the "reader" or "readers" normally focuses on the reading tradition and/or the place of contemporary interpreters and reading communities. Indicating this propensity contemporary conversations tend to travel along the very bottom of the triangle, between text and reader and very near the bottom horizontal line representing human agency. The figure below shows this:

---

[10] Werner Jeanrond, *Theological Hermeneutics* (New York, 1991), chapters 4 and 5.

[11] Bradford E. Hinze, "Reclaiming Rhetoric in the Christian Tradition" *Theological Studies* 57 (Sept., 1996), p. 491.

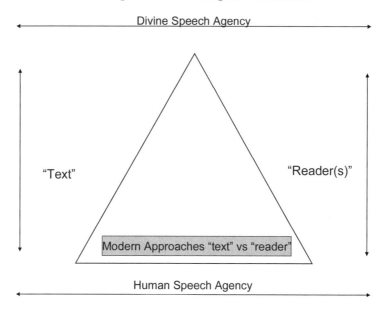

Fig 2.1   The Triangle and Modern Hermeneutics: Coordinating Divine and Human Action

However, if beliefs related to divine agency are, as we have suggested, ingredient in these debates then the presently accepted construal of the problem which travels the bottom of the triangle between "text" and "reader" neglects and ignores this vertical dimension. Further, it will not suffice to reply simply that the role of divine agency is "assumed." It is certainly true that pre-critical writers and readers casually approached the question of reading Scripture with a robust view of God's causal accompaniment. However, the time when this could be taken so easily as given has long been eclipsed, and the careful and intentional articulation of the place and role of divine agency in the hermeneutics of reading Scripture is now, as much or more than any time in history, requisite.

The composition of the text of Scripture, as well as the act of reading and interpreting Scripture, are complex activities; complicated in the interrelationship of so many facets of action which involve both divine and human agency. The role the church plays in the reception and acknowledgment of a select group of writings comprising the canon is one more obvious example of one facet of this complex activity that can only be adequately accounted for from within such a framework.[12] In fact, there ultimately is no adequate account of the unity of the canon apart from

---

[12] See John Webster: "The Dogmatic Location of the Canon" in *Neue Zeitschrift Für Systematische Theologie* 43 (2001): 17-43, and "Hermeneutics in Modern Theology" in *Scottish Journal of Theology* 51 (1998): 307-41.

its divine underwriting. Further, all of the coincidental activities which comprise the composition and reception of the text of Scripture are only adequately analyzed with respect to the interaction between the divine and human agents.

The typology we are constructing seeks to offer a clarification of the broader issues involved in the reading and interpretation of Scripture as it is located and enacted in this space between the two horizontal planes of divine and human action and between the vertical planes of text and reader. To illuminate this relationship we construct a typology in the shape of a triangle which sits inside these four planes. The first two corners of the triangle rest on the bottom plane of human action and indicate our first two "types." The bottom left corner is occupied by approaches that give greatest weight to human agency in the "text" in the act of reading. The bottom right corner, as the second type, likewise, gives greater weight to the "reader" or "readers." The third corner of the triangle as the third type is near the top plane representing divine action. Preference for divine agency in one's hermeneutics dictates that one is located in this corner, and the degree to which the emphasis is made, the more extreme one's location. Each of these three present a distinct yet indispensable aspect of the agency invested in any and all accounts of the act of reading Scripture. This is illustrated below.

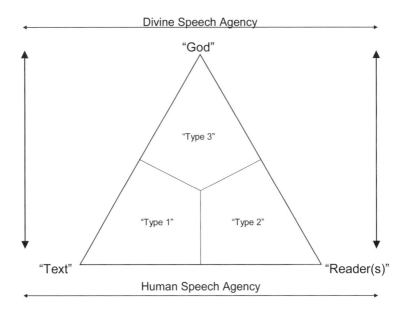

Fig 2.2 The Triangle Typology: Mapping the Three Types

The issues that animate each type can be also mundanely represented by three questions respectively: the bottom left corner by "What does the text enact or contain of human speech action?"; the bottom right corner by "What does the reader or reading community enact?" or "How is the text read or appropriated?"; and the top corner by "What does God do or say in the composition and/or reading of Scripture?"

Type One: Human Agency in/through the text of Scripture

The bottom left corner of the triangle is our first "type" and is related to the question of what the text of Scripture enacts or contains. This corner rests near the plane representing human action and indicates the various synchronic and diachronic human activities which reside in and express themselves through the text of Scripture. This includes any and all activities which comprise the composition of the text whether by a single author or by a "community." Type one also includes issues related to any subsequent arranging and editing of the text as well as the reception and identification of the books included in the Christian Canon. The majority of post-enlightenment biblical scholars would be a variety of this type.

Chapter 3 will be devoted to surveying some of the more influential recent hermeneutic proposals of type one which indicate a tendency to prioritize or emphasize the content or action of the text over against or above the issues related to the other two types. Late twentieth century theological figures whose work will be surveyed in Chapter 3 include the early work of Hans Frei,[13] Kevin Vanhoozer,[14] and Francis Watson.[15] These three were selected because they remain influential, they show development and movement in the course of their writing and also because they each possess distinctive emphases within the variety of options available to type one. They, then, illustrate some range within this corner and the ability of this typology to account for a greater level of subtlety.

Type Two: Human Agency in the reading and reception of Scripture

The bottom right corner of the triangle is our second type and is related to the question of how Scripture is read or appropriated. It also resides on the plane of human action and indicates a similar preoccupation in giving preference to the range of human activity involved in the interpretation, and appropriation of Scripture in its being read. Studies which examine the implications of a "reader-response" approach

---

[13] Hans Frei, *The Identity of Jesus Christ* (Philadelphia, 1975); *The Eclipse of Biblical Narrative* (New Haven, 1974); and *Theology and Narrative*. See bibliography for other relevant works by Frei.

[14] Kevin Vanhoozer, *Is There a Meaning in This Text?* (Grand Rapids, 1998), and *First Theology* (Downer's Grove, 2002). See bibliography for full details of Vanhoozer's hermeneutical writing.

[15] Francis Watson, *Text, Church and World* (Edinburgh, 1994) and *Text and Truth* (Edinburgh, 1997).

to Scripture or which focus on how the reader "uses" Scripture are two better known recent examples of this type. Also included are recently popular approaches that explore the role the community plays in the reading of Scripture. Questions that will further assist us in representing this second type include "What do readers do?" or "how is the text read and/or appropriated?" In Chapter 4 we will survey varieties of this second type. They include David Kelsey, (the later work of) Hans Frei, Werner Jeanrond and Stephen Fowl.

Summarizing to this point, both types one and two stand at bottom right and left corners of a triangle respectively. They both rest on the bottom plane representing human action. Type one is approaches which enter into the reading of Scripture by giving methodological and authoritative priority to some aspect of human activity present in the text or presented by the text. Type two perceives the definitive aspect of the reading as residing in the human agency identified in the function, use or appropriation of the text. This agency and action is determined by the reader or community of readers.

The epistemological ideas we described in the first chapter resulted in two tendencies which both have had a strong influence on these first two types. First, there is an increased focus on immanent objects of attention; on things that are immediately accessible to the human senses as being the best or sole focus for study. Second, there is a decisive and exacting bias against antecedent judgments; especially those deriving from the influence of another agent on the act or investigation of the knowing agent. Both of these influences combined to repress any attention to the constructive role for God's agency in either the agency contained and enacted by the text as well as the divine agency that influences the reading of Scripture. This resulted in modern readers and interpreters of Scripture becoming increasingly preoccupied with the study of human actions present either in the text and/or in the reading while, at the same time, increasingly neglecting divine actions that precede and accompany each.

Both of our first two types are characterized by this preoccupation. Both the subject-reader and the object-text are immanently proscribed in ways not unlike Kant in his epistemological model for obtaining knowledge. They approach their description of the reading of Scripture as if it is ideally done by knowing subjects in the absence of the influence of any other agent, human or divine. It is in this idealized mode that type one gives preference to the human activity that is enacted within or is contained within the text of Scripture while type two gives preference to the human acts of reading and interpreting the text. There is an analogous relationship between this hermeneutical propensity in modern approaches to reading Scripture with ways of doing theology. So: just as there is a tendency to do "Christology from below" or "natural theology" so also to do "hermeneutics from below" and "natural hermeneutics."

We have suggested that the first two types are characterized by having been influenced by the preoccupation with human agency and action as advocated by epistemological preferences in the Enlightenment tradition. This should *not* be interpreted to mean that these aspects and the range of issues represented in these types are inappropriate or incorrect. On the contrary, these two both represent necessary features of reading Scripture. Approaches which occupy either of these first two types are only partially adequate, however, and incomplete in two senses: first, insofar as they neglect the relevant issues that they represent to each other; second, insofar as they neglect the fundamental hermeneutical dynamics that are only properly considered within the auspice of divine agency.

Type Three: Divine Agency in the Hermeneutics of Scripture

The top corner of the triangle is the third type. The question "What does God say or do in, with, and under both the text and reading of Scripture?" indicates the priorities of this type. Divine agency is normally considered to be the theological, dogmatic, or confessional concern and is typically viewed as being a separate or subsequent consideration in hermeneutical and theological methodologies. Representatives of this type, however, resist this characterization and describe Scripture and its reading initially or primarily from the standpoint of divine activity and, in turn, subordinate questions about the human action present in the text and in the reading. They emphasize Scripture insofar as it is the result, and continuing instrument, of God's self-involved speech action. This third type will be represented in our survey by two philosophers and a theologian: Karl Barth,[16] Nicholas Wolterstorff, and James K. A. Smith.

It might initially seem odd to associate these thinkers. Although the views of these Christian dogmatists and philosophers differ greatly on the legitimacy of the referential function and capacity of language to describe divine action, they do share a common commitment to acknowledging the appropriate direction and shaping that human action receives from divine activity or transcendent agency—transcendent action which in some sense precedes and encompasses human action. They will also demonstrate some variance in the *degree* to which they express this emphasis.

Finally, a few words of caution should be offered here about what many may fear is an inherently violent or hegemonous character of typologies. In mapping these thinkers I am *not* suggesting that any individual, as a member of any "type," indicates the issues represented by that type to the absolute exclusion of the others. What I *am* saying is that these three facets represent aspects of reading of Scripture which are necessarily interwoven in *any and all* readings of Scripture. So the location within the taxonomy that the various accounts of reading the Bible will be given are measured and mapped by how they negotiate and mix together these facets and how they prioritize and arrange them. Each "type," then, is simply the grouping that shares the preferencing of one of the three aspects over the other two. Further, a strength of this way of doing a typology is that we will be able to show movement in many of the individuals that we will survey: movement that in several cases actually takes them to the border of, or into, one of the other types.

In some cases an approach in one type may be proximately closer to approaches in one of the other two types than to the more extreme positions in their own "type." For example, we will see Hans Frei, in his later writing, emphasize human agency in both the text and the reading community. This places him in type two but very near

---

[16]   Karl Barth, *Church Dogmatics*, 14 Volumes (Edinburgh, 1956-1975).

the midpoint between the bottom right and left corners. In this position he will be closer to some type ones who are located just across this midpoint to the left than to extreme type twos who occupy positions at the extreme end of the right corner.

This is another way that this typology has an advantage over others which tend to arrange their types along a linear, one dimensional axis. A two dimensional field is more flexible and better equipped to allow the particularity of individual approaches to be seen and is less prone to distort the particular nuances of individual work while still assisting us in seeing the relationship of one approach to another.

A Clarifying Conversation With Four Other Typologies

We will now briefly discuss four other typologies which will assist us in illuminating some of the features of our triangle. First we will discuss Niebuhr's *Christ and Culture* and Frei's *Types of Theology*. One feature we will highlight in relation to these is that the more extreme position one occupies in a typology the more that approach is removed from a more constructive and balanced relationship to the other issue or issues. Thus the extreme corners of our triangle, as well as the outer edge, are positions that few, if any, really occupy. The edge of the triangle should not, then, be seen as a position that can be assumed, but rather as a limit. Niebuhr and Frei both have linear typologies and both also saw the two positions at the far ends of their typologies as extremes and not truly viable as actual positions as compares to the moderate and mediating positions between them. [17]

To begin: both Niebuhr's *Christ and Culture* and Frei's *Types of Theology* trade on a similar idea; the negotiation of two metaphorical entities pertaining to the doing of theology. Niebuhr names this the tension between "Christ" and "culture" as "the double wrestle of the church with its Lord and with the cultural society with which it lives in symbiosis."[18] He has five types, two of which are "extreme" and "non-mediating". These two non-mediating types are "Christ of culture" and "Christ against culture". He, again, sees the strict occupation of either of the non-mediating positions as realistically impossible. If Christ and culture are coincidental then it makes no sense to talk about the church of Christ as a distinct entity. Conversely, the church cannot exist in absolute abstraction from culture in that Christians invariably interact with those who are not Christians and the production of human culture is a process by which influence between Christians and non-Christians is simultaneous and co-operative. The real options for Niebuhr, then, lie with the three mediating types which assume constructive positions relative to *both* Christ and culture.[19] The

---

[17] Frei was clear on this point. In a letter to William Placher dated the 11th of March, 1986, he writes "I haven't made much progress, I regret to say, on my typology, but I hope you'll at least discuss the possibility I tried to raise in it, viz., that theologians may have a *range* of possibilities for relating theological (or Christian) to other instances of rational argument and other instances of 'truth', and not simply *one*." (emphasis his) New Haven, Yale University Library, Divinity Library Special Collections, Record Group No. 76, Box 4, Folder 78.

[18] Niebuhr, *Christ and Culture,* p. ix.

[19] Yoder's well known blustery and largely ad hominem attack of Niebuhr's typology should be mentioned here—John Howard Yoder "How H. Richard Niebuhr Reasoned: A

issue Niebuhr wants to confront us with is, then, not *whether* one negotiates them but *how* one negotiates the relationship between the two in particular theological circumstances. It is important to note that, for Niebuhr, the approach one assumes may not be the same every time. He is careful to acknowledge that specific thinkers will variably, in an ad-hoc fashion, express themselves in ways which will sometimes make them more representative of one type and at other times another.[20]

Similarly Frei's types one and five stand at either end of the spectrum of his typology, in relative positions to Niebuhr's non-mediating extreme types. Frei's analysis is focused on the tension between the Christian community's internal self-understanding and self-description and the descriptions of Christianity which originate externally to it. He uses spatial metaphors of internal and external to represent the two alternate milieus to be related in the typology.[21] Frei's five types represent different weightings of the internal and external descriptions. Types two and one give greater and greatest weight respectively to the external. Likewise types four and five increasingly rely in Christianity's self-descriptions to the exclusion of those that come from outside it. Frei's type three attempts something of a balancing act between the two.

Both Frei and Niebuhr see the coordination of the two facets they each describe as necessary. Likewise, our triangle typology sees all three facets we describe as necessary. Niebuhr sees the relationship of the two as requisitely related entities for the Christian engaging ethical and political issues. Frei argues for the necessity for the Church to wrestle with both its internal and external descriptions. Our triangle typology suggests that all three: the human action that constitutes and is enacted by the text, the human action of reading and appropriating the text, and the divine action that accompanies and constitutes both the text and the reading are all necessary features of a Christian biblical hermeneutic.

One notable difference between our typology and theirs is that they create sub-types within the range between their two extreme types. Both Niebuhr and Frei describe three moderate types. Our typology will not do this but will allow the individuals we survey to demonstrate the uniqueness of each of their positions within the triangle, each uniquely relative to the three facets. In this important sense this triangle typology is *only* comprised of mediating types. Further, while we will still retain the language of "type" one or "type" two this operates as shorthand language

---

Critique of Christ and Culture," pp. 31-90 in *Authentic Transformation: A New Vision of Christ and Culture* edited by Glen Stassen (Nashville, 1996). One of Yoder's primary concerns is that the entities "Christ" and "culture" are too abstract and inevitably distort the particular historical expression. However the question remains whether Niebuhr himself understood the *ad hoc* nature of his typology, which I believe he did, and, despite the abstraction, whether there is still value in using metaphors like "Christ" and "culture" and setting them in various kinds of relationships in order to engage people's critical imaginations. Is the apostle John no less abstract in his use of metaphors and setting in critical relationship the notions of "light" and "darkness"? Or Paul with "flesh" and "spirit"? Or Jesus with the "kingdom of earth" and "kingdom of heaven"?

[20] Niebuhr, *Christ and Culture,* pp. 43-4.

[21] Frei, *Types,* pp. 20-21.

for a *range* and *space* within the triangle whereas for Frei and Niebuhr the "type" is more a punctiliar idea; a point on a line.

We will now discuss two other typologies which influence the creation of the triangle typology in that they both offer analysis that is suggestive of the unique focus of this book; the accounting of both human and divine action in the hermeneutics of Scripture. They each contribute to this in different ways. They are George Lindbeck's *The Nature of Doctrine* and James Buckley's article "Beyond the Hermeneutical Deadlock."

George Lindbeck's *The Nature of Doctrine* is an attempt to reorient the perception of doctrines in a way that is both faithful to the broader Christian tradition and that would help in easing unnecessary tension in ecumenical disagreements.[22] He sees these tensions as arising more from commitments to modern philosophical ways of thinking and arguing than from real or confessional disagreements. In response he advocates viewing the nature and function of doctrine as a controlling grammar for confessional language. This, in turn, will create a less encumbered way of assisting ecumenical participants in moving toward more constructive ground in their discussions. In *The Nature of Doctrine* Lindbeck identifies those contemporary terms which unduly hamper the ecumenical discussion.

On the one hand, he is critical of those bogged down in questions about the referential nature of language; the "propositional" approach. On the other, he criticizes those who rely too much on anthropological or existential categories; the "experiential-expressivists." He sees both as being invested in philosophical frameworks owing more to the Enlightenment than to the Christian tradition.[23]

Lindbeck suggests that both of these are indebted to the Kantian "turn to the subject."[24] Considering how these groups would advocate the selection and implementation of their methodology, Lindbeck hints that they both, in this sense, can seen as variations of the same tendency.[25] Drawing from his discussion we extend this observation to discuss the implications of each approach in the way they read Scripture as well.

They both share certain critical features in their thinking about Scriptural hermeneutics. They embrace the unique meaningfulness and authority of the original Christian religious utterances. They locate with or within the original expressions a

---

[22] This locates Lindbeck's book in a particular location which is almost always disregarded. Lindbeck once remarked to me both that he was disappointed in how strongly the book has been read as a "grand epistemological proposal" or "philosophy of religion" (which was not his intention) and, given how dominant this reading had become, that he has come to be influenced to read the book that way himself. On this see the important correctives to the reading of *The Nature of Doctrine* that Lindbeck has recently made available to English audiences: "Foreward to the German Edition of *The Nature of Doctrine*," in *The Church in a Postliberal Age* (Grand Rapids, 2002), pp. 196-200; also George Lindbeck's "Response to Avery Cardinal Dulles," *First Things*, January, 2004, pp. 13-5.

[23] So Reinhard Hütter, *Suffering Divine Things* (Grand Rapids, 2000), p. 45 ff.

[24] Lindbeck, *Nature*, pp. 24 ff.

[25] Lindbeck, *Nature*, p. 20, 51. Lindbeck discusses here the common heritage that these types share in being variously indebted to modernity and specifically Immanuel Kant's influence. Below I suggest that Lindbeck's cultural-linguistic model also shares in the debt.

unique quality or content of that meaningfulness which is decisive for later Christians. Critical, historical, philosophical and sociological investigative methods are used by both to unearth or distill that unique meaningfulness or content. These methods are employed in a host of ways and means to study facets of immanent human activity related to either the origin of the text or reading of the Bible. Finally, certain Enlightenment ideals about the "objective" context for the study and derivation of this content are embraced as normative.

The point where the two differ is that propositionalists see the definitive and authoritative content as being deposited in the words and text of Scripture, usually as this relates to the specific intentions of the human authors of Scripture while experiential-expressivists locate the authority in the experiences of Christ and by extension in that of those who were with Him and see the expressions of Scripture as symbolically related to those experiences.

Lindbeck's alternative to these approaches to doctrine is his well known "cultural-linguistic approach" where "emphasis is placed on those respects in which religion resemble languages ... and are thus similar to cultures." The function of doctrine is how they function as "communally authoritative rules of discourse, attitude, and action."[26] Lindbeck is convinced that the groups indicated above have all conceded to authorities external to the Christian faith the power to indicate and adjudicate the content and expression of the faith of the Christian community. He sees his alternative as a way to constructively rehabilitate a properly constructive role for traditional doctrine in ecumenical engagements without disturbing the hornet's nests of issues that are normally pressed by the other two approaches.

There is an omission in Lindbeck's account which is indicative for the development of our hermeneutical typology and, in particular, for the creation of a two dimensional space which overtly seeks to account for divine action in the third "type." In his proposal he considers the function of doctrine abstracted from theological particularities,[27] particularities which he himself is dependent in making his proposal. Reinhard Hütter describes this:

> Here [between the model's universal character and the notion of intratextual theology] a central element of tension emerges in Lindbeck's model between form and content. Although the model presupposes this tension on the one hand in order to function as

---

[26]   Lindbeck, *Nature*, p.18.

[27]   The critical remarks that follow are substantially in agreement with Hütter, *Suffering Divine Things*, (Grand Rapids: Eerdmans, 2000) pp. 40-69. Lindbeck wrote in a review that Hütter's account "contains the best description and most interesting criticisms of my own postliberalism that I have seen." (back cover). George Hunsinger criticizes Lindbeck along somewhat similar lines in "Truth as Self-Involving: Barth and Lindbeck on the Cognitive and Performative Aspects of Truth in Theological Discourse" *Journal of the American Academy of Religion 61* (1993), pp. 41-56. Hütter better accounts for the limited scope of Lindbeck's argument than Hunsinger. As a result Hunsinger's criticisms can border on exaggeration. Nevertheless, because Lindbeck tends to be widely read as if he is making a larger more comprehensive methodological proposal, Hunsinger's criticisms are generally more pertinent. Also see Hütter's discussion of Hunsinger's criticisms, pp. 54-6 and endnotes.

a formal and universal model, that very tension is undermined by the impossibility of abstracting the descriptive activity from the text itself.[28]

Adopting the terms from our analysis above, we suggest that Lindbeck does not adequately address the ingredient and necessary role that antecedent judgments as beliefs about God's action plays in the doing of theology.[29] In other words, the "grammar" of doctrine derives its directive power from a network of confessional and dogmatic claims that ultimately reside in certain beliefs about God's nature and agency. Hütter is concerned with the ecclesial dimensions of these beliefs: the more fundamental issue, we suggest, resides with the "hidden" beliefs about God. This tension is expressed in Lindbeck's writing in a way that is congenial to our efforts to rehabilitate the essential question of divine agency in biblical hermeneutics. Lindbeck has a tendency to talk in certain ways about doctrine that parallels the way that our types one and two talk about reading Scripture. For example, throughout *The Nature of Doctrine* he writes as if religions, cultures, languages, doctrines and creeds are agents. Here are a few examples:

[A]t least part of the task of doctrines is to recommend and exclude ... What is innovative about the present proposal is that this becomes the only job that doctrines do ....[30]

[A] religion can be viewed as a kind of cultural and/or linguistic framework of medium that shapes the entirety of life and thought. It functions somewhat like a Kantian *a priori* ... Like a culture or language, it is a communal phenomenon that shapes the subjectivity of individuals rather than being primarily a manifestation of those subjectivities.[31]

Thus while a religion's truth claims are often of the utmost importance to it (as in the case of Christianity), it is nevertheless, the conceptual vocabulary and the syntax or inner logic which determine the kinds of truth claims the religion can make.[32]

Lindbeck is certainly not alone in talking this way, that is, in attributing agency to abstract entities apart from acknowledging the particular personal agents which give them their shape and impetus. Likewise, it is fashionable in literary, biblical and theological circles to talk as though things like books and doctrines act.[33] There is a glaring opacity in this, however. Books and doctrines don't really "do"

---

[28] Hütter, *Suffering*, p. 60. In the original text the entire quote is italicized.

[29] So Hütter who writes, "[T]he substantively and ecumenically qualified formal character of Lindbeck's proposal precludes any explicit, concrete development of theological discourse as a church practice and of the substantive pathos characterizing the church itself." *Suffering*, p. 41.

[30] Lindbeck, *Nature,* p. 19.

[31] Lindbeck, *Nature,* p. 33.

[32] Lindbeck, *Nature,* p. 35.

[33] "Meanings are not simply lodged within a text to remain there inert until they are extracted by readers; the meaning of a text is not something that is cut off from and made independent of the actions involved in producing and interpreting a text." Clarance Walhout, "Narrative Hermeneutics" In *The Promise of Hermeneutics* (Grand Rapids, 1999). pp. 66.

anything. Agents do things by means of books and doctrines.[34] In Lindbeck's case this vocabulary facilitates the consideration of the function of doctrine in ecumenical discussions, keeping at bay the persistent and often distorting modern debates about language and reference. We should and do sympathize with his intention. These debates have certainly often contributed to oppressive and violent ways of thinking and acting.

However, the discussion of "what religions or doctrines do" if left there, is only an abstract metaphor, a shorthand way of talking about an activity that involves both human and divine agents. It assumes some form of this agency but fails to describe this more fundamental and important issue: what God, human creatures and the Church are doing with religions and doctrines. A series of questions impose themselves at this juncture. Is the community using them in the way he describes? Is God? If both, then how do these actions relate to each other? If God is not uniquely active in electing this community's action, then what makes *this* community's use of doctrines preferable or authoritative over an alternative community's use of these or other doctrines? And most importantly, how does the understanding of how these activities relate direct one's own, in this case Lindbeck's, thinking about the nature of doctrines? If we cannot ask and (albeit imperfectly) answer these questions then how or why should we even attempt to negotiate between conflicting views of various religious and non-religious communities and their various uses of doctrine? To neglect the underlying issue of divine agency in discussing the nature and function of doctrine potentially undermines the very rationality for engaging in ecumenical discussions in the first place.

However, despite Lindbeck's efforts to keep his analysis unencumbered by this sort of dogmatic complication, his way of talking about what religions and doctrines do nevertheless demonstrates a particular shape of divine agency.[35] Thus, at a minimum, he would affirm the ongoing action of God in the work of the Holy Spirit in the tradition of the church, particularly when that tradition reaches some degree of collective consensus, such as the case with the canon and the ecumenical councils. Nevertheless, insofar as Lindbeck neglects to name divine agency as such or account for the presence of divine agency in the nature and function of doctrine, he leaves open the possibility of readers of his work proscribing and attributing that agency strictly to immanent human spheres. Therefore, without an accounting of divine agency his proposal does not *necessarily* effect anything more than a shift from an individual synchronic subjectivity exhibited in the "experiential-expressivists" and "propositionalists" to a collective diachronic subjectivity in the "cultural-linguistic."[36] In the end, the more exacting critique of the Kantian turn to the subject in the eclipse of *divine* agency is missed.

---

[34]   James Buckley, *Seeking the Humanity of God* (Collegeville, 1992), p. 58.

[35]   So Hütter; "Lindbeck offers an explanatory model that must leave implicit his own specific context of justification, namely, a 'theology of the church,' so that it may remain a theologically neutral model and thus be ecumenically acceptable to everyone." *Suffering Divine Things*, p. 46.

[36]   Hütter writes, "If intratextuality is not to break up reflexively and become fixed in formalized intersubjectivity (as the continuation and differentiation of the logic of subjectivity),

Lindbeck's own vocabulary in describing the nature and function of doctrine hints at a constellation of constructive theological assumptions, not least of which is a view of God's empowering and facilitating activity in the living tradition of the church. These are the operational and notional antecedent judgments underwriting Lindbeck's proposal.[37] At the heart of these is a healthy theology proper and it is here (insofar as it can be discerned) that one can and should begin to negotiate the differences between his and other approaches.[38] For the purposes of our typology Lindbeck demonstrates both the impossibility of abstracting one's talk about theological questions from a horizon of articulable dogmatic commitments and the centrality of questions about agency, particularly God's agency, as a foundational and determinative feature of that horizon.

Insofar as this is true for the discussion of theological method and the nature and function of doctrine it becomes an even more compelling issue in the consideration of proposals for the reading of Scripture. So when Christian theologians, biblical scholars and hermeneuticians talk about what the "text does" and neglect the implicit dogmatic shape of that talk, they ignore the same fundamental issue that Lindbeck neglects in talking about what "doctrines do" even as they risk even greater theological perils as Scripture's authority is of a higher order than doctrine.

At this point James Buckley provides some helpful guidance. Buckley, a student of Frei and Lindbeck's, in his article "Beyond the Hermeneutical Deadlock" presents what was a singular muse in the construction of the argument of this chapter. In it he sets up a typology which bears a formal affinity to Lindbeck's yet points in the direction of some of the theological sensitivities regarding divine agency which Frei and Lindbeck neglect. His article also brings the discussion directly to the point of our typology; the reading and interpretation of Scripture.

Buckley presents as an advocating voice between three groups of theories in hermeneutics: "revelationalists", "functionalists" and "textualists."[39] He seeks to reorient the shared assumptions about the debate between these groups. They tend to, he suggests, reduce the discussion of hermeneutics to the questions of "what is Scripture about?" (revelationalists), "what is Scripture?" (textualists), or "how is Scripture used?" (functionalists).[40] He insightfully argues that those who seemingly commit themselves to one as opposed to the other two positions have necessary commitments to all three, and so the real question should not be seen as choosing among mutually exclusive options but rather of relatedness and priority among

---

then only a substantively developed pneumatology as a salvific-economic explication of the doctrine of the Trinity will be able to examine thematically the poiesis underlying the pathos of consistent, that is, soteriologically explicit, intertextuality." *Suffering Divine Things*, p. 63.

[37] This is not a criticism. It is the unshakeable commitment to orthodoxy that Lindbeck indicates here that should be appreciated as being the primary motivation behind his work.

[38] George Lindbeck, "The Bible as Realistic Narrative" in *Consensus in Theology?* (Philadelphia, 1980), pp. 81-5.

[39] Buckley, "Deadlock," pp. 187-203. These three do not have a strict relationship with our three types.

[40] Buckley, "Deadlock," pp. 194-5.

them.[41] His discussion of the revelationalists group is of particular relevance. There he suggests that the common characterization of the intramural debates[42] among revelationalists tends to define their differences as views of the mode of the presence of the *same* God. He provocatively suggests, however, that

> In reality, these are not different ways of describing or imagining God. They are…different gods. Indeed, I think it would be even more accurate to say that these are not only different gods but different religions….[43]

As Buckley moves on to discuss functionalists and textualists he does not raise this point again but he could and, we argue, should. The triangle typology pushes this argument it to its full logical conclusion. Thus the differences that he denotes among revelationalists as being ascribable to their having different gods in view also applies for functionalists and textualists. So, the differences between representatives of each who focus on "what Scripture does" and "what Scripture is," can also be directly attributed to their differing perceptions about what God does and who God is respectively. The intramural differences among the three groups can then be coordinated at a more encompassing and fundamental level. That is, in discrepancies attributable directly to their varied, and sometimes conflicting, antecedent judgments about God's nature and agency.

This is a natural consequence of Buckley's discussion and reinforces the argument we have been building in relation to the triangle typology. Thus the beliefs pertaining to divine activity that underwrite these accounts becomes a kind of "confessional" logic that accompanies all accounts of reading Scripture. As this relates to our typology the reading of the Bible just as in the doing of dogmatics or theological method, there is always a confessional aspect at work, standing in, with, and under the reading and interpretation. This confession is rooted in and includes both affirmations and denials concerning the nature of God and claims regarding divine activity: beliefs pertaining to whether and how God reveals Himself in and/or through this book, beliefs about Jesus Christ and His relationship to the various facets involved in the production and reading of the Bible, and the activity of the Holy Spirit in the formation and maintenance of the Christian church particularly in the composition, collection, preservation and interpretation of Scripture. In saying this I do not mean to make the additional claim that the church "gives" these qualities to the Bible or to its reading. Rather, that our employment of this or that method in reading Scripture is directed by what we understand and acknowledge as qualities of this book which includes, at the most basic and formative level, a confessional stance towards the nature and origin of divine agency and the patterns by which we assume God relates to all the aspects of the production and reading of Scripture in all of its salient features. This brings us back to confirm an important feature of the triangle typology; that approaches to reading Scripture will indicate a position relative to both human and divine action and, thus, to all three corners of the triangle.

---

[41] Buckley, "Deadlock," pp. 189 ff.

[42] Buckley, "Deadlock," pp. 190-2.

[43] Buckley, "Deadlock," pp. 190-1.

Summary: Looking Back and Looking Ahead

The rationale and shape of the triangle typology is now established. We have constructed a triangle with three "types," positions, facets, or orientations at each of its corners. These three facets are represented by the three questions: What does Scripture say and do? What do readers do?, and What does God say and do? The first two questions (and types) are characterized by preoccupations with immanent fields of human action. The last question, as the third type, is indicated by attentiveness to God's action in, with and under both Scripture's character as divine speech and the action of the reader(s).

The primary defining attributes of types one and two are reflexively related to the limiting features of the Enlightenment as indicated in the Kantian epistemology we described in Chapter 1. Thus the modern biblical interpreter (insofar as he or she indicates a tendency toward either type one or two) ideally views his or her task as one which should set aside dogmatic or confessional predisposition, which, by definition, includes any prior acknowledgment of God's action in shaping the reader and the reading moment. Insofar as this is true they accept the Enlightenment's criticism and limitation of antecedent judgments. Presuppositions, they would say, should be set aside, or kept as minimal as possible.

Modern biblical scholars, to the degree that they fall into these two types, then, perceive the initial and/or decisive task of reading Scripture as focusing on various modes or byproducts of human activity which comprises aspects of either the biblical text as a human expression (type one) or in the human activity constituent in the interactive use, function, reception or reading of the book (type two). Whether their initial focus is on the compositional efforts of the human author; the editorial work of a redactor; the social, cultural, or rhetorical setting of the occasion of the text; the underlying core religious experience of the original or contemporary community or individual; or the response to or use of the text by the reader or the community of readers; all of these approaches pursue the question of making sense of the text of Scripture primarily, initially, decisively, or exclusively in immanent anthropological spheres of activity as immanent objects seen as either a feature in the text or human byproducts of the text, or in human reactions to or uses of the text.

The question of the particular shape of God's activity in, with, and under those processes is typically "set aside" as a secondary (at best) question, or irrelevant (at worst). The net result is that they find themselves, at the end of their task, in the well known position of having to make some sort of "leap" in order to make the material suitable for preaching or relevant as they are faced with having to join together their work with some overt aspect of divine agency as a shaping influence on the lives of God's people. The greater the perceived need for a leap at this point, the greater is the real possibility that the particular work is organically unrelated (or irrelevant) to the task of proclamation or spiritual formation. The origin and nature of the "great gulf fixed" between not only professional biblical studies and the life of the Church, but also between it and all the various specialty theological areas makes perfect (albeit tragic) sense if both the character of the Enlightenment epistemological limitations and their influence continues to be as pervasive as is suggested.

These tendencies in biblical studies are, from one standpoint, understandable. It is difficult to conceive of describing God's action in these arenas without appealing to confessional or dogmatic language. To make such a claim about the shape of the action of "supersensible objects" prior to the act of investigation is, according to Kant, the highest form of treason to the freedom of reason. Christian scholars are naturally sensitive to charges that their work is of lesser consistency or value in relation to their non-Christian counterparts and would want to avoid this accusation, assuming it to be valid.

Additionally, throughout history, religious and political issues have been inextricably interrelated in unhealthy ways. For the Reformers, as for Descartes and Spinoza, as for many others, the invocation of dogmatic language had grave (literally) political implications. The setting aside of dogmatic language and the separation of questions of faith and reason, like church and state, was viewed as a political move to assist in relieving the bloody political tensions, and was also seen as potentially alleviating the social oppression which was often the result in the wedding of religious dogma and political rule.

Taking up theological questions again, often in political terms, so-called postmodern developments in the reading of Scripture helpfully remind us of these problems, but insofar as they pursue their work in acceptance of the Enlightenment's criticisms of antecedent judgments they most often represent a kind of high modernity and only offer partial (at best) help.[44] As long as they ignore the issue of the proper and necessary role for antecedent judgments of *both* types they inevitably repeat the errors of the oppressive systems which they denounce in that they deny the very descriptive capacity of language necessary to rhetorically indicate, contrast, and effect reform and change. There are, however, hopeful hints and murmurs in some recent writings which attempt to constructively engage postmodern thought and be faithful to Christ.[45]

In addition to the typologies and works named and discussed above, this work also stands constructively indebted to the work of John Webster[46] and Nicholas Wolterstorff.[47] Wolterstorff and Webster want to acknowledge the formative role that divine or transcendent action plays in the event of reading Scripture even as they do so from various perspectives and in different manners (Wolterstorff is a philosopher

---

[44]   On this point see the two excellent studies by Linda Hutcheon, *A Poetics of Postmodernism* (New York, 1988), and *The Politics of Postmodernism* (New York, 1989).

[45]   *Renewing Biblical Interpretation* (Grand Rapids, 2000), and *After Pentecost: Language and Biblical Interpretation* (Grand Rapids, 2001), both edited by Craig Bartholomew, Colin Greene and Karl Möller; *The Rule of Faith: Scripture, Canon and Creed in a Critical Age* (Harrisburg, 1998), edited by Ephraim Radner and George Sumner; *Theology and Scriptural Imagination* (Oxford, 1998), edited by L. Gregory Jones and James J. Buckley; *Reclaiming the Bible for the Church* (Grand Rapids, 1995), edited by Carl Braaten and Robert Jenson; *Theological Exegesis: Essays in Honor of Brevard S. Childs* (Grand Rapids, 1999), edited by Christopher Seitz and Kathryn Greene-McCreight; and Stephen Fowl and L. Gregory Jones, *Reading in Communion: Scripture & Ethics in Christian Life* (Grand Rapids, 1991).

[46]   John Webster, *Word and Church* (Edinburgh, 2002).

[47]   Nicholas Wolterstorff, *Divine Discourse* (Cambridge, 1995) and *Art in Action* (Grand Rapids, 1980).

of Dutch Reformed background; Webster an Anglican dogmatic theologian). It is this instinct in their work in particular that I want to push a bit harder to its more resolute conclusion. I want to argue that *all* readings, as well as descriptions of the reading, of Scripture implicitly assume a position or stance with respect to the accompanying action and agency of God. Demonstrating the presence of beliefs pertaining to divine action which accompany the approaches named in the three types above will be one of the chief aims of the chapters that follow. In the process the author's own preferences and views will gain a sympathetic location within the work of these thinkers even as we seek ground beyond them. In pushing beyond and in the survey that follows it will become clear that some of the figures we will discuss have not fully resolved the limiting role of the Enlightenment's epistemology. This is often indicated in the continued hesitancy exhibited in exploring and acknowledging the constituent relationship of a "rule of faith" in, with, and under all accounts and enactments of reading Scripture. For our purposes, the traditional role of the rule of faith and how it was perceived also assists us in challenging the Enlightenment limitations on antecedent judgments described above and would be a fruitful direction to pursue in constructing an alternative way to construe the reading of Scripture.[48]

To gauge the indebtedness to a "rule of faith" in the approaches we survey in the following three chapters we will identify the confessional, theological, doctrinal, and dogmatic implications of their use of language about agency, both human and divine, in their hermeneutical descriptions. As contra indications we will also attend to the various appeals they may make to a broad range of general theories of literary hermeneutics. These theories normally do not have the Christian reading of Scripture in mind. Thus they are only variously (at best) compelled to deal with the question of transcendent agency and action and even when they do so, for example in a work like George Steiner's *Real Presences*,[49] tend to in strictly non-specific categories, which does little in assisting the confessionally Christian reader to understand the particular shape that the influence that prior divine action has in the human responsive act of reading Scripture.[50] Appeals to theories such as these often reinforce the tendency to neglect the unique shaping role of divine action in relation to the reading of the Bible. Thus the appeals Christian scholars make to such work, and the degree to which they rely on them undifferentiating their approach from the uniqueness that the reading of Christian Scripture entails will substantiate the continuation of the chief problem.

In the end our analysis advocates the idea that the proper way to view the reading of Scripture is under a rule of faith, keeping in mind that

> Neither the Rule of Faith nor the creed was in fact a summary of the whole biblical narrative…They provided, rather, the proper reading of the beginning and the ending, the focus of the plot and the relations of the principal characters, so enabling the 'middle' to be heard in bits as meaningful. They provided the closure which contemporary theory

---

[48]   Augustine, *Teaching Christianity: De Doctrina Christiana* (New York, 1996) is a formidable example.

[49]   George Steiner, *Real Presences* (Chicago, 1989).

[50]   Steiner, then, can be seen as resisting Kant's limitation of antecedent operational judgments, while still accepting the limitations of notional antecedent judgments.

prefers to leave open. They articulated the essential hermeneutical key without which texts and community would disintegrate in incoherence.[51]

The claim that we necessarily stand in a constant relatedness to God's prior shaping action, and that that action *can* be described, would generate two notable challenges: that this does not imply either that it should be described; nor that it should be brought intentionally to bear on the act of reading Scripture.

In response to these I suggest the following. If, as part of what it means to be created, dependent, timed and placed beings, we always stand within a horizon of beliefs,[52] and cannot talk about a specific aspect of God's action within that horizon or describe the responsive human activity within that horizon without appeal to some kind of confessionally charged language, then what makes unconscious or unarticulated beliefs more tolerable or acceptable in the reflection on questions of prolegomena than conscious or expressed beliefs? One cannot make a qualitative preference simply on the terms that once identified, the influence of confessional beliefs should be arrested, but that unconscious beliefs which may still inform the descriptive act are inescapable, and so just a reality of the situation and in some way acceptable. Why must that follow? The range of potential influence that conscious or unconscious beliefs are able to exert is the same in either case. So if the situation is inescapable would not thoughtfully and carefully presenting one's conscious assumptions in the end prove both safer, with respect to controlling the unconscious heretical urges we all share and harbor, on the one hand, and, on the other, simply be more honest?

In the presence of modernity's expectations we all feign degrees of objectivity greater than our capacities allow with respect to how our passionately embraced faith commitments inform our work. In a moment of honest reflection how many actually arrive at conclusions in their work which, in the end, strongly contradict those commitments? Certainly there is wisdom in being scrupulous about how we let our rules of faith direct our reading of Scripture and theological expressions. However, if we wish to maintain an appropriate attitude of *semper reformanda* toward our dogmatic constructs, it is arguably much preferred that they are unveiled, and presented as constituent aspects of our lives and actions so that they can be reformed in the process of hearing and wrestling with God's Word. There must be something present *to* reform. This, ultimately, is the task that this work intends to promote and assist.

[51] Frances Young, *Biblical Exegeses and the Formation of Christian Culture* (Cambridge, 1997), p. 21.

[52] I am, again, indebted at this point to the work of Charles Taylor, particularly *Philosophical Arguments* (Cambridge: Harvard University Press, 1995).

Chapter 3

Type One: Human Agency in the "Text"

In this chapter we begin to fill in the typology we sketched out in the last chapter. The first type, discussed here, occupies the bottom left corner of the triangle. Those who represent this type have, to various degrees, two characteristics. First, they see the decisive issues in determining the meaning of Scripture as being derivative of some aspect of the question "What does Scripture say, contain, or enact?" Second, in answering this question, they focus their investigation on some dimension of human activity contained in, referred to, or enacted through, the text. Accompanying this is a correlating relegation of the role of the reader or reading community (type two) or the divine action constituent to both (type three) to secondary or subordinate status.

The degree to which the second characteristic is present in type one approaches is also the degree to which they observe the immanent epistemological limitations discussed in Chapter 1. Once the tendency towards "objective" readings gained prominence, reading Scripture from this (exclusive) vantage point of immanent human authorial agency made the most sense. The investigation of the construction of the text itself is the most obvious and immediate "thing" available within immanent domains. The alternative is to look to the immanent human activity in the reading. This is the option for which type twos opt, often in response to the hegemony of type one approaches. This second option is viewed with suspicion by type ones insofar as it is perceived to be inevitably corrupted over time in the sedition of tradition and by the whims of prevailing cultural subjectivity and bias: it violates the integrity of the authority of the Bible itself.

Despite these differences types one and two share the characteristic of giving preference to immanent fields which translates into a preoccupation with immanent human agency as the sole indicator of textual meaning. At the same time, types one and some type three approaches share the characteristic of focusing on the specific aspect of what the text enacts or contains. The difference between them on this point is that type threes approach the question by giving priority to the shape and form of *divine* speech action constituting the text of Scripture, while type ones give priority to the text as a vessel of *human* action or expression. Anticipating later discussion this is illustrated in the difference between the approaches of Karl Barth and dominant paradigms among twentieth century Evangelicals in the USA.

It might be helpful at this point to reiterate the qualification suggested above; that no one can occupy one of the three types to the exclusion of also assuming a constructive position relative to the aspects represented by the other two. The service offered here is to uncover what are often unseen tensions within particular approaches to reading Scripture; tensions that are better understood as one perceives the stance one assumes between the two fields of human and divine action on one hand, and between human agency in the text or the reader, on the other.

This first type is the paradigm that has been dominant in the last two centuries. Almost any modern commentary belongs to this type. It would be difficult to identify modern commentaries which do *not* reside in this type. Regardless of whether one's stripes are Evangelical, mainline Protestant or (belatedly) Catholic, the tendencies in biblical studies have been towards seeing some variety of the historical critical methods employed as tools of immanent inquiry into a humanly formed and enacted text as the exclusive or decisive grounds in determining the meaning of Scripture. For our typology we have selected representatives of each type who are both distinctive and influential contemporary examples of each. For type one, these will include the early work of Hans Frei, Kevin Vanhoozer, and Francis Watson.[1]

The Evangelical Tradition

The Evangelical tradition is a common conversation partner for the three writers we survey in type one. We will very briefly broach the subject of how Evangelicals exemplify type one to set a backdrop for the rest of the chapter. Evangelicals are rightly considered preeminent defenders of the Bible's right to speak "for itself." Evangelicals have also been among the more active groups in both appropriating and critiquing modern biblical critical methods. This sometimes produces ambivalence in their stance towards Scripture; double mindedness that helps to illustrate some of the tensions of more extreme forms of type one.

William Abraham defines two definitively modern approaches to understanding the nature of the inspiration of Scripture which, he suggests, underwrite classic Evangelical approaches:

> A deductive type of theory begins with a basic theological claim about the meaning of inspiration and attempts to deduce from this what Scripture must be or contain. An inductive type of theory begins with Scripture as it is and attempts to arrive at a vision of inspiration that will be compatible with this. The former is often attractive to the systematic theologian while the latter is very attractive to the exegete or historian.[2]

Abraham suggests that the hermeneutical principles of the deductive approach are inconsistent; that dogmatic interests are employed covertly in defense of an assumed theory of inspiration. The hermeneutic principles advocated in deductive approaches are, however, quickly set aside when the charge of subjectivism is raised by opponents and critics. When confronted by this "Conservative Evangelicals argue that Jesus and the apostles believed in verbal inspiration [and] it is taken for

---

[1]   Other examples that were considered for this work that illustrate some of the diversity of type one included the work of Brevard Childs and Anthony Thiselton. Also the writings of Christopher R. Seitz (see bibliography); Grant R. Osborne, *The Hermeneutical Spiral* (Downer's Grove, 1991); and Clark Pinnock, *The Scripture Principle* (New York, 1984).

[2]   William Abraham, *The Divine Inspiration of Holy Scripture* (New York, 1981), pp. 11-12.

granted that any 'neutral' observer can see this from a plain and natural reading of the text."[3]

This move is interpreted by Abraham as being motivated by the perception that the inductive ground is firmer. The deductive claims that Abraham names function much like *notional* antecedent judgments in Kantian epistemology: some quality or feature of God or the text is presented as a kind of backdrop for the subsequent consideration of purely immanent spheres of inquiry.

To the degree that this shift from deductive to inductive arguments continues to be prevalent in Evangelical biblical scholarship is an indication of the continuing tendency to accept the *values* of Enlightenment epistemology; particularly those which locate greater authority in inductive modes of investigation that proceed in immanent fields of inquiry. These also place greater trust in the purity of the "objective" independent self-sufficient agent apart from the corrupting influence of other agents. Thus: the idea that "any reasonable person" should also recognize these features of the text aside from any "help" from other persons (or from God?).

The definitive collections of articles which both indicate this tendency and represent the best Evangelical expressions to defend and develop the heritage of B.B. Warfield et al. in the late twentieth century grow out of, and in literature are subsequent to, the meetings of the *International Conference on Biblical Inerrancy* held in Chicago in 1978. A few of the more prominent examples are *Hermeneutics, Inerrancy & the Bible: Papers from ICBI Summit II*,[4] as well as a series of books sponsored by the ICBI: *Inerrancy*,[5] *Biblical Inerrancy: Its Philosophical Roots*,[6] *Challenges to Inerrancy*,[7] *Inerrancy and the Church*.[8] Also in this tradition are *Scripture and Truth*[9] and *Hermeneutics, Authority and Canon*.[10] These last two books were originally published in 1983 and 1986 respectively and, as a telling indication of their influence, remained in print into the next millennium.

Many of the articles in these books are prototypical examples of type one insofar as they have both of the two tendencies above: they embrace immanent fields and modes of inquiry as the decisive grounds for determining the meaning of Scripture and tend to confine this field to domains of human authorial agency in abstraction from divine agency. This is so for two reasons. First: that their theological deductive claims tend to be truncated in that they affirm things about the text of Scripture *as if* they are independent qualities of the text, thus existing in relative abstraction from the active milieu of divine agency as God's speech action. I emphasize *as if* because for many in this group there is likely some difference between what they believe or would say in an offhanded clarification and what they actually articulate and do

---

[3]   Abraham, *Inspiration*, p. 21. See bibliography for Abraham's two subsequent relevant works.

[4]   Edited by Earl D. Radmacher and Robert D. Preus, (Grand Rapids, 1984).

[5]   Edited by Norman L. Geisler (Grand Rapids, 1979).

[6]   Edited by Norman L. Geisler (Grand Rapids, 1981).

[7]   Edited by Gordon Lewis and Bruce Demarest (Chicago, 1984).

[8]   Edited by John Hanna (Chicago, 1984).

[9]   Edited by D. A. Carson and John Woodbridge (Grand Rapids, 1983).

[10]   Edited by D. A. Carson and John Woodbridge (Grand Rapids, 1986).

in their methods and writing. In this they faithfully adhere to the epistemological limitations set forth by the Enlightenment's devaluation of antecedent judgments.

The second reason grows out of the first; that the theological claims that they do employ as either support for, or results of, their investigation tends to be treated as notional judgments and not as operational judgments.[11] Thus appeals to God's agency, when they occur, tend toward either the underwriting of human language by God's original act of creation,[12] or focusing exclusively on God's contemporaneous activity in the composition of the text in influencing the human authors/editors apart from the consideration of any consequent or subsequent activity. The theological picture emerges that the only relevant activity (and thus the *only* activity?) that is to be considered in the reading of the Bible is in God's setting the stage for human speech action in creating the world and/or in God acting specifically and locally in the "inspiration" of the human authors. In this they accept in methodological spirit, if not in letter, the Enlightenment advocation to reading Scripture that same way as one would read any book.

We go on now to consider the proposals of several contemporary writers who have engaged Evangelicals on these issues. In the process they both indicate a variety of stances toward the three aspects of our typology while remaining committed to modes of thinking that locate them within this first type. Thus they advance upon the extremes of the Evangelical tradition while remaining committed to the primacy of human authorial agency. It is telling that we will see each thinker evolve in the course of their writing to move to a more nuanced position on these issues; sometimes even to move to type three or two. Our survey begins by considering the early work of Hans Frei.

The Early Hans Frei: The Eclipse of Modern Biblicism

Hans Frei is the first figure surveyed in this chapter. He will also be the first figure discussed in the next chapter. This is so as the development of Frei's work follows a trajectory from type one to type two. Frei is compelling for our study for two reasons. First, his early work remains influential as a paradigmatic example of a type one that engages Evangelical theories but provides a distinct alternative. Second, the later shift in his thinking illustrates some larger shifts in hermeneutical thinking and is, in this sense, helpful in demonstrating the advantages of our triangle schema.

We will see that the issues that compelled him in his shift from the first to the second type are also compelling for those who continue to observe the epistemological limitations as we outlined in Chapter 1. Frei is a model of the modern hermeneutical tendency in that the only options he envisioned was the tension between the human agency in the text and the human agency in the reading. We will see how he illustrates the limitations and weaknesses of trying to reduce the hermeneutical issues to these.

---

[11]   I am indebted to conversations with John Webster at this point. Also see Abraham, *Inspiration.*

[12]   See our discussion of Vanhoozer's early work below for an example.

Frei's earliest hermeneutical work consists of pieces including, and related to, his book *The Identity of Jesus Christ*[13] In *Identity* he has two goals. His first goal is to refute what he sees as injurious approaches to reading Gospel narratives. These, he contends, are too invested in establishing methods and schemas *prior to* reading thus *imposing them on* the text. They read with the preconceived idea that the text is referentially related to some other entity which is the real location of its "meaning." In response he gives his well known criticisms of attempts to "get behind" the text.

The getting behind of which he is critical takes two forms. First: those who understand the Gospel texts to refer in a directly ostensive and measurable fashion to "public" historical events. In this case the meaning of the text is a byproduct of the investigation, determination and affirmation of those events. Frei sees here an inappropriate shift of the location of the meaning from the text itself to the investigation of "public" events to which the text "refers."

Second: those who view the texts as referring to "private" religious experiences of Jesus or his followers. Frei sees this as similarly improper as it relocates the meaning from the text to the internalized experiences of human beings. Both of these are suspect in that the meaning of the Gospel narratives only has a derivative relationship and does so only *insofar as we can distill it from the text*.

The emphasis in the sentence above on the human reader's ability to distill meaning highlights the nature of the problem in terms of agency. Cast this way we can paraphrase Frei's main contention with these other approaches in that they are dependent on A) *human actions* to determine where, other than the text, meaning is located, and B) *human actions* to enact an investigation that uncovers the meaning in that location. Frei's first goal relates to these activities and their heavy handed treatment of the text in imposing the bias of the reader on the text by dictating a location for the meaning of the text and the means of uncovering that meaning. We go on to note Frei's response to this problem as seen in his second goal in *Identity*.

His second goal is to defend the self sufficiency of the "text" as the enactor and container of its own meaning. He does this by advocating the use of *ad hoc* tools of identity description to discern the literary patterns present in the text. Insofar as he is rigidly committed to these two goals in his early work he stands as a paradigmatic example of a type one approach. This is so as the text of Scripture in *Identity* is systematically removed and isolated from questions which Frei sees as unnecessarily impinging on it from outside. The text as the realized intention and expression of human authorial agency becomes the sole agent and container of its own meaning.[14] His definition of the Gospel stories as "realistic narrative" in *Identity* sums up Frei's early position in this regard:

> Realistic narrative reading is based on one of the characteristics of the Gospel story, especially its later part, viz., that it is history-like … In other words, whether or not these stories report history (either reliably or unreliably), whether or not the Gospels are other things besides realistic stories, what they tell us is a fruit of the stories themselves. We

---

[13]   Hans Frei, *The Identity of Jesus Christ* (Philadelphia, 1975).

[14]   Frei, *Identity*, p.87, p. 133. (The first number here, and throughout, will be according to the original pagination in the Fortress edition. The second number is the page number in the Wipf and Stock reprint).

cannot have what they are about (the 'subject matter') without the stories themselves. They are history-like precisely because like history-writing and the traditional novel and unlike myths and allegories they literally mean what they say. There is no gap between the representation and what is represented by it.[15]

Frei frames the contending issues for the proper reading of the narrative in Scripture in *Identity* as the competition between two fields of human agency; the human authorial agency contained in the text and the agency of the contemporary reader. With respect to the former he defends the text as being adequately self-contained so as to be fully capable of rendering its meaning. With respect to the latter he wants to proscribe the overambitious reader by advocating the use of textual kit gloves: *ad hoc* descriptive schemes. The unintended result of both of these moves is the creation of a gap between the perfectly self-contained text and the quarantined and emasculated reader. The difficulty that arises for Frei is to explain the process of how meaning traverses the gap from the one to the other.

His early work is mapped in the extreme lower left corner of the triangle in type one. We will see in his later work that he will inevitably be confronted by this problem. This is shown in the chart below:

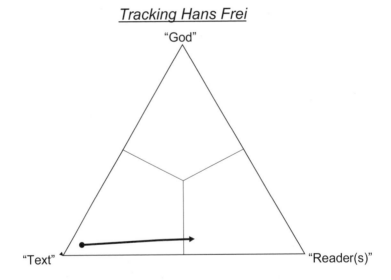

Tracking Hans Frei

"God"

"Text"   "Reader(s)"

Fig 3.1   Mapping Hans Frei: His Early Position and Trajectory

There are three pairs of terms that Frei uses that capture the gist of his argument in *Identity*. First, "identity" and "presence": Frei believes that notions about Christ's presence have tended to have an unnatural influence on the reading of the Gospels. He suggests, instead, that identity description should take priority thereby allowing Christ's identity, as presented in the narratives, to determine its own mode of

---

[15]   Frei, *Identity*, p. xiii-xiv, p. 59.

presence.[16] Second, "meaning" and "truth": Frei wishes to make a clear distinction between the two because of a similar difficulty: notions of how or what constitutes "true" statements tend to be employed and imposed on the reading in ways that undermine the integrity of the text as a self-sufficient vessel of meaning. Reading for meaning, then, proceeds independently of truth schemas and is thus allowed to determine its own truth implications. Third, "descriptive" and "explanatory" schemes: Frei advocates the ad hoc use of purely descriptive schemes prior to and apart from explanatory schemes.[17] These three pairs of terms can be aligned. "Descriptive schemes" seek to elucidate Christ's "identity" insofar is it is ingredient in the "meaning" of the Gospel narratives. This results in the indication of the mode of Christ's "presence" as well as possible "truth claims" while also being suggestive of "explanatory schemes."[18]

In *Identity* Frei describes two modes of ad-hoc identity descriptive schemes which he sees as being conducive to this process: "Intention-action description" and "Self-manifestation description."[19] These *ad hoc* tools insulate the text from the distorting questions which compel investigation beyond the text. Frei's use of identity description results in a segmenting of the narrative framework of the Gospels into three "stages"; the birth narratives, the ministry narratives and the passion narratives. The chief difference between the stages is that only in the last stage does Jesus finally become the "unadorned, singular" ascriptive subject which he is not in the first stage and only partially in the second stage. This shift occurs in relation to the actions of other characters strictly as it is discerned *within the narrative*. In the first two stages, especially the first, Jesus, his titles, and identity are defined by "the identity of the people of Israel" and not by Jesus himself: "He, the infant king, is little more than a symbol of Israel."[20] In his infancy Jesus is passive. His identity is not yet "unsubstitutable" in the way that it will be when he redefines the titles by taking initiative in self-manifestation in the latter stages. Jesus' assertion of his agency begins in the second stage and culminates in the third. The third stage begins in the scene at the garden of Gethsemane. This is one intact narrative sequence, which, according to *Intention-action* description, is uniquely suited to reveal the identity of a person.[21] The culmination of the third stage is the crucifixion-resurrection.[22]

---

[16]   Frei, *Identity*, p. 101, p. 144.

[17]   "The nature of the narrative therefore imposes a limit on theological comment. It is not likely that we shall be able to get beyond the descriptive accounts presented to us in the Gospels concerning the resurrection and the relation of God's and Jesus' actions. And if we do go beyond them in explanatory endeavors, we are clearly on our own and in speculative territory, just as we have suggested that we are in speculative realms when we look beyond the narrative for the writers' and Jesus' own inner intentions. In that instance, our speculation would be historical; in the present, metaphysical. But it is never easy and usually not desirable to transform a literary description, such as a narrative sequence, into an *explanatory* scheme using abstract concepts and categories." Frei, *Identity*, p.125, 163.

[18]   Frei, *Identity*, pp. 46-7, p. 102.

[19]   Frei, *Identity*, p.127, p. 165.

[20]   Frei, *Identity*, pp. 128-9, p. 166

[21]   Frei, *Identity*, p. 110, p. 151.

[22]   Frei, *Identity*, pp. 135-6, pp. 171-2.

Frei's descriptive analysis of Jesus as a character in the Gospel narratives thus portrays him in the context of his relationship with the variety of other human agents in the text. Frei is interested in the transition among these relationships within the Gospel narratives which begin, in earlier stages, by others imposing on Jesus titles and categories. In the last stage, the situation reverses: Jesus now determines and defines the titles which were defining him. In this active mode Jesus also, thereby, establishes and reveals his identity. It is also at this point that Jesus not only defines *his own identity* but also begins to both define the identity of his followers and share his presence with them.[23]

> Indeed, in the Gospel story the human person of Jesus of Nazareth becomes most fully himself in the resurrection. Moreover, the focusing of his full identity in the resurrection is what enables him to turn and share his presence with his disciples.[24]

The question naturally arises here as to how Jesus' sharing of his presence with his disciples *in* the narrative also extends to others *outside* the narrative,[25] and if so, how? Here we have an obscurity in the nature of Jesus' "turning" which highlights a limitation of a purely intratextual approach. How does Jesus' presence emerge from the text? How does it present itself to subsequent believers? Whose agency causes this to occur? Frei answers: "When the Christian speaks of Christ's presence, he means that Jesus *owns his own presence and yet turns and shares it with us*."[26] He elaborates,

> In the case of Jesus Christ ... Christians claim we cannot even think of him without his being present. But it is not the power of our thinking that makes him present; it is he who presents himself to us. Furthermore, we do not have the capacity within ourselves to hold the unity of his identity with his presence in our minds. If he is effectively rendered to us in this unity when we think of him, it is due to his powerful goodness.[27]

Frei continues to reign in *our* agency, the agency of the reader, in either making Christ present to us or in our making ourselves present to Him. It is only Jesus who can turn and make himself present to us. But, again, how does this happen in Frei's schema? How does Jesus, whose agency was at first carefully proscribed within the textual narrative, apart from issues of reference to the world beyond the text, now transcend the text? How does Christ's sharing of his identity and presence to his disciples, within the gospel narratives, now become a sharing with us? This is not an ability that all characters in narratives possess. Jesus is somehow unique in possessing this capacity. Why?

Frei's answer is that Jesus can refer his identity beyond the text because his identity is not simply that of a human character in a narrative but co-incidental with God's identity. Jesus then either originally possesses or obtains (Frei does not

---

[23] Frei, *Identity*, p. 133, p. 169.
[24] Frei, *Identity*, p. 49, p. 104.
[25] David Demson, *Hans Frei & Karl Barth: Different Ways of Reading Scripture* (Grand Rapids, 1997), is instructive on this point.
[26] Frei, *Identity*, p. 33, p. 91.
[27] Frei, *Identity*, p. 14, p. 76.

spell this out) divine capacities which account for the extratextual rendering of his presence. Frei sees this as an outcome of the climactic third section of the Gospel narrative.[28]

At this point Frei appears to violate the intratextual rules that he sets up at the beginning. In order to establish the identity of Jesus' and God's identity *within* the narrative Frei must bring God in as a character in that narrative despite there being no explicit textual reference to God. Frei justifies this by *extratextual* arguments, appealing to John's Gospel, to other New Testament passages, and to the testimony of the early church. Based on this he then concludes, regarding the third stage in the synoptic Gospels, that

> [I]t is surprising that the absolute and direct initiative of God, reaching its climax at this point and stressed in the early preaching of the church, is completely unmentioned in the narrative itself. It is *Jesus*, and Jesus alone, who appears just at this point, when God's supplantation of him is complete ... where the initiative of God is finally and decisively climaxed and he alone is and can be active, the sole identity to mark the presence of that activity is Jesus. God remains hidden, and even reference to him is almost altogether lacking. Jesus of Nazareth, he and none other, marks the presence of the action of God.[29]

At this very point we are in the midst of Frei's unnoted transition from purely intratextual categories of agency to extratextual categories. God is not indicated in the Synoptic Gospels as a character or agent in the manner Frei suggests. Nevertheless, Frei *needs* divine agency at this point if Jesus is going to be able to turn and share his presence and identity with his disciples in and after the resurrection and to the Church. It is here, in this transition that we discern clues as to how the early Frei does (and does not) account for how the intratextual meaning asserts itself beyond the text to the reader.

Frei asks "Did Jesus raise himself?" and answers "Obviously, he did not."[30] He demonstrates that the narratives claim continuity between the pre and post crucifixion Jesus according to the identity description schemes. He assumes at that point, that the narrative cannot be read as suggesting that Jesus resurrected himself. He also acknowledges that no other human agent can be responsible and concludes that only God can raise a human being from the dead back to life. This line of argument is, he admits, not present *in* the Synoptic narrative. Yet Frei presents this extratextual divine agent into the reading at this all important point. He knows he is pressing his descriptive/explanatory scheme pretty hard here and quickly qualifies his argument suggesting that

> The nature of the narrative therefore imposes a limit on theological comment. It is not likely that we shall be able to get beyond the descriptive accounts presented to us in the Gospels concerning the resurrection and the relation of God's and Jesus' actions. And if we do go beyond them in explanatory endeavors, we are clearly on our own and in

---

[28]   This is detailed in Frei, *Identity*, chapter 11.

[29]   Frei, *Identity*, p. 121, p. 160.

[30]   Frei, *Identity*, p. 124, p. 162.

speculative territory, just as we have suggested that we are in speculative realms when we look beyond the narrative for the writers' and Jesus' own inner intentions.[31]

Despite Frei's original dogged intention to stay within the narrative, at the point when he introduces God as the agent of the resurrection in the Synoptic Gospels he has no choice but to go outside it.[32] The introduction of God as an extratextual agent into the narrative coincides, not with Frei's hermeneutics or view of texts, which is so stringently concerned with preserving the integrity of the text qua text, but from his theological assumptions, his "antecedent operational judgments", about the relationship of God and human history.

> History is public history—the intention-action pattern formed by the interaction of the church with mankind at large; and it is this history which forms the mysterious pattern of meaning to be disclosed by the presence of God in Jesus Christ in the future mode. We are saying that this presence to history means that history is neither chaotic nor fated, but providentially ordered in the life, death, and resurrection of Jesus Christ, who is Lord of the past, the present, and the future.[33]

Also,

> God's work is mysteriously, abidingly mysteriously, coexistent with the contingency of events. The history of his providence is one that must be narrated. There is no scientific rule to describe it and eliminate the need for narration. Nor is there any historicist perspective or universal claim that can eliminate history's narrative form.[34]

Frei's appeal to extratextual divine agency is also shown in the last chapter of *Identity* when he nuances the nature of Christ's presence within the church in terms of the agency of the Holy Spirit. Frei also discusses the role of the Spirit in conjunction with his treatment of Calvin in *Eclipse*.

Among the figures Frei discusses in *Eclipse* he is the most agreeable with Calvin.[35]

Frei is so sympathetic that his description of Calvin's hermeneutic begins to sound very much like his own approach in *Identity*.[36] Frei acknowledges the role of the Holy Spirit in Calvin's reading:

> The internal testimony of the Spirit, then, is neither a peripheral edifying appendage to the actual reading of the biblical text nor an explanatory theory that alone would warrant the unity of the objective claims made in the text with the personal life stance of Christian faith. It is the effective rendering of God and his real world to the reader by way of the text's appropriate depiction of the intercourse of that God and that world, engaging the reader's mind, heart, and activity.[37]

---

[31] Frei, *Identity*, p. 125, p. 163.
[32] See Frei, *Identity*, Chapter 14, "The Pattern of Christ's Presence."
[33] Frei, *Identity*, p. 123, p. 161.
[34] Frei, *Identity*, pp. 124-5, 163.
[35] Frei, *Eclipse*, pp. 34-5.
[36] See Frei, *Eclipse*, pp. 121 ff. for his discussion of Calvin.
[37] Frei, *Eclipse*, pp. 24-5.

Frei goes on to isolate two questions around divine agency that gained prominence through the deistic controversies of the eighteenth century that rendered this way of thinking about biblical hermeneutics untenable. The first "concerned the inherent rationality or credibility of the very idea of a historical revelation."[38] Are historically revelatory intervening acts of God even possible? The second follows from the first. If historical revelation is possible (a "yes" answer to question one) then how likely is it that such a thing took place, and beyond that, how could we ever know even if it did?

Frei sees these questions as dominating the discussion from the eighteenth century onward. These questions also underwrote the eventual "eclipse of biblical narrative." Negative response to these questions result in "Lessing's ditch." Now access to God is a "problem". God becomes conceived as locally distant. God's speaking is only a possibility that we must now work hard to prove or show. The "reversal" that Frei discusses, which we looked at in Chapter 1, hinges on these questions. The direction can no longer be from God and text to us, we are cut off by culture and "history." The onus of all agential responsibility, ethical and hermeneutical, falls now to us and our efforts at building bridges across the ditch; apparently, thereby, allowing or enabling the historically distanciated text, and a domesticated and distant God, to speak. The interpretive direction is thus reversed from precritical times ideally represented by Calvin. Frei summarizes the net effect of these developments in the eighteenth and nineteenth century in terms very similar to those which we described in Chapter 1 in relation to Kant.

> It is simply impossible to exaggerate the self-conscious novelty and power of the full-orbed conviction at the end of that century, no matter how far one may see its roots extending into previous history, that a free and self-conscious self-positioning toward the world is an independent and indispensable factor in shaping the depiction of that world with its bearing on the self. It matters little whether this self was the Pietist's self dispositioning itself religiously, that of the Romantic dispositioning itself aesthetically in acute awareness of its own sensibility, that of the philosophical Idealist dispositioning itself in conceptual self-reflexiveness, or that of budding Existentialist, dispositioning itself in self-committing agency.[39]

These are perceived to be the only available options for the responsible reader at the end of the nineteenth century. *Two* "ditches" can actually be discerned; one between the text and the reader and another between the text and its referent. In his early work Frei only redresses the problem of the second ditch. He strives to reunite the text with its referent. The problem of the agency which renders this unity to the contemporary reader across the second gap, however, is still there.

One considerable factor in this remaining problem is that Frei's intratextual hermeneutic seeks to discern the meaning of the text as a separate and distinct act apart from any explanatory scheme. The chief difficulty with this is that this also removes the reading from any account of the *agency* which is responsible both for the presence of meaning *in* the text and for its maintenance and transmission to the

---

[38] Frei, *Eclipse*, p. 52.
[39] Frei, *Eclipse*, p. 201.

reader *beyond* the text. In point of fact it is impossible to conscientiously read any text without employing some prior understanding of how these agencies interact. Frei's appeal to the agency of God in *Identity* and the work of the Holy Spirit in Calvin's hermeneutic of Scripture in *Eclipse* are two indications that explanatory schemes pertaining to the interaction of divine and human agency, in this sense, are unavoidable.[40]

Whereas Frei insists on abstracting the meaning of the text apart from "truth" schemes in his early work, he remains committed to the Enlightenment limitations we described in Chapter 1. Frei's persistent separation of meaning from truth claims in the independent, self-sufficient reader, and making the latter strictly subsequent to the determination of the former, trades on a similar abstraction. It is analogous to Kant's criticism of antecedent judgments and continues to subscribe, indirectly, to the proscription of "religion within the boundaries of mere reason."

It is no surprise, then, that Frei encounters a problem when he attempts to negotiate the movement from the meaning *in* the text to its presentation to the reader. As we mentioned above Frei was aware of this problem even before *Eclipse* was available. He indicates this in a presentation to the Barth Society meetings in Toronto in the spring of 1974. His lecture is entitled "Scripture as Realistic Narrative: Karl Barth as Critic of Historical Criticism."[41] In the latter half of the lecture Frei focuses on passages in the *Church Dogmatics* where Barth compares characteristics of Scripture to those of the literary saga and takes this as a departure point to make his own, now familiar argument, that Scriptural narrative bears some analogy to the modern novel. At the very end of the question and answer period, Frei, responding to a question regarding his comparison of Scripture to the novel, says:

> There is an ambiguity that I slipped in. I hoped that you might not notice it but be kind about it. I said at least once that the meaning in a novel, the meaning of a story, is the story itself. I said also that it emerges *from* the story and that ambiguity is one that I simply cannot solve.[42]

If we pause and reflect on this seemingly innocuous comment we see that his insight gestures in the direction of questions regarding agency we have raised. Frei's own work, from this date forward, is compelled by the attempt to resolve this ambiguity between the meaning of a story being "in the story" and somehow

---

[40]   See the very helpful discussion in Kevin J. Vanhoozer, *The Drama of Doctrine* (Philadelphia, 2005).

[41]   Hans Frei, "Scripture as Realistic Narrative: Karl Barth as Critic of Historical Criticism", a paper delivered to the 2nd Karl Barth Colloquium, Emmanuel College, Toronto, Spring, 1974. Transcript made and edited by Mark Alan Bowald. Thanks to David Demson for graciously giving me access to an audio tape of this meeting.

[42]   Frei, "Scripture as Realistic Narrative," p. 23 of the transcript. Francis Watson points out the related problem of how Frei accounts for the movement from literary observation to faith and/or from meaning to truth: "Frei is right to acknowledge that recognition of the irreducibility of narrative should not serve as a substitute for the question of truth. The problem is that he appears to have no means at his disposal whereby to reintegrate this question into the narrative framework." *Text, Church and World*, p. 25.

"emerging from the story." His early work reflects the investment in the former while his later work, by way of the influence of David Kelsey and in conversation with George Lindbeck's "cultural-linguistic" framework, is an attempt to account for the latter. In doing so, Frei was intuitively addressing the weaknesses of a pure intratextualist position which lacks the ability to account for the extratextual agency in the emergence of meaning.

Once this issue is cast this way he has two possible candidates from which to provide this agency; humans or God. These are not mutually exclusive.[43]

We have surveyed Frei's early work on hermeneutics with an eye toward discerning how he relates the three facets that represent the three corners of our triangle. With respect to the "text" Frei has clear and decisive commitments to defending its capacity to determine its own meaning. The text means what it says. It contains its own meaning. There is no need to "go behind it" and look for meaning in some opaque region of human authorial intention or obscure cultural location. Meaning emerges from the text by means of our careful attention to the interplay of characters within the story, allowing them to reveal the shape of their identity. Frei's commitment is unwaveringly to the text. God, as a divine agent, does not factor into his theory of texts apart from providing a created setting within which human speech actions have a predictable and stable expression. Frei's location in the triangle reflects this, being very near the bottom left corner.

Despite Frei's theological reticence, we saw at a key juncture he was compelled to bring divine agency into his account in order to provide the means by which Jesus Christ can turn and share his identity and presence with his disciples. There are two things we can note about Frei's awkward use of divine agency in relation to our typology. First, it is telling that Frei requires divine agency despite his meticulous theory of narrative which turns on the absolute self sufficiency of the text in providing its own meaning. Second, the theological position Frei indicates regarding the relationship of divine and human agency in his early work emphasizes only two aspects of God's action: 1) God's structuring the world in such a way that the cause and effect events in the narrative can be accounted for; 2) God as an agent within the narrative at key points where Jesus' extratextual agency is required to share His presence. Beyond this Frei does not comment on divine agency in the early writings. The mapping of Frei below, again shows where he begins in his early work and where these questions will take him:

---

[43] Wolterstorff's *Divine Discourse* is instructional on this point.

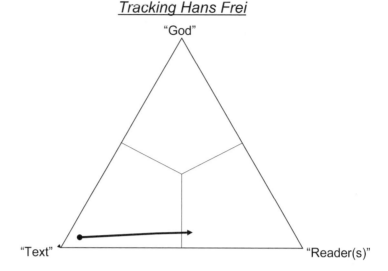

Fig 3.2   Tracking Hans Frei: His Late Position and Movement in the Triangle

The work of Kevin Vanhoozer and Francis Watson illustrate two other important and paradigmatic examples of type one. The early writings of both occur in conversation with Evangelicals and with Frei. They are similar to both in that they address the question of the agency of meaning strictly in terms of immanent human agency invested in the composition of the text of Scripture. Vanhoozer reinvests in the agency of the author while Watson will, not unlike Frei in his later work, explore the agency of reader(s) as co-operative agents with the text. The complexity of the question of the agency of meaning will compel them to begin to account for divine agency. Both Watson and Vanhoozer will eventually drift up in the triangle towards the boundary with (and even into?) type three.

Kevin Vanhoozer: From *General* Hermeneutics to General *Christian* Hermeneutics to Divine Canonical-Linguistics

Vanhoozer's earliest published paper on hermeneutics was called "The Semantics of Biblical Literature: Truth and Scripture's Diverse Literary Forms."[44]

---

[44]   In D. A. Carson and John Woodbridge (eds), *Hermeneutics, Authority and Canon*, (Grand Rapids: Zondervan, 1986) pp. 49-104. Hereafter "Semantics".

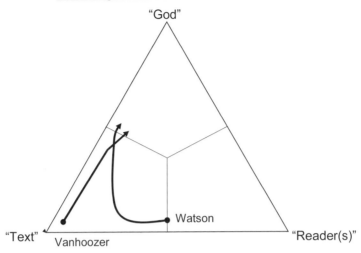

Fig 3.3 Mapping Kevin Vanhoozer and Francis Watson

This article contains seeds of his subsequent thinking and demonstrates certain bias which allows us to clearly locate his early position in type one. We will see a development and trajectory in his writing from a more extreme version of type one toward a nuanced position in which he attempts to more carefully negotiate the corollary issues of the human and divine agency which produce the meaning of the text. In this development divine agency takes on a greater and greater role.

To begin: in "Semantics" he challenges Evangelicals to become more sensitive to issues related to the diversity of literary forms in Scripture. He suggests that they have been preoccupied with propositional theories of language. In contrast he sets out to "provide a model of biblical revelation that will preserve the substance of 'propositional' revelation…while at the same time allowing for greater appreciation of the 'ordinary' language of Scripture and its diverse literary forms."[45]

He discusses the problem of imposing prefabricated systems or theories on Scripture; frameworks that get in the way of "letting Scripture's literary forms be literary forms."[46] He discusses the American New Critics and praises Hans Frei's *Eclipse of Biblical Narrative* as examples of a defense of the integrity of the text.[47] He takes issue with Frei, however, in the latter's assertion that "meaning" and "truth" should be distinguished. Vanhoozer takes up a similarly radical, but opposite

---

[45] Vanhoozer, "Semantics," p. 67.
[46] Vanhoozer, "Semantics," p. 69.
[47] Vanhoozer, "Semantics," pp. 67-75.

position; that meaning and truth are utterly united in God and that, therefore, all textual expressions of meaning necessarily carry with them a variety of truth claims which can and should be described:

> Because God is all-knowing and omnipresent…Truth must be comprehensive and unified (at least for God, if not always for us). Truth, like Reality, is in one sense One. However, Reality is so rich and multifaceted that it, like white light, can only be conveyed (verbally) by an equally rich "spectrum"—diverse literary forms.[48]

Vanhoozer displays the influence of his Evangelical heritage in which claims about God and God's participation in the world and in the communication of Scripture function more as notional judgments than operational judgments. This is not unlike the way notional ideas about God, as Creator, Preserver, and Judge, function for Kant in the second *Critique*: they underwrite human activity but do not necessarily influence, interfere, or actively participate with that action. Vanhoozer's selection of which of God's attributes to emphasize reinforces the point: God is everywhere and God knows all. But is God *doing* anything? Further, his argument for the unity of "Truth" is founded on the infinite unity of God's presence and knowledge. However, truth is not only a state or essence but also an action. Questions arise; who enacts truth? Do we? If we do, is there a corollary and accompaniment in God's action? The issue of divine agency is not addressed anywhere in this early piece. Vanhoozer is not necessarily being intentional in this omission but rather is exhibiting the learned epistemological tendencies. He is influenced by the shape of the contemporary debates which all tend to set aside the consideration of divine agency. He will demonstrate a growing sensitivity to the issue as his writing evolves until he comes to examine it in great richness in *The Drama of Doctrine* (2005).

Again: theological statements about God function for Vanhoozer in his earliest work as notional judgments—like a backdrop for a play. The activity in a play occurs against, but not with or in, the backdrops. Similarly Vanhoozer's general hermeneutical theory displays the tendency of type one which gives methodological preference to the diverse human action played out in the text of Scripture apart from the question of God's action, which remains hanging like printed tapestries in the wings or in the background.

This is demonstrated, for one, in the way Vanhoozer takes his cue from speech act theory by way of the work of J. L. Austin and John Searle.[49] It is not necessary to rehearse the features of speech act theory at this point.[50] Indicating one of the features of type one, Vanhoozer's sole interest in his appropriation of speech act theory is in demonstrating how it assists us in perceiving the integrity and diversity of *human* authorial speech actions. Although, to be fair, at one point in "Semantics" he does briefly discuss divine action, writing,

---

[48] Vanhoozer, "Semantics," p. 85.

[49] Vanhoozer, "Semantics," pp. 86 ff.

[50] The best introduction to Speech Act theory and its implementation in theological hermeneutics is Richard S. Briggs, *Words in Action* (New York, 2001). Also Timothy Ward, *Word and Supplement* (Oxford, 2002).

God makes Himself known through what He does and through what He says … God personally confronts us by means of the scriptural propositions that He propounds in various ways for our consideration. God spoke to Israel in Scripture, and Scripture itself is a collection of divine speech acts, which have been inscribed by human authors.[51]

This is the only consideration of divine activity in this early piece. It too, however, could be read as indicating some distanciation between God's speech action and human speech actions; as if God acted, and the composition and formation of Scripture is a purely human action in response to God's actions. After this brief comment, his attention shifts immediately back to attend to the use of human speech act theory to discern the human communicative actions comprising Scripture. The potential role for divine agency in this early piece is limited to that which is witnessed to and enacted within the text of Scripture. This limitation is also reflected in a telling comment: "What Scripture says, God says." "Scripture" becomes a metaphor for the admixture of human and divine agency which arises from the reading and even assumes God's character and agency: "Scripture is, then, indefatigable in its illocutionary intent. It encourages, warns, asserts, reproves, instructs, commands—all infallibly."[52]

Vanhoozer's early work is sympathetically located close to the base and in the far left corner in proximity to the early work of Hans Frei. Despite their hailing distance at the outset, however, Vanhoozer and Frei subsequently chart very different courses:

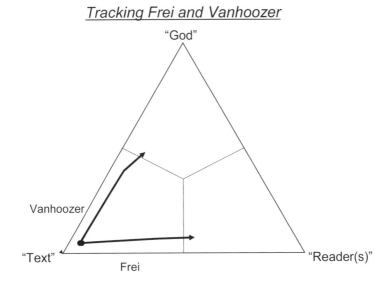

Fig 3.4   Comparing the Hermeneutical Development of Kevin Vanhoozer and Hans Frei

[51] Vanhoozer, "Semantics," p. 93.
[52] Vanhoozer, "Semantics," p. 95, see also pp 102-3.

The next phase of Vanhoozer's hermeneutical writing is represented by a collection of articles written between 1993 and 2001 published as *First Theology*[53] and a book, published in 1998, *Is There a Meaning in this Text?*[54] One of the strongest points of continuity from the early piece into the writings in this period is the use of notional claims about God to set the stage for a lengthy consideration of human speech acts. Chapter 6 of *First Theology*, "From Speech Acts to Scripture Acts," originally read at a conference in 1998, reads much like an updated and expanded version of "The Semantics of Biblical Literature."

In "From Speech Acts" he proposes ten theses for the consideration of a development of theological hermeneutics:

1. Language has a "design plan" that is inherently covenantal.
2. The paradigm for a Christian view of communication is the triune God in communicative action.
3. "Meaning" is the result of communicative action, of what an author has done intending to certain words at a particular time in a specific manner.
4. The literal sense of an utterance or text is the sum total of those illocutionary acts performed by the author intentionally and with self-awareness.
5. Understanding consists in recognizing illocutionary acts and their results.
6. Interpretation is the process of inferring authorial intentions and of ascribing illocutionary acts.
7. An action that aims to produce perlocutionary effects on readers other than by means of *understanding* counts as strategic, not communicative, action.
8. To describe generic (or canonic) illocution is to describe the communicative acts that structure the text considered as a unified whole.
9. The Spirit speaks in and through Scripture precisely by rendering its illocutions at the sentential, generic and canonic levels perlocutionary efficacious.
10. What God does with Scripture is covenant with humanity by testifying to Jesus Christ (illocution) and by bringing about the reader's mutual indwelling with Christ (perlocution) through the Spirit's rendering Scripture efficacious.[55]

In a development since "Semantics" he now sees *the triune action of God* as the "paradigm" for human speech action. This appeal to the Trinity, nevertheless, continues to function as a notional claim about God which, in turn, underwrites a general theory about human speech acts much as the doctrines of God's omniscience and omnipresence did in "Semantics."

Further, upon initial inspection of the list above, one might expect the first two theses to be full-bodied theological comments pertaining to divine agency. Instead, he displays the trinitarian characteristics of God only as an analogous paradigm from which to build an anthropology of communicative action. It remains unclear if or how God's trinitarian action and human action are interrelated.[56] This is reinforced in two ways; first, in that he seeks to

---

[53] Kevin Vanhoozer, *First Theology* (Downer's Grove, 2002).

[54] Kevin Vanhoozer, *Is There a Meaning in this Text?* (Grand Rapids, 1998).

[55] Vanhoozer, *First Theology*, pp. 202-3.

[56] R. W. L. Moberly notes "'Transcendence' is defined by Vanhoozer in terms of the encounter with any other through a text. What it means that that other should be not just Isaiah of Paul but also God is only cursorily, and rather unpersuasively, addressed." Review

[D]evelop a theological understanding of communication on the basis of the "economic," not the immanent, Trinity. "The economic Trinity" is the technical term for the way the triune God progressively reveals himself in human history. The economic Trinity is the name for God in communicative (and self-communicative) action.[57]

Limiting the analogy to the economic trinity in this way has two effects. First, insisting on the distinctiveness and opacity in the relationship between the economic and immanent Trinity could imply a similar distance and opacity as related to our immanent theological and confessional expressions regarding God. Second, his discussion of the use of the economic Trinity continues to leave the relationship of God's economic speech action to human speech action ambiguous.

This trinitarian model is utilized because the "missions of the Son and Spirit, authorized by God the Father/Author, bear a certain resemblance to the economy of the 'sender-receiver' model of communication."[58] Once this is noted he gives exclusive attention to human speech action. We could conclude from this that a proper way to establish the general conditions of human speech action is to do so with the model of God's economic self-relation and self-communication in the background and apart from the consideration of their inter-relationship.

Another point of continuity in his work is related to his radical identity of meaning and truth. This identity is reflected in his persistent interest in constructing a general theory of hermeneutics. He proposes that we modify the adage "Scripture should be read like any other book" in two ways. First, that the way Scripture is read is underwritten by the unity of truth in God and that the conditions of all language in general are also, then, inherently theological. Second: that, therefore, "every other book should be read like the Bible"[59] and that "the best general hermeneutic is a *theological* hermeneutic."[60]

All hermeneutics, not simply the special hermeneutics of Scripture, is "theological." Does special revelation need a special hermeneutic? On the contrary, I am advocating a trinitarian hermeneutic for all interpretation; better, I am arguing that general hermeneutics is inescapably theological. Our polluted cognitive and spiritual environment darkens understanding of *all* texts … Understanding —of the Bible or of any other text—is a matter of ethics, indeed of spirituality.[61]

This argument reaches a climax in his book *Is There a Meaning in This Text?*[62] In it he, again, sets out to defend the integrity of the author and the text. His opponents

---

of "Is There a Meaning in This Text", *The Expository Times*, Vol. 110 No. 5, February 1999, p. 154.
  [57] Vanhoozer, *First Theology*, p. 168.
  [58] Vanhoozer, *First Theology*, p. 168. There also may be theological problems with the identification of the communicative actions of the different members of the Trinity with the three modes of speech act theory. Thus he suggests Father = locution, Son = illocution, Spirit = perlocution. *First Theology* pp. 154-6; 162-3.
  [59] Vanhoozer, *First Theology*, p. 208.
  [60] Vanhoozer, *First Theology*, p. 213.
  [61] Vanhoozer, *First Theology*, p. 231.
  [62] Vanhoozer, *Is There a Meaning*.

are the "undoers" represented primarily by Jacques Derrida and including Richard Rorty, Stanley Fish, and others who share their outlook. Part one of the book outlines the problem he sees with their undoings. The integrity of the human author is under siege: the human reader is left vulnerable to the whims of human ideology and violence.

Vanhoozer responds in part two. He begins by suggesting that the issues they raise are inherently theological; that "secular literary theories are anti-theologies in disguise."[63] The proper response to these attacks, he concludes, should be theological as well. The theological defense here, however, continues to exhibit the ambiguities of his earlier writing pertaining to divine agency. For example, among the three, author, text, and reader, the place where we would most likely expect a discussion of *divine* action is with the author. However, Vanhoozer pursues the issue of authorship with strict attention only to the general conditions of *human* language and authorship. The theological component is missing, yet assumed to be pivotal to his larger argument. So he begins by telling us "the fear of the author is the beginning of literary knowledge," hinting at the theological analogy, yet proceeds to argue that "to inquire after the nature of the author is also to ask what it is to be human."[64] We have shifted, as before, to anthropological categories and the logic of his argument proceeds to defend the capacity of language strictly as an immanent creaturely activity. He writes, "Language is a God-given capacity that enables human beings to relate to God, to the world, and to one another." Language is "designed" and "endowed" by God and given to human beings to "produce true interpretation."[65] The theological component is the creational integrity of language but does not indicate any further or related action by God. We also see this in his specific response to Derrida:

> If we begin not from Derrida's Doubt but from Christian doctrine, we can formulate the following thesis: *the design plan of language is to serve as the medium of covenantal relations with God, with others, with the world.* There are two dimensions to this covenant of discourse … First, language is the medium in which we relate to others … Second, language is the medium in which we relate to and seek to understand the world.[66]

Language is an instrument used by human beings according to its "design plan". It remains unclear how divine action fits into this plan apart from the planning phase. Vanhoozer tends, then, to approach these issues in his earlier writings honoring post-Enlightenment terms which isolate the immanent spheres of human action from the accompanying influence of transcendent agency.

He does address the issue of divine agency in the last four pages of the chapter on "resurrecting the author" where he discusses the *sensus plenior* of Scripture. He suggests that "the canon as a whole becomes the unified act for which the divine intention serves as a unifying principle. The divine intention supervenes on the

---

[63] Vanhoozer, *Is There a Meaning*, p. 200. Vanhoozer appeals, here, to John Milbank's work.

[64] Vanhoozer, *Is There a Meaning*, p. 201.

[65] Vanhoozer, *Is There a Meaning*, p. 205.

[66] Vanhoozer, *Is There a Meaning*, p. 206. Emphasis his.

intention of the human authors. Inspiration, that is, is an emergent property of the Old and New Testaments."[67] This does not help very much, though, in that it could be read to imply that divine agency is *only* "emergent" and *only subsequently* "supervenes" on the intention of the human authors.

Vanhoozer closes *Is There a Meaning?* with a clarification of one of the developments in his thinking, that "the best general hermeneutics is a *trinitarian* hermeneutics." He clarifies how the Trinity functions in this:

> The thesis underlying the present work takes God's trinitarian communicative action as the paradigm, not merely the illustration, of all genuine message-sending and receiving … The triune God is therefore the epitome of communicative agency.[68]

That the Trinity is not simply an "illustration" but rather the "paradigm" and "epitome" does not provide much clarification, however. All this suggests is that the Trinity is not *a type* but *the archetype* of human communication. There is still no clear indication for how the actual influence or participation of God's speech action occurs with human speech action. He also indicates this ambiguity when he suggests that "Disputes about the nature of interpretation are ultimately theological, therefore, insofar as they revolve around the *possibility* of transcendence"[69], and that,

> The Trinity thus serves the role of what Kant calls a "transcendental condition": a necessary condition for the possibility of something humans experience but cannot otherwise explain, namely, the experience of meaningful communication.[70]

This quote needs no unpacking in light of our discussion in Chapter 1. It serves to highlight the location of Vanhoozer in a conservative position within the corner of type one. In discussing this middle phase in his writing we, finally, return to discuss his proposal that "all books should be read like Scripture." At the end of *Is There a Meaning* he further clarifies what he means by this:

> On the one hand, then, we should read the Bible like any other text, though due consideration must be given to those factors that set it apart (e.g., its divine-human authorship, its canonical shape, its function as Scripture). On the other hand, we should read every other text with the same theological presuppositions that we bring to, and discover through, our study of the Bible.[71]

We see here hints that divine action will be the point at which the uniqueness of Scripture is established. Unfortunately he leaves this undeveloped and can even be read as immediately taking back what he gives. It may be that the difficulty with his proposal that we read every book like Scripture is that it tends to react too strongly to the attack of the adequacy of *human* authorial action creating restrictions that are heavy handed in dealing with the complex issue of the uniqueness of *divine* action.

---

[67] Vanhoozer, *Is There a Meaning*, p. 265.
[68] Vanhoozer, *Is There a Meaning*, p. 457.
[69] Vanhoozer, *Is There a Meaning*, p. 455. Emphasis mine.
[70] Vanhoozer, *Is There a Meaning*, p.456.
[71] Vanhoozer, *Is There a Meaning*, pp. 455-6.

In other words, Vanhoozer is so determined to defend *human* speech acts in the reading of Scripture that he tends to skirt over the distinctiveness of that reading in terms of *divine* speech action.

As a result it is difficult to identify a mechanism or line of argument in Vanhoozer's general theology of *all* texts by which we would justify giving Scripture any preferential reading. Should we read all books like Scripture? If so then how is reading Scripture different than reading Dante or Shakespeare or the Koran? The answer to this question may, in the end, not be available from the consideration of the general conditions of human language via a theological anthropology but may only be established by an overt consideration of the priority and distinctiveness of divine action.[72]

Vanhoozer may be fighting a worthy battle but spends too much time and resources on the wrong front. He wages his war in defense of Scripture against the undoers primarily in terms of human communicative action. However, it may be that the more important front is located in the question of the uniqueness of divine action in, with, and under Scripture. The unique claim of Christianity regarding God's action in the Canon is impossible in Derrida's eyes and not within the purview of textual possibilities he discusses. In other words, Derrida is discussing the problems of human agency in reading texts but there is a point at which the uniqueness of Scripture, as related to divine agency, completely escapes the sphere of his attention and the relevance of his criticisms. Maybe, then, we can let Derrida's criticism of the fallenness and violence of human interpretation stand. We may even applaud the theological implications of the violent depravity of human action which results. We still respond that nevertheless, and despite the perseverance and pervasiveness of sinful and violent human speech acts, God has spoken and still speaks graciously and redemptively in His Word, in, with, and under the reading of faithful readers. A better response to Derrida in defense of the stability of the meaning in Scripture properly begins, then, with God's speech action.

We go on to see how Vanhoozer's thinking, beginning in the late 1990s, begins to explore the nature of reading Scripture by overtly considering divine speech action in more expansive terms. One indication of this development in his thinking is found in Chapters 2-4 of *First Theology* which were published between 1996 and 2001. They deal explicitly with different questions pertaining to the doctrine of God and specifically with laying out a trinitarian theology of communicative action. There is also a shift in his vocabulary in these writings. For example, before, in "Semantics" he defined the diversity of human speech acts in Scripture as diverse literary forms. Now he sees that same diversity as "a rainbow of divine communicative acts."[73] This is also demonstrated in a more dynamic exposition on the relationship between God and Scripture. He writes:

> I submit that the best way to view God and Scripture together is to acknowledge God as a communicative agent and Scripture as his communicative action. The virtue of this construal ... lies in its implicit thesis that one can neither discuss God apart from Scripture

---

[72] Moberly makes a similar point in "Review" p. 154.

[73] Vanhoozer, *First Theology*, p. 35.

nor do justice to Scripture in abstraction from its relation to God. For if the Bible is a species of divine communicative action it follows that in using Scripture we are not dealing merely with information about God; we are rather engaging God himself—with God in communicative action. The notion of divine communicative action forms an indissoluble bond between God and Scripture.[74]

He also clarifies the role of theology proper and of divine action as antecedent judgments in how one views and approaches Scripture.

One's view of Scripture is always correlated to one's view of God: no doctrine of Scripture without a doctrine of providence. Most theologians, I argue, gravitate toward a particular genre of Scripture in their construal of how God is involved with Scripture.[75]

We also see in "Body Piercing, the Natural Sense & the Task of Theological Interpretation" (2000) a modification of the "ten theses" we noted above to "five theses:"

1. The ultimate authority for Christian theology is the triune God in communicative action.
2. A text's "plain meaning" or "natural sense" is the result of a person's communicative action (what an author has done in tending to his or her words in this way rather than another).
3. To call the Bible "Scripture" is to acknowledge a divine intention that does not contravene but supervenes on the communicative intentions of its human authors.
4. The theological interpretation of Scripture requires us to give "thick descriptions" of the canonical acts in the Bible performed by both the human and the divine authors.
5. The norm of theological interpretation (what an author has intentionally said/done) generates an interpretive aim: to bear competent witness to what an author has said/done.[76]

The ubiquitous coupling of human and divine action in these as compared to the early list is a confirmation of his growing investment in divine agency.[77] In introducing this list he also offers the qualification that he had "sought to derive these theses from Christian doctrine; the use of speech act philosophy is merely ancillary to my theological purpose."[78] Whether speech act theory was, in fact, auxiliary in his early work is unclear.[79]

There are other signs of the growing sophistication in his implementation of divine agency. For example, "covenant" in "Semantics" (1986) is not predicated on God's trinitarian covenantal action but arises from the covenantal state of creation.

---

[74] Vanhoozer, *First Theology*, p. 35.

[75] Vanhoozer, *First Theology*, p. 131.

[76] Vanhoozer, *First Theology*, p. 293.

[77] Vanhoozer, *First Theology*, p. 12-3.

[78] Vanhoozer, *First Theology*, p. 291.

[79] His earlier use of speech act theory suggested the following analogy: "Father = locution, Son = illocution, Spirit = perlocution". He now softens this to "God is the initiator of this action (agent), the Word or content of this action (act) and the Spirit or power of its reception (consequence)." Vanhoozer, *First Theology* , p. 292.

Then, in "From Speech Action" (1998) the covenantal status of human speech is predicated on the economic Trinity. Finally, in this Preface to *First Theology* (2002), our speech action is more closely linked to God's economic *and* immanent (in both senses) speech action. This shift is a clear indication of the trajectory of where his hermeneutical thinking is going.

This becomes most overt in a paper he gave in Toronto in 2002 at the annual meeting of the Institute for Biblical Research and, finally, in his recent book: *The Drama of Doctrine* (2005). In the former he responded to a paper given by I. Howard Marshall[80] entitled "Developing a Biblical Hermeneutic for a Developing Theology." Vanhoozer's thinking has become so attuned to the issue of divine agency that he directs his critical remarks toward the role that antecedent judgments pertaining to God's agency play in Marshall's proposal.

Vanhoozer makes his critical comment by way of highlighting the implicit theological judgments about God, and in particular the judgments about God's *immanent* actions that underwrite Marshall's proposal.[81] He does not challenge the validity of bringing such judgments to the conversation but only suggests that those that Marshall brings may be inadequate in light of Scripture's own witness. In response he affirms the necessity and priority of antecedent judgments about God:

> Now what might this paper have looked like had it been written by a theologian- by me, for example? First, the title would have to be slightly adjusted: "Developing a *Theology* for a Developing Biblical Hermeneutic". The point is that the way we read and use the Bible already depends on certain theological assumptions, say, about the character of God (as we have just seen) or about the trajectory of redemption. There is circularity here, to be sure, but it need not be vicious because these assumptions are corrigible.[82]

He then picks up on the notion of the "trajectory of redemption" that Marshall proposes and highlights the primary problem he sees with it in similar terms.[83] Vanhoozer sees Marshall as usurping aspects of the authoritative action of God in Christ and relocating it in the present interpretive actions of the Christian community. His proposed corrective highlights how it is God's action in Christ that is uniquely definitive for shaping the life and interpretive practices of the Church and how it is proper and necessary to be led into the reading of Scripture with doctrinal judgments about God's action in Christ.[84]

Vanhoozer's comments demonstrate two points relative to the greater argument standing behind the construction of our typology. First, in his response to Marshall Vanhoozer directs our attention to a host of other theological issues that accompany it.[85] Second, Vanhoozer's relocation of the point of issue from third article theology

---

[80]   I. Howard Marshall, *Beyond the Bible* (Grand Rapids, 2004).

[81]   Kevin Vanhoozer, "Comments on 'Developing a Biblical Hermeneutic for a Developing Theology'", p.3.

[82]   Vanhoozer, "Comments", p. 4.

[83]   Vanhoozer, "Comments", pp. 6-7.

[84]   Vanhoozer, "Comments", pp. 9-10.

[85]   Vanhoozer, "Comments", pp. 9-10.

of the Holy Spirit to first article, theology proper, demonstrates the inextricable nature of beliefs regarding divine action that accompany Marshall's plan. This reinforces one of the main arguments underwriting our typology; that all debates over the hermeneutics of Scripture need to consider the negotiation of human and divine action and that this ultimately resides in claims related to theology proper.

Vanhoozer's trajectory of development can now be summarized. His early articles located him nearer to the bottom of the triangle. He has now moved up towards the top of the triangle. His work demonstrates increasingly acute and careful attention to the problem of adequately accounting for both divine and human agency and the complexity of their relationship. Vanhoozer also continues to show reservations about the role of the reader as potentially usurping the authority of Scripture. He is consistently skittish about issues related to the constructive or productive role of the contemporary action of the reader in his hermeneutic. These are the issues represented in type two, the bottom right corner of the triangle. We see this in Chapter 6 of *First Theology,* "From Speech Acts to Scripture Acts" when he proposes his ten theses for the appropriation of Speech Act Theory for biblical interpretation. The article covers 45 pages yet the issue of the readers action comes only at the end and is quickly summarized in two pages. His discomfort is indicated in the awkwardness of the following comment:

> Indeed this is essentially what interpretation is: bearing witness to the meaning of the authorial intentions enacted in the text. That is why it is important to attend to the history of interpretation. God has spoken to previous generations through his word, and we need to hear what God said to them as well as the original readers. It may be, in fact, that God speaks to us in Scripture by way of the tradition of its interpretation. This would be the case, however, only if previous generations had rightly discerned God's canonical action in Scripture.[86]

The qualifier "only if" is significant. This tone leans toward a hermeneutic of tradition that is initiated in suspicion rather than trust. His uneasiness is also shown in Chapter 7, "The Spirit of Understanding," where he responds to the shift in Hans Frei's definition of the literal meaning in his later work in which he began to explore the role of tradition as co-operative with the text, suggesting that

> Two consequences attend this new definition: first, the literal sense is no longer a feature of the 'text in itself,' but rather the product of the community's interpretive practice … No conflict between letter and spirit here: it is spirit, or community reading conventions, all the way down. Has Hans Frei exchanged his hermeneutical birthright for a mess of pottage, or rather, Fish—stew? It was Fish, Hauerwas's muse, who first suggested that meaning is a product of the way it is read. It is the community, ultimately, that enjoys interpretive authority. Must all hermeneutic roads lead to Rome?[87]

We will discuss this development in Frei in the next chapter. Frei's later position is, in fact, both more nuanced and less extreme than Vanhoozer's characterization. That Vanhoozer reacts so strongly to Frei on this point is an indication of just how

---

[86] Vanhoozer, *First Theology*, p. 202.
[87] Vanhoozer, *First Theology*, p. 219.

nervous he remains about the constructive role of reader(s) synchronic or diachronic action in hermeneutical process. His movement within type one, then, remains removed type two and along the left edge of the triangle.

Nevertheless: recalling basic geometry, the furthest distance within a triangle from the extreme of any one corner of a triangle will be in the outer extreme of the other two corners. As Vanhoozer moves up and away from the extreme of the first corner within the triangle he inevitably moves closer proximately to *both* of the other corners. This illustrates another advantage of using a triangle for this typology. I have suggested that no one can occupy a position relative to only one of the three issues represented by the three types and corners. I would further suggest that as one nuances one's thinking with respect to any combination of two of the three corners that the third issue inevitably and naturally becomes more pressing. We see this in Vanhoozer when the issue of the role of readers gets a cautious treatment in Chapter 8 of *First Theology*, entitled "The Reader at the Well" (1995). In it he casts the role of the reader in relation to the text primarily in responsive terms; "following," "feeding on" and "drinking from" as accepting, receiving, and appropriating the text.[88] Likewise, Vanhoozer acknowledges but carefully proscribes the role of the reading community in Chapter 10, "Body Piercing, the Natural Sense & the Task of Theological Interpretation" (2000):

[W]e must recognize the ecclesial and hermeneutical priority of God, specifically, the priority of his speech agency or "authorship" of Scripture. To interpret the Bible theologically is to interpret it as the verbal communicative action of God that bears witness to God's historical communicative actions in the history of Israel and of Jesus Christ. There are indeed many possible interpretive aims and interests, but the people of God must above all concern themselves with what God is saying, and doing, in and through Scriptures.[89]

The reading community is important insofar as they maintain the "norm" of theological interpretation: a "canonical rule" which is always understood as "God's say-so that enables the church's say-so"; a Rule of Faith consciously drawn from the text of Scripture itself.[90] We see Vanhoozer appropriating and accounting for issues relative to the second corner, type two, concurrently as he seeks to relate the issues presented by the salient features of types one and three. The trajectory of his work is confirmed then as moving from a more extreme position within type one up toward a position with a more balanced relationship between one and three (but still, at this point, closer to one).

This trajectory continues in his most recent work *The Drama of Doctrine*.[91] *Drama* is a watershed book in the evolution in Vanhoozer's hermeneutical and theological thinking. The subtitle is "A Canonical-Linguistic Approach to Christian Theology." This is a deliberate play off George Lindbeck's "cultural-linguistic" approach in *The Nature of Doctrine*. By replacing "Nature" with "Drama" and "Culture" with

---

[88] Vanhoozer, *First Theology*, p. 255-6.
[89] Vanhoozer, *First Theology*, p. 290.
[90] Vanhoozer, *First Theology*, p. 293.
[91] Kevin J. Vanhoozer, *The Drama of Doctrine* (Philadelphia, 2005), hereafter *Drama*.

"Canon" he signals both the indebtedness he attributes to Postliberal theology as well as his key points of difference.[92]

Key to his proposal is that the biblical Canon possesses the unquestioned hermeneutical authority. This is in contrast to what he sees as a kind of ambiguity or even ambivalence in Lindbeck, who he sees as ultimately giving it, instead, to the community of faithful readers. Likewise, in contrast to an abstraction he sees in Lindbeck's approach, he frames his discussion of theological methodology by way of drama theory in order to emphasize theology's active, practical and participatory nature. Thus a "canonical-linguistic theology" must be "prosaic, prophetic, and phronetic."[93]

One other important point of continuity that remains in *Drama* is his ambivalent relationship with his Evangelical forebears regarding the role of propositions in interpreting the Bible. On one hand he continues to affirm a necessary role for a degree of propositional content as a necessary ingredient in the truth that Scripture presents. On the other he reiterates his call for a greater sensitivity to the diversity of biblical genres that indicate a myriad of truth forms in addition to propositions.[94] This argument is original to his earliest article, which we discussed above. He goes much further, however, in *Drama* by locating the diverse aspects of biblical truth assertions within the more expansive milieu of *divine* speech action: "The macrogenre of Scripture is divine address."[95]

This is the culmination of the trajectory and development in his integration of divine and human agency in his thinking. So, whereas before he anchored the meaningfulness and truthfulness of Scripture abstractly in the speech actions of its human authors and sought to create a hermeneutic for all texts which unpacked this against the backdrop of the stability of language inherent to creation, he now emphasizes divine agency to the point that he dismisses his earlier assertion that all texts should be read like the Bible. Now he argues that "The Bible is not like other texts; it has been commissioned by Jesus and prompted by the Spirit. It is part and parcel of God's communicative action that both summons and governs the church."[96] And: "Both the gospel and the ensuing work of theology involve words and acts, thought the divine speech and action are prior to and take precedence over the human response."[97]

The Bible is now unique among texts due to its being caught up in the divine canonical-linguistic speech action. It is this divine speech act that also now "takes precedence" over both the human authorial speech action expressed in Scripture, and likewise over the speech-act of the theologian. These two developments are sufficiently sophisticated and certain in *Drama* that Vanhoozer would now be located just across the line into type three.

---

92   Vanhoozer, *Drama*, See introduction.
93   Vanhoozer, *Drama*, p. 441 et al.
94   Vanhoozer, *Drama*, p. 88 ff. Also see pp. 266-305.
95   Vanhoozer, *Drama*, p. 224.
96   Vanhoozer, *Drama*, p. 202.
97   Vanhoozer, *Drama*, p. 35, also see p. 114.

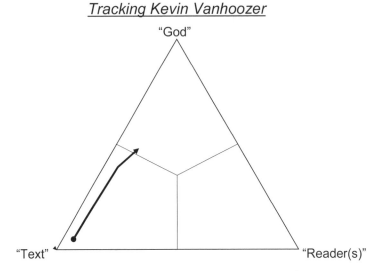

Fig 3.5 **Tracking Kevin Vanhoozer's Late Hermeneutical Development**

His commitment to the authority of Scripture in both its hermeneutical and doctrinal functions continues, but is now overtly acknowledged to be solely derivative of its relationship to God's prevenient and accompanying gracious revelatory activity. There is also a slight shift to the right in his location in the triangle. This is due to a heretofore unmentioned new emphasis in *Drama* that insists on the necessity and value for the role of responsive readers in a canonical-linguistic hermeneutic and theology. So:

> What comes first—that to which doctrine is primarily accountable—is triune communicative action. In the beginning was the word—the *promissio*, a communicative act—not propositions or religious experience or community practices. To the extent that Scripture has been taken up into the economy of triune communicative action, it has meaning *before* it is used by the interpretative community or socialized into the church's life.

So far this sounds very much like his earlier writings. However, now he continues:

> At the same time, Scripture is incomplete in the sense that, as an authoritative script, it calls for appropriation on the part of the believing community—in a word, *performance*.[98]

This new emphasis receives extensive treatment in *Drama* and is one of few Evangelical attempts to dwell deeply with the question of the role of tradition and reading communities without getting anxious and nervous and aborting the dialogue

---

[98] Vanhoozer, *Drama*, p. 101, also discussion on pp. 161-185.

too quickly. In the end Vanhoozer approximates one of the few contemporary approaches to biblical hermeneutics that attempts to fully account for all three aspects that are represented by our typology. It will be curious to see whether Evangelicals follow his lead or dismiss him as a prodigal son.

We will now go on to discuss the work of Francis Watson, as a biblical scholar who shares type one characteristics but who demonstrates a different initial balancing of the three correlate issues and thus a different track of development: a trajectory that eventually brings him into a sympathetic location relative to Vanhoozer.

Francis Watson: Negotiating Text, Church, and World

Francis Watson has wrestled deeply with issues related to all three of the component issues of our typology. Much of his development has taken place in dialogue with the work of Frei and Vanhoozer. His first attempt to systematically discuss his hermeneutic position is found in the book *Text, Church and World*.[99] In the preface he recognizes that the argument he is presenting may not be congenial to the status quo in his field insofar as he makes a case for "the primacy of theology within biblical interpretation."[100]

Like Vanhoozer he advocates a trinitarian hermeneutic. However, in contrast to Vanhoozer, the Trinity for Watson does not serve to underwrite a general hermeneutic of all texts but is uniquely relevant for the interpretation of Scripture. Without explicitly citing Vanhoozer he seems to have him in mind arguing against a general theological schema of all texts suggesting that "the idea that a literary perspective is, as such, already 'theological' seems to me to be without foundation."[101] He is also sympathetic to Frei's as shown in his argument that it is "impossible to separate the extra-textual content from its textual form."[102] In order to coordinate his distinctly Christian trinitarian hermeneutic along with his commitment to the final form of the text he constructs a framework of three concentric circles: text, church, and world. In the innermost circle stands the text in its final, canonical, form.

There are three possible justifications for taking the Bible in this final form. First, "under the influence of perspectives derived from literary studies"; second, "communal usage" appealing to the work of Brevard Childs; third, and "most compelling" is that it is "the form of the text most suitable for theological use." This last idea takes central place in *TCW* and is really a larger single argument which finds support from the other two. Thus the theological use of Scripture "is an ecclesial discipline and must therefore take seriously the ecclesial form of the text, but also from the theological judgment that the subject-matter of content of the biblical texts is inseparable from their form."[103] This theological judgment is justified by both contemporary literary studies which confirm the identity of form and context and

---

[99]   Francis Watson, *Text, Church and World* (Grand Rapids, 1994).
[100]   Watson, *TCW*, p. vii.
[101]   Watson, *TCW*, p. 1.
[102]   Watson, *TCW*, p. 3.
[103]   Watson, *TCW*, pp. 16-7.

by its place in the community of readers. Frei and Childs assist him on these points. This dual justification is prominent in his definition of "text":

> [C]urrent usage of the general term 'text' remains important in its emphasis on the relative autonomy or self-sufficiency of the written artifact. 'Text' is not synonymous with 'work', a term referring to productions which remain perpetually within their author's sphere of influence. To think of a 'work' is to imagine an author with a particular range of intentions and meanings to be communicated; it is to focus on the process and the circumstances which brought the work to birth. To think of a 'text', on the other hand, is to focus on the finished product, abstracted from its relation to a progenitor and considered in terms of its *use*.[104]

On the one hand, following Frei, he wishes to remove the text from the problematic preoccupation with the human author which he sees as underlying the problematic approaches of historical critical methods in biblical studies. On the other hand he forefronts the question of the agency which produces the reading in its use and function in its reading in the community:

> The contemporary concept of the 'text' is not without its own blindness and contradictions. Theologically, it can take us no further unless we counterbalance its claim to autonomy by asserting the fundamental hermeneutical significance of the reading community as the location from which the text derives its being and its rationale.[105]

The reading community, specifically the church, is the second concentric circle which encompasses the final form of the text of Scripture. Watson is attempting to balance the issues relative to types one and two; the text and the reader. His initial location on our triangle reflects this: his early work is near the middle of the base of the triangle between them. Like Vanhoozer he is both sympathetic to Frei's reaction to the imposition of prefabricated frameworks of meaning and, at the same time, critical of Frei's distinction between meaning and truth. However, he addresses this weakness differently.[106] Whereas Vanhoozer opposes Frei's differentiation of meaning and truth by affirming the unity of truth in God as reflected in the creational/ covenantal status of language Watson is wary of attributing too much of a role to the human author as he sees this preoccupation as underwriting the abuses he has witnessed in biblical studies. Instead, he responds to Frei by investing that agency in the church.

> [Frei's] perceived need to protect the text from the world may stem from the failure adequately to address the church's proper concern with the fundamental truth of the biblical story of salvation: for if, and only if, this story is true, then all worldly reality must be understood in the light of it. The claim that the text is fundamentally true liberates it from self-containment and enables it to shed its light on worldly realities.[107]

---

[104] Watson, *TCW*, p. 2.

[105] Watson, *TCW*, p. 3.

[106] I agree with David Ford that Watson's position in *TCW* is closer to Frei's actual position, especially in light of his later work, than Watson believes. See David Ford's Review of *TCW*, *Journal of Theological Studies*, Vo. 49, No. 1, April, 1998, p. 502.

[107] Watson, *TCW*, p. 29.

In this activity the church performs a ministerial function as the intermediary between text and world; an orientation that is inherently relational and communal.[108] Watson clarifies the function of "church" in his schema in conversation with Brevard Childs. He appreciates the emphasis Childs places on the community as a necessary and limiting framework for the consideration of the reading of Scripture. However, he believes Childs has employed too ideal a notion of community; one that seems to set up a reading context apart from the ideological and violent complications of the world. Watson is also concerned that the ideality of the community that Childs upholds, in the end, may undermine the authority of Scripture. Watson, rightly, walks the fine line here between affirming the constructive role of the church as the Bible's community of readers and maintaining Scripture's own prerogative to speak to the sinfulness of the church as it is implicated in its necessary interrelationship with the world.

He appeals again to his concentric circle framework and asserts that the community is the appropriate category to denote the space within which Scripture should be read but that the "'truthful witness' offered by the canonical text cannot simply be read off its surface but must be given and discovered in the midst and in the depths of the conflict-ridden situations in which the church is inevitably entangled."[109] This larger context and largest concentric circle in Watson's schema, is "world."

This is not some "neutral" sphere conceived in non-theological terms that needs to be negotiated with the text. Against this he insists that

> There is … no need to correlate text, church and world in such a way that the academy, representing the world, offers an independent location for the text over against the church … In correlating text, church, and world, the term 'world' must instead be understood theologically.[110]

Understanding the world theologically means recognizing that the world will ask certain questions that may result in the need for the church to evaluate what it holds to be the plain meaning of Scripture. His commitment to the final form of the text is not, therefore, transposed into a *carte blanche* commitment to the literal sense of Scripture. Watson appeals to Martin Luther's hermeneutic for support:

> The criterion by which the 'plain meaning' of certain texts must be resisted and rejected is the gospel itself; but since the gospel is not accessible to us in transparent, uninterrupted form, the process of discrimination will not be a mechanical one but a constant struggle for discernment, taking place above all in dialogue with others.[111]

Watson's commitment to the text is nuanced, then, in light of the text's location within the church and the world. Between these there are a series of dialogues: between the text and the church, between the church and the tradition, between the contemporary church and the world, and between text and world. All of these

---

[108] Watson, *TCW*, pp. 28-9.
[109] Watson, *TCW*, p. 45.
[110] Watson, *TCW*, pp. 8-9.
[111] Watson, *TCW*, p. 236.

dialogues are constructed in dialectical fashion. However the *agency* responsible for initiating and resolving the dialogues resides with the interpreter in the context of the church community. This is indicated in *TCW* when he outlines more extensively the "theological dimension" suggesting that

> The term 'theological' is of course contested, but implies in my usage an ability and a willingness to operate within a determinate form of ecclesial discourse: the tradition of self-critical reflection generated by the claims to truth, validity and adequacy inherent in Christian faith, or, more traditionally expressed, *fides quarens intellectum*. A hermeneutic which claims to be 'theological' must therefore explore the possibility of an interpretive practice oriented towards self-critical reflection on Christian truth claims.[112]

There is, here, no overt role for divine agency within the dialogues or in the process of their resolution.[113] This obscurity is also indicated in the nature of the agency which refers vis-à-vis the text of Scripture. How does the text refer beyond itself? Whose agency instigates this referral? Watson's circles would suggest that it is some combination of the human author and the church as a community of readers. In *TCW* it is, nevertheless, unclear how these agencies are related.

Watson's gesture toward the community of readers in *TCW* is based, in part, on his appreciation of the work of poststructuralists.[114] However, he is wary of losing the integrity of the person which he reads as an outcome of their work. He responds that "what is required in response to poststructuralism is an approach which sees the human person as constituted and not eliminated by its socio-linguistic framework."[115]

> [This] view is grounded in a relational, dialogical understanding of the image of God … In its vertical dimension, the concept of the image represents humankind as called by God's address to the autonomous response appropriate to dialogue … In its horizontal dimension, the image of God is closely related to the creation of humankind … as essentially relational.[116]

He appeals to the creation narratives in Genesis and the work of Jürgen Habermas to support his case. Similarly the early work of Vanhoozer Watson also seeks to ground his hermeneutic in a theology of creation. This grounding is characteristic of the epistemological terms we discussed in Chapter 1 in the wake of the Enlightenment's proscription of antecedent judgments about God. Watson's appeal to Habermas[117],

---

[112]   Watson, *TCW*, p. 79.

[113]   So Ford who suggests "To take just the doctrine of God, to which he gives priority: for all the presence of a trinitarian framework there is relatively little theological thinking about how who God is…affects interpretation, or about the nature of God's activity in interpretation, or about the ways in which knowing this God and being known by this God are related." "Review of *TCW*," p. 503.

[114]   See Watson, *TCW*, chapter 5.

[115]   Watson, *TCW*, p. 107.

[116]   Watson, *TCW*, pp. 107-8.

[117]   See Watson, *TCW*, chapter 6. It is no secret that Habermas is committed to maintaining the limits to reason which Kant advocated.

whose work is also committed to the exposition of human agency within immanent categories and spheres, also suggests that Watson's early work travels in similar circles. When we combine these two points we could conclude that there need not be any accompanying action by God in Watson's early schema other than that which Kant would also allow; in creating the world which includes the intersubjective social frameworks within which we receive our constitution and direction. Thus the theological claims function for Watson much as they do in Vanhoozer's early work; as notional judgments and scenery backdrops for human action. This is particularly evident when Watson moves from Habermas' general description of communicative communities to the case of the church.

> It is ... preferable to retain ... the more conventional notion of the church as a specific historical community which not only incorporates (like any other community) the possibility of relatively undistorted communication derived from creation and fall but also relates its existence primarily to the eschatological vision of universally undistorted communication which lies at the heart of its gospel of the kingdom of God.[118]

Like Kant, the notional theological claims which underwrite the ethical efforts of the individual are anchored in the created past and directed towards a yet unknown future. Watson, following Habermas, in contrast to Kant, defines the ethical integrity collectively instead of individually. The agency, however, is exhaustively human and immanent. This is reinforced when Watson goes on to clarify the nature of the vertical and horizontal dimensions of image we noted above. "The vertical dimension of the divine image is not prior to the horizontal ... the horizontal and vertical dimensions are posited as equally original, with the result that each is the mediation of the other."[119] If there is any divine agency present in this framework it operates strictly in identity with the dialogue established and maintained by and between the individual and community.

> God speaks only by way of one human person addressing another in intelligible language, for the vertical relation to God implied in the concept of the image is mediated in the horizontal form of an essential relatedness among human beings.[120]

This limitation of divine agency underscores Watson's location near the bottom of the triangle in this early work. Watson also claims an identity of the vertical and horizontal dimensions of image not simply in creation but also in the Trinity.[121] His emphasis is on Scripture's representation of God as one who seeks community. Humanity, as image of God, reflects this. The Trinity functions as a formal analogy to human communication similar to the way it does for Vanhoozer in *Is There a Meaning*; as an archetypal model with analogous features.[122] Watson also appeals to the activity of the "Spirit" to underwrite the validity and value of insights originating

---

[118] Watson, *TCW*, p. 114.
[119] Watson, *TCW*, p. 115.
[120] Watson, *TCW*, p. 119.
[121] Watson, *TCW*, pp. 149 ff.
[122] Watson will come to reject this use of the Trinity in his subsequent book *Text and Truth*, p. 304, fn. 26.

from outside the church as correctives to the potentially oppressive ways that the church reads the text as well as in providing insights into when and how the "plain sense" of Scripture should be resisted.[123]

Watson, in contrast to Vanhoozer, however, will emphasize the importance of keeping both the economic and the immanent Trinity in view.[124] Insofar as Vanhoozer is reluctant about the productive role of readers he has a vested interest in maintaining some distance between God's speech action and that of the contemporary community: a more formal appeal to the features of the economic Trinity affords him this safe distance. Conversely, Watson seeks to affirm the constructive immanent role for the church as users and readers of Scripture and, likewise, the emphasis on the inclusion of the immanent Trinity assists this.

On the whole Watson demonstrates a strong ambivalence about the role of community in the reading of Scripture. There are probably good and wise reasons for this. On the one hand we are inevitably formed within communities and traditions and to simply assert the problems associated with this leads to the profound sorts of skepticism and pessimism typical of poststructuralists. Watson insists, however, that the community is not only an instrument of violence but of justice and redemption as well.

He summarizes his own position in *TCW* and indicates awareness of the implications of this as well as the potential problems that arise:

> The decision to work with the final form of the biblical text is in keeping with its use of the narrative genre and with its functioning an ecclesial context ... Although there is a danger that the text will now be construed as a self-contained and self-sufficient narrative world, it is possible to combine elements of a literary approach with a critical realism aware of the text's existence within the public, socio-political domain.[125]

Some of the broader points of agreement and disagreement between Watson and Vanhoozer's early positions can now be succinctly noted. Vanhoozer is first a theologian who comes to hermeneutics indebted to the Evangelical commitment to the primacy of the biblical text and in particular to the integrity of the human author. He enters into the broader hermeneutical debates and confronts the "undoers", Derrida et al, and responds to their subversion of the human author. Vanhoozer uses speech act theory coupled with a strong assertion of the inherent theology in all literary theories (with nods to the work of John Milbank). He thereby intends to defend the agency of the human author as the determiner of meaning.

Watson is first a biblical scholar. He is less sanguine about prevailing notions of "author" and "text" as he sees the restrictive way that his field has used these categories to shut off the transformative power of Scripture. He is, conversely, more sanguine towards Derrida and poststructuralists in that they help him open the text and wrest it from the iron grip of biblical scholarship overly indebted to methods of historical criticism. Watson's early position in *TCW* advocates a nuanced version of Childs's canonical reading which is more sympathetic to the church's use and

---

[123] Watson, *TCW*, pp. 236-240.

[124] Watson, *TCW*, p. 6.

[125] Watson, *TCW*, p. 77.

reading of Scripture. Watson's affirmation of the agency of the church corrects what he sees as Frei's abstraction of the text from the world. We will now go on to see his subsequent work take him further to the left in the triangle and becoming a more moderate type one as well as up in the triangle, towards type three as he develops a more sophisticated understanding of the relationship between divine and human agency.

Watson's second book *Text and Truth* shows a distinct movement away from his early positions. In the introduction he writes in a way that could be seen as a criticism of some aspects of the position he previously assumed in *TCW*.

> In opposition to [a] one-sided reader-oriented hermeneutic, the [chapter] 'Literal Sense, Authorial Intention, Objective Interpretation' offers a 'Defence of Some Unfashionable Concepts'. These unfashionable concepts are important not because a 'conservative' hermeneutic is inherently preferable to a 'radical' one but because the notion of the readerly creation of meaning is incompatible with the role of a particular set of texts as Christian scripture. This role requires the communication of determinate meaning to readers. Although the elaboration of that meaning will always be shaped by the context of its reception, it remains possible to argue that texts have a 'literal sense' dependent on 'authorial intention', and that their ambiguities may be contained (if not eliminated) by a set of 'objective', non-context-dependent interpretive procedures.[126]

The role of Scripture, here, is to communicate meaning *to* readers. He has, then, qualified the assertive agency of the reader and community in co-creating meaning in *TCW* and more clearly gives the authority and primacy to the agency of the text. Like Vanhoozer, he now employs speech-act theory to assert that a "determinate communicative intention is embedded in the text" and, still following Frei, that "it is not to be found 'behind the text' in an authorial psychology or in an 'original' historical context." Also, he appears to be repentant in his response to his earlier work and has once more embraced a more typical stance as a biblical scholar with regard to the tools of their trade when he writes that "In so far as textual-critical and exegetical procedures make it possible to determine more precisely what a text does and does not *say*, they are indispensable for all interpretation, irrespective of its communal location."[127]

His shifting emphasis is also demonstrated in that his appeal to Habermas in *TCW* is replaced with an appeal to Gadamer and Ricoeur in *TT*, who are both more accommodating and appreciative of the agency ascribed to the text in contrast to Habermas who places greater emphasis on the community. Regarding the value of Gadamer for his proposal he writes,

> If the gospels are regarded as canonical, communally-authoritative texts, then there can be no question of confining these texts to an immobilized past into which one enters through the fictive activity of the empathetic imagination. As classic texts, *they bear with them a truth-claim*, and the primary task of interpretation is to come to terms with that truth-claim in a context which will always be different from past contexts in which the truth-claim has

---

[126] Watson, *Test and Truth*, p. 11.
[127] Watson, *TT*, p. 11.

been heard, to struggle with the difficulties that it may pose, and to bring to light its disclosive possibilities for the present.[128]

Gadamer's thought needs supplementation, however, in that he can be read to insulate the community and tradition from criticisms that may arise externally to it. Thus whatever authority Scripture is ascribed by the church must be mitigated by criticisms brought by the world.

> [T]he sphere of the church and its proclamation is not hermetically sealed against the rest of the world, and to confine the significance of the gospels within narrow communal limits would betray the universality of their truth-claim. We must search for a conceptuality which mediates between the ecclesial and the non-ecclesial spheres..[129]

We see some continuity here with the three circle arrangement in *TCW* even as he has given greater determinative agency to the text over above the interpretive actions of the community and the world. The agency of the text is also now discussed in terms of the agency of the author. Thus there is a fairly substantive shift in his attitude toward the author from *TCW* to *TT.* He begins; "Writing, like speaking, is a communicative action. It is an *action*, carried out by human agency."[130] However, he is quick to reinstate the Freian limits on the investigation of that agency:

> An oral speech-act can initiate various forms of communicative interaction ... In contrast, the author will normally be absent from the reception of the written communication and will therefore be unavailable to answer questions. The extendedness of writing in space and time makes most authors more or less inaccessible, and, where a text is deemed significant enough for answers to questions of meaning and truth to be important, a surrogate for the absent author is installed in the form of an *interpreter*.[131]

Nevertheless, interpreters "can only *receive* meaning, they cannot *create* it."[132] Watson now insists that the author is the creator of the meaning in the text and that this can be conceived in terms of speech act theory, which invests the text with potential illocutionary and perlocutionary force in the future, even in the absence of the author. A leftover theme of *TCW* remains in that it is the community which sustains and preserves that perlocutionary action.[133] The communal tradition also restrains the perlocutionary force in the case of violent plain meanings.[134]

His new emphasis on the positive role for the author in *TT* is also accompanied by overt gestures to the anchoring of that agency in divine action.

> While certain parallels may be drawn between the general phenomenon of the classic and Christian holy scripture, they break down at the crucial point—which is that Christian scripture bears witness, in many and various ways, to the decisive series of events in

---

128   Watson, *TT*, p. 50. Emphasis mine.
129   Watson, *TT*, p. 51.
130   Watson, *TT*, p. 98.
131   Watson, *TT*, p. 102.
132   Watson, *TT*, p. 104.
133   Watson, *TT*, pp. 116 ff.
134   Watson, *TT*, pp. 120-1.

which God is held to have uniquely disclosed Himself, and to the pattern of life shaped in response to that self-disclosure.[135]

Thus in addition to the main qualification of *TT* from *TCW* which involves Watson's renewed, but careful, confidence in the agency of the author of Scripture, there is added a stronger link of the author's action as a responsive witness to God's actions of self-disclosure.[136] In *TCW* his emphasis was placed on the agency of the reading community with hints about the underwriting of that action in the economic/ immanent Trinity. In *TT* he qualifies and supplements that emphasis with a more overt consideration of the relationship of divine and human agency. His effort to balance these two aspects is evident in *TT* when he advocates three rules for the theological interpretation of Scripture:

> 1. The *literal sense* of the biblical texts comprises (*i*) verbal meaning, (*ii*) illocutionary and perlocutionary force, and (*iii*) the relation to the centre … The criteria by which scriptural communicative actions are assessed derive from God's definitive communicative action in the incarnation of the Word. 2. To grasp the verbal meaning and illocutionary and perlocutionary force of a text is to understand the *authorial intention* embodied in it … . 3. A text's verbal meaning, illocutionary and perlocutionary force, and relation to the centre precede and transcend the additional meanings or significances it may acquire as it is read in different communal contexts. *Objective interpretation* concerns itself with the primary and determinative aspects of a text's existence. While local, contextual concerns will often and rightly leave their mark on interpretive practice, they should not deprive the text of its proper vocation, which is to represent, in frail human language, a divine communicative action which does not arise from among ourselves but addresses us from without.[137]

Watson's position on our typology, then, moves from the middle of the bottom of the triangle towards the left. His position also moves up from near the base line of the triangle towards the top corner of the triangle insofar as he more clearly anchors the agency of both the author and the reader in divine action. Despite these emphases the exact relationship of human and divine action remains undeveloped.

So: while Frei and Vanhoozer's ships begin at a hailing distance in the extreme corner of type one and move off in different directions, Frei to the right towards type two and Vanhoozer up towards type three, Frei and Watson are like ships that pass in the night. Watson begins at the crossroads of types one and two. Watson moves to the left and then with Vanhoozer up toward type three. He does this even as Frei in his later work explores the role for the reading community in the determination

---

[135] Watson, *TT*, pp. 97-8.

[136] It is here that Watson affirms a constructive role for a kind of rule of faith for reading Scripture as part and parcel of accepting the final form as canon. He writes, "The real question is whether or not it is granted that the Christian canon exists, that it has a centre, that this centre is the self-disclosure in Jesus of the triune God who is creator, reconciler and redeemer, and that an exegesis of a particular text cannot be regarded as *theologically* normative if it conflicts with what must be said at this centre." TT p. 248.

[137] Watson, *TT*, pp. 123-4.

of the text's meaning, moving past Watson's early position and into a moderate position within type two. The difference between Frei's later work and Watson's early work, we will see, is that Frei emphasizes the role of the *diachronic* community (by way of Kelsey and Lindbeck) while Watson initially emphasizes the agency of the *synchronic* reading community.

Watson's new position in the triangle reflects a new set of commitments regarding the relationship of divine and human agency in the reading of Scripture. In contrast to his earlier position he has come to be much more reserved and even critical of the imposing agency of the present reader and reading community. At the same time he is more sanguine about the role of the received tradition of reading. Further, there is a much more overt signaling of the primacy of divine agency in composing, guiding and preserving the meaning of the biblical text. His new position on the triangle reflects these.

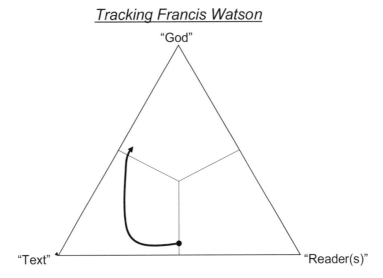

Tracking Francis Watson

Fig 3.6 Mapping Francis Watson's Hermeneutical Trajectory

The Implications of Type 1: Benefits and Detriments

We close this chapter with a brief consideration of some of the positive and negative implications of type one approaches. The more extreme forms of type one will correspondingly indicate greater propensities for the problems and, conversely, will share less in the benefits. Likewise, the more moderate type ones will be more immune to the detriments and possess greater benefits. The three figures we surveyed above are all more moderate expressions of type one.

There are two benefits or strengths and two weaknesses for type one approaches to reading Scripture that we will discuss here. Certainly there are others which could be included as well, if space allowed. The first strength, as well as the first weakness, is methodological; the second, likewise, in both cases, is theological. First, the methodological benefit of this type is that the text itself receives serious consideration and attention on its own terms.

Type one approaches, including a majority of the work of modern biblical scholars, theologians and hermeneuticians, have given great service in providing access to language and cultural resources which shed light on the richness and diversity of the language of Scripture. The study of the linguistic, social, and historical background of the text is tenaciously pursued with the result that a great many nuances and subtleties within the text are revealed. These both assist in anchoring the literal meaning of the text, assisting us in recognizing borders between readings which can and cannot be read off the surface of the text. The nuances also reveal the variety and flavor of the text, like exotic spices, which the able expositor can take and apply in the recipes of their exposition and proclamation of the Gospel.

The second, theological, benefit accompanies the methodological; that Scripture is acknowledged as the primary locus of authority for Christians. The utmost commitment to this principle in type one is negatively indicated by the fact that those within this type, in the face of disagreements with other type one scholars, will often accuse them of neglecting the true authority of Scripture: as if their differences can be reduced to their level of commitment to the authority of the text. We saw that Hans Frei, as one of the purest examples of type one, is highly critical of other type one approaches that he sees as bringing to the reading of the text frameworks for meaning that tend to distort the meaning in the text. Watson and Vanhoozer are both sympathetic to this criticism. Likewise, the most provocative accusations and debates in the history of biblical interpretation often take place between biblical scholars and theologians who all share a methodological commitment to the priority of the text but disagree about how the task of discerning that meaning should best be undertaken.

These intramural debates, as well as criticisms that come from outside type one, certainly have points of validity. Nevertheless, the *intention* of this approach is to give the text itself the utmost attention and priority in the establishment of meaning and any truth claims that we see as attributable to the text. Thus from a *theological* standpoint type one approaches all perceive themselves to be committed, albeit in often times conflicting manners, to the unique authority of the text of Scripture. This theological strength remains despite the differences. This is so in that the neglect of the uniquely authoritative role of Scripture in forming and sustaining the life of the Church carries greater potential harm than the problems they potentially present. In other words, it is theologically preferable to read Scripture as being authoritative with inadequate methodological tools for dealing with divine agency and the role of diachronic and synchronic reading traditions, than to either read it as if it is without any unique authority or to not read it at all.

There are, conversely, two detrimental aspects of type one, which are also methodological and theological. Each of these detriments has an identifiable relationship with the methodological and theological strengths, respectively, above. These detriments can be seen as the other side of the coin of the strengths. The weaknesses of this type are also the byproduct of the inherent strengths in the position being pushed to too far of an extreme. This results in the proper relationship and negotiation of divine and human agency in reading Scripture being thrown out of balance and skewed.

The methodological detriment of type one occurs when the focus on the text in terms of immanent spheres of human authorial and editorial actions becomes too abstracted from the correlate issues in the typology represented by type two. This is the result when biblical scholars and theologians fail to recognize that their own handling, reading and study of the text of Scripture are always variously traditionally and contextually shaped and biased. This bias, in the extreme type one approach, is viewed with absolute suspicion and as something which should be eliminated. In this case the practitioner is the most faithful proponent of the Enlightenment terms we laid out in Chapter 1. The failure of these more extreme type one approaches to accept and account for their locatedness often produces the perception that their work can, and does, completely transcend location and influence. There then arises an overestimation of reason's capacity for objectification and an overinvestment in the ability of human investigation to proceed with objectivity and comprehensiveness regarding the various minutiae of issues and details that arise in the course of the study of the text. This is, ultimately, a house of cards, which, if tethered too closely to one's faith, can have disastrous results. All of us know sincere persons who, after traversing the rigors of a PhD program in biblical studies, have their house knocked down when they discover that the foundation of their house is not as sturdy as believed.

The net result of this is tendency in scholarship is exemplified in the well known cottage industries of biblical studies which wrestle with historical questions pertaining to the composition, modification and transmission of the biblical text in increasing abstraction. The abstraction takes place in two respects. On one hand, the work becomes more and more unrelated to any concrete contemporary purpose of Scripture. Scripture's primary role, as the communication of the good news of Christ and as the witness and conveyance of God's Word to God's elect people, shaping them toward their salvation and to His glory, is increasingly irrelevant to the questions as they are pursued. On the other hand, the pursuit of the question becomes abstracted from the inherent limitations of historical critical investigations. Thus the propensity for proposals related to specific textual questions to assume less and less of a descriptive stance and more and more of a creative, speculative tone. The ubiquitous and variously irreconcilable proposals for discerning the historical Jesus is one of the most obvious examples of this principle at work. The work of the reader and scholar of Scripture, to the degree that it is characterized by one or both of these abstractions, will be increasingly in an unproductive and irrelevant relationship with the function of Scripture in its formative role for the contemporary community. Just because a questions *can* be asked does not entail that it *should* be asked or that it could ever be answered. Therefore, the more extreme one's location in the bottom left corner of type one, the more one's work will not be constructively related to the reading of Scripture in the church.

The first *methodological* detriment tends, then, to neglect the corollary issues represented to the reading by type two as demonstrated in two kinds of abstractions; the abstraction from the contemporary reading context and the abstraction from the inherent limitations of the nature of the historical question. The second, *theological,* detriment of type one also relates to these two abstractions but does so as they are abstractions from the correlate issues represented by type three; divine action.

The first abstraction relates to understanding the contextual nature of the act of reading. In methodological terms, this involves neglecting the complex nature of the influence and bias of the reader within a reading community. In theological terms this abstraction is a neglect, denial or removal of the reading of Scripture from the divine action that underwrites and accompanies the reading of the text. This includes both the accompaniment of the Spirit in guiding the diachronic tradition and in leading the synchronic church in the reading and appropriation of Scripture.

The second abstraction is the neglect of the inherent limitations of historical question asking in the pursuit of specific textual issues and questions. In theological terms the abstraction runs the danger of pressing human inquiry into service beyond its limited created capacity to perform. This relates to the construal of the task of reading Scripture and the influence of the Enlightenment epistemological restrictions we discussed in Chapter 1. The more extreme forms of type one will assume, along with Kant, that the more objective and ethically responsible reading of Scripture will be initiated and maintained by the self-sufficient reader apart from the corrupting influence of any other agent, human or divine.

Pre-critical readings of Scripture assumed the action of God alongside and with the reader. As we suggested above the more the act of reading Scripture is construed as taking place apart from the assistance and attendance of divine agency, the more a vacuum forms. The problem arises as to who guarantees and controls reading, guiding to a correct end. Enlightenment epistemology reinforces the perception that God does not share in this responsibility as this relieves human agents of their ethical and moral obligations. The human action of reading is, then, perceived as solely responsible for providing the impetus and action as well as the controls for the reading. Once this perception is accepted the felt need to account for every methodological jot and tittle, as well as the compulsion to ask and answer every possible question that arises in regard to the text, become overwhelming.

This produces an analogy to the original temptation represented by the fruit of the tree of good and evil in the Garden of Eden; when the creature felt the desire and need to know what the Creator knows. The difference between the temptation in the garden and the temptation of the modern reading of Scripture is that in the latter case the creature seems to have no choice; that the creature is alone in producing meaning and knowledge and so *must* eat the apple and pursue textual questions *ad infinitum* so as to ensure the correct meaning and the exhaustive knowledge of good and evil.

The discussion of the two detriments of type one should not be read to imply that all approaches will be equally or similarly guilty of promoting or producing these two weaknesses. For example, Frei, Watson and Vanhoozer are moderate approaches by comparison and demonstrate developments in their work which tend to avoid the extreme effects of the detriments. It is nevertheless generally the case that the tendencies of type one approaches will arise, when they do, in forms resembling one of, or a combination of, these two weaknesses.

Chapter 4

Type Two: Human Agency in the "Reading"

In this chapter we will continue to develop our typology looking at examples of type two. Those who represent this type have two characteristics. First, they see the initial, primary, or decisive issues in reading Scripture as being derivative of some aspect of the question "How is Scripture used or read?" Second, in answering this question, they employ methods and focus their investigation decisively or exclusively on some dimension of human activity or human quality present in the reading. Accompanying this emphasis is the subordination of the roles of human agency contained in, or constituting the text (type one) and of the divine action prior to and constituent in both (type three).

This second characteristic is common to both types two and type one. The first characteristic, of focusing on the specific aspect of how the text is used or read, is a common concern of type twos along with some type threes in that the question can be approached from either the standpoint of human or divine agency. There are mediating positions along the spectrum. Where one would be placed along that line would be determined by the weighting and relationship of divine and human agency.

There are also two distinct variations within type two. The first variant attends to that aspect of the human reading which is developed in the *diachronic* community's role in reading of the text. The role that tradition plays in much of Catholic interpretation is an example of this. The second variant is the role and function of the *synchronic* reading and attends to the shaping of the reading that is produced in the contemporary engagement of the community or reader with the text. Werner Jeanrond and Stephen Fowl are examples of this second variant and will be surveyed below.[1] In philosophical hermeneutics the work of Hans-Georg Gadamer and his

---

[1]   Other examples of this type include Walter Brueggemann, *Texts Under Negotiation: The Bible and Postmodern Imagination* (Minneapolis: 1993); Robert M. Fowler, *Let the Reader Understand: Reader Response Theory and the Gospel of Mark* (Minneapolis, 1991); Mary McClintock Fulkerson, "'Is There a (Non-Sexist) Bible in the Church?' A Feminist Case for the Priority of Interpretive Communities" in *Theology and Scriptural Imagination* (Oxford, 1998); Claude Geffré, *Christianity and the Risk of Interpretation*, trans. David Smith (New York, 1987); Darrell Jodock, *The Church's Bible* (Minneapolis, 1989), and "The Reciprocity Between Scripture and Theology," *Interpetation* 44 (October, 1990), pp. 369-382; Wesley Kort, *Story, Text and Structure* (University Park, 1988), and *"Take, Read": Scripture, Textuality and Cultural Practice* (University Park, 1996); Stephen D. Moore, *Literary Criticism and the Gospel* (New Haven, 1989), *Mark and Luke in Poststructuralist Perspectives* (New Haven, 1992), and *Poststructuralism and the New Testament* (Minneapolis, 1994); Lewis Mudge, *Rethinking the Beloved Community* (New York, 2001); *The Open Text: New Directions for Biblical Studies?*, edited by Francis Watson (London, 1993); *The Postmodern Bible*, edited

view of the "fusion of horizons" tends towards the first variant; Jürgen Habermas is an example that has a strong tendency toward the second.[2] These two aspects of type two are not mutually exclusive or necessarily opposed. Thus one can attempt to bring both aspects into constructive tension, as Paul Ricoeur does with Gadamer and Habermas, although in the actual concrete moment of reading one is inevitably given preference over the other.

Our analysis will focus on how a diverse sample of thinkers approaches the prioritizing of immanent human readerly agency. These examples use a variety of terminology and language to describe Scripture and the act of reading. We will see that, regardless of how a type two emphasizes the role of the reader, there is always something also assumed with respect to the nature of the text as a human speech action as well as the divine action that accompanies *both*. These assumptions appear as either positive or negative claims about the text or about divine agency.

The writings which belong to this second type have often developed in explicit response to the dominance of type one approaches in modern biblical hermeneutics. Recalling Buckley's groupings from Chapter 2 we suggest that debates about reading Scripture early in the twentieth century were dominated by the interchange between textualists and revelationalists. Both textualists and revelationalists tended to focus on the question of reading Scripture in relative abstraction from the specific and particular relationship the reading has to its function in the community of readers. In this abstraction there is a tacit commitment to the sufficiency and independence of the reader. The issue of how the location of the individual or the role of the interpretive community should carry interpretive weight was, *at most,* a subsequent and secondary issue. The primary issues for biblical scholars during this time tended to be reduced to questions related to what Scripture contains or enacts. For example, whether the very words should be taken as the essential content, as they had some kind of determinable relationship to the events they depict, or that the essential thing the words had was a relationship to a transhistorical referent or religious experience. As time granted biblical scholars and theologians perspective on this debate the flaws in the commonly held assumptions became apparent. Inevitably, as with all historical and traditional developments, there was a reaction. The reaction came as a shift away from individualist textualist readings to collectivist functionalist readings.

---

by Elizabeth Castellli, Stephen Moore et al. (New Haven, 1995); *The Postmodern Bible Reader,* edited by David Jobling et al. (Oxford, 2001); Kathryn Tanner, "Scripture as Popular Text," in *Theology and the Scriptural Imagination* (Oxford, 1998); Frances Young, *The Art of Performance* (London, 1993); *The Bible and Its Readers,* edited by Wim Beuken, Sean Freyne and Anton Weiler (London, 1991); J. Severino Croatto, *Biblical Hermeneutics: Toward a Theory of Reading As the Production of Meaning* (Maryknoll, 1987); David Tracy, *Blessed Rage for Order* (Minneapolis, 1975), and *Plurality and Ambiguity* (San Francisco, 1987); George Aichele, *Sign, Text and Scripture* (Sheffield, 1997). Also see Edgar McKnight, *Post-Modern Use of the Bible: The Emergence of Reader Oriented Criticism* (Nashville, 1988).

[2]   Other non-theological examples would include Stanley Fish, *Is There a Text in This Class?* (Cambridge, 1980), and the writings of Richard Rorty.

David Kelsey: Using Scripture

David Kelsey's book *The Uses of Scripture in Recent Theology*[3] stands as a seminal writing in this development. This book has both characteristic features of type two approaches. First, his analysis gives greater determinative weight to the actions of reader(s) over the text as determining its meaning. Second, there remains a notion of neutrality underwriting his work that reinforces a bias to looking to immanent human fields of action to explain this. This is underwritten by the claim to enter a "theologically neutral" sphere as the proper location from which to examine the reading of Scripture.[4] He admits: "I have tried in this essay to devise a way of commenting on quite different theological procedures without relying on a general theory about the nature of theology."[5] Kelsey is committed both to this neutral theological space and also assumes a similar meaning/truth distinction as Hans Frei:

> [B]efore questions about a theological position's "adequacy" can be addressed, or even its "truth" Christianly speaking, it is necessary to make some judgments about the kind of intellectual enterprise it is, the way it is "put together."[6]

This meaning/truth distinction carries over into his analysis of the particular positions in *Uses*.[7] Frei's stance toward the text in *Identity* viewed the text as having an opaque integrity. Its integrity is the unity of "meaning" and "truth" in its composition. The opacity is the inability of the reader to discern "truth" apart from its embeddedness in and with the "meaning." Thus the stance of the reader that Frei advocates is one which simply attempts to describe the text; as a kind of neutral observer of the ingredient unity of truth and meaning. Kelsey advocates a similar stance towards the reader/"user." Thus whatever truth claims the readers make in regard to their approach to reading Scripture, they are relativized in the same way that the truth claims in the text are for Frei. In other words, both Kelsey and Frei determine to undertake a purely (objective?) descriptive task (of the text and the reader, respectively) apart from explanatory frameworks (antecedent judgments?). In this they are both similarly observant of the Enlightenment limitations from Chapter 1.

We will see further below that Frei eventually came to see his own earlier employment of this meaning/truth distinction as being just as culpable in its heavy handed imposition of truth or explanatory schemes as those to which he was responding. Frei also came to see that his claim about the self-referentiality of the text was, in fact, a general theory, and indebted to theological judgments. There are also similar developments in Kelsey's subsequent thinking. But these will not

---

[3] David Kelsey, *The Uses of Scripture in Recent Theology* (Philadelphia, 1975), reprinted as *Proving Doctrine* (Harrisburg, 1998). Kelsey subsequently qualified certain aspects of his thinking in *Uses* in "The Bible and Christian Theology," *JAAR* 48/3, 385-402.

[4] Kelsey, *Uses*, p. 2.

[5] Kelsey, *Uses*, p. 8.

[6] Kelsey, *Uses*, p. 10.

[7] Kelsey, *Uses*, p. 14.

concern us here insofar as *Uses* stands as such an important text in the evolution of type two approaches. We will look at it in its own terms, in the manner in which it remains influential,[8] as a way of introducing this group.

Kelsey identifies seven types of approaches to reading Scripture. Six of the seven exhibit tendencies which make them examples of type one approaches in our typology. Kelsey denotes a first grouping of three as attributing authority to the *content* of Scripture.[9] They construe the determinative content either as "doctrine"[10] (B. B. Warfield), as "concepts"[11] (Hans-Werner Bartsch), or as "the narrative of salvation history"[12] (G. Ernest Wright). Kelsey identifies two conceptual agreements between these.

> First, it is agreed that scripture has a body of context that is "authoritative" for all Christian theology *in the sense that* it is the context which modern theology must simply restate … Second, there is agreement … that scripture is authoritative in virtue of the fact that its authoritative content is identical with the content of divine revelation.[13]

The second group of three attributes authority based on the *expressions* of Scripture:

> The authoritative elements [in this case] may be called "images" or "symbols" or "myths."… Men have verbally expressed their experience of that event in very concrete, iconic ways. Scripture is a collection of those expressions.[14]

These three view the authority of scripture in terms of the "mystery" expressed in its "images"[15] (L. S. Thornton), its "religious symbols"[16] (Paul Tillich), or the "myths" of the "Christ event"[17] (Rudolf Bultmann). Kelsey also identifies a rationale for linking them:[18]

> We lump them together in order to stress how much they have in common just at the point at which they also so deeply differ. They all stress the radically "event" character of revelation and share a common decision to construe the Bible as a collection of expressions of the occurrence of that event. Hence what is authoritative about scripture is not its surface content of doctrine, concept, or narrative, but its non-informative *force* as expression.[19]

---

[8] To this date the book is still in print under the new title *Proving Doctrine*.
[9] He includes a fourth, Barth, in this group. However our reading of Barth locates him in type three so we set him aside for now.
[10] Kelsey, *Uses*, pp. 17-24.
[11] Kelsey, *Uses*, pp. 24-9.
[12] Kelsey, *Uses*, pp. 33-8.
[13] Kelsey, *Uses*, p. 38.
[14] Kelsey, *Uses*, p. 56.
[15] Kelsey, *Uses*, pp. 57-64.
[16] Kelsey, *Uses*, pp. 64-74.
[17] Kelsey, *Uses*, pp. 74-83.
[18] Kelsey, *Uses*, p. 83.
[19] Kelsey, *Uses*, p. 85.

These three, along with the first three, are all variants that belong to our type one. They all attribute authority to some aspect, agency or "force" within the text of Scripture. Kelsey models a quintessential methodological alternative to these six. His book is, in this way, a classic and remarkably consistent expression of a type two. It should not be underestimated how seminal and pure an example his book *Uses* is in the development and growth of type two approaches in the twentieth century.

How this is the case deserves some careful unpacking. First, Kelsey assumes that the approaches he is discussing have a common internal integrity which can be explained by his theory of "uses." This has an important and profound impact on the nature of the apparent disagreements between the six. Among and between these writers, their differences are irreconcilable: they each are committed to the text as the proper location or medium of meaning but have clear and mutually exclusive views on what that entails. However: by surveying them under the coordination of a theory of uses these differences are no longer seen as irreconcilable views on the nature of the biblical *text* but are now viewed as variable views on the nature of *reading*.

Second, in this he assumes the ability to stand above, observe, describe, and choose among these uses. The net effect of these two moves combines to negate the determinative thing which is the common point of agreement in all six. That common point is their commitment to the authority ascribed to some aspect of the text as the key to the location of its meaning. Kelsey, by describing all six simply as options available to any reader, shifts the location of authority from the agency in the text to the agency of the reader. In essence, he has completely redefined the nature of the problem. The six are mistaken or naïve to think that these problems are about the "text"; they are, in fact, about the "reading." This is clearly indicated in his four point response to the six approaches.

> 1) Part of what it means to call a text or set of texts "scripture" is that its use in certain ways in the common life of the Christian community is essential to establishing and preserving the community's identity ... 2) Part of what is said in calling a text or set of texts "scripture" is that it is "authority" for the common life of the Christian community ... 3) To call a text or set of texts "scripture" is to ascribe some kind of "wholeness" to it ... 4) The expression, "Scripture is authoritative for theology" has self-involving force. When a theologian says it, he does not so much offer a descriptive claim about a set of texts and one of its particular *properties*; rather, he commits himself to a certain kind of activity in the course of which these texts are going to be *used* in certain ways.[20]

In each case, the reader is now construed as having the primary responsibility as the agent who attributes and gives scripture its authority and meaning as such. This is also seen in the way that Kelsey summarizes each of the three main sections of *Uses* in terms of "decisions" that the reader makes. He writes:

> In Part I we saw that when a theologian appeals to scripture in the course of doing theology he is obliged to make at least three decisions about how to *construe* the texts ... In Part II we saw that our theologian is also obliged to make decisions about how to *use* the texts he construes ... in Part III ... [I will discuss] a decision a theologian must make about the

---

[20] Kelsey, *Uses*, p. 89.

point of engaging in the activity of doing theology, a decision about what is the subject matter of theology.[21]

The reader, again, has the responsibility for the "decision" and the determination of each aspect.[22] This reader is reminiscent of the self-sufficient moral agent in Kant. The reader enjoys this capacity unencumbered by any restriction imposed by the human agency contained in the text or by divine agency in the text or tradition. The question raised at this point is how it is that the reader in the specific act of reading selects and orients his or her approach. How do we negotiate between the options at our disposal? Kelsey, in an apparent lapse from his theological neutrality, offers a prescriptive answer:

> These decisions [regarding how to construe Scripture] are decisively shaped by a theologian's prior judgment about how best to construe the mode in which God's presence among the faithful correlates with the use of Scripture in the common life of the church.[23]

This observation may be methodologically at odds with Kelsey's own claims about his analysis, however it reinforces claims made in our typology and also concurs with Buckley's argument in "Deadlock" that it is ultimately "different Gods" that are at work in the variances of approaches to reading and authority.[24] The same can also be said for Kelsey. That despite his initial claims otherwise, Kelsey's own analysis also trades on notions of divine agency that can be discerned and described in overt theological categories. For example, in Kelsey's methodological shift, which attributes greater agency in the determination of the meaning of Scripture to the decisions of the reader, there are also implicit judgments that pertain to God's agency. His proposal gives greater authority to *synchronic* (or contemporary) divine action. It does so primarily to underwrite and serve as a backdrop for all the discriminatory decisions the *present* reader makes. God does not, however, specifically participate in that discrimination, nor does God's diachronic (past) action provide any special guidance to the contemporary reading. Kelsey writes,

> Therefore, instead of taking "God saying" as the overarching image for all the various things Christians are inclined to say God "does" with the Bible, we have proposed "shaping identity". Speaking *theologically*, God "uses" the church's various uses of Scripture in her common life to nurture and reform [her] self-identity … Theological proposals are to elucidate what that identity is and ought to be, and what reforms are called for and why. However, "shaping" is abstract. Every actual set of theological proposals … is given its peculiar shape by some concrete construal of the mode in which that "shaping" takes place. And that, we have suggested, is an imaginative act, not an exegesis of the "meaning" of what God "says" through the Bible.[25]

---

[21] Kelsey, *Uses*, pp. 166-7.
[22] Although Kelsey qualifies this in "The Bible and Christian Theology".
[23] Kelsey, *Uses*, p. 167.
[24] Buckley, "Deadlock," see discussion in chapter 2.
[25] Kelsey, *Uses*, p. 214.

Also,

> "Control" is simply a misleading term to use … No "hermeneutic" and no doctrine of the
> authority of scripture could hope to discover the key to that perfect employment … No
> "theological position" would presume to tell us how to use scripture so as to "guarantee"
> that God will be present to illuminate and correct us. Theological proposals are concerned
> with what God is now using scripture to do, and no degree of sophistication in theological
> methodology can hope to anticipate that![26]

Kelsey only negatively cautions us about the influence of prior agents and
theological constructs as well as any assumption (antecedent judgment) about God's
assistance in and with that reading. God's contemporary action underwrites, but does
not influence or participate with, this reading in any way which can be described
beforehand. This way of setting the stage for the reading of Scripture is common to
other type two approaches as we will see below. All of them share a debt to Kelsey's
definitive work.

We suggested above that despite Kelsey's warning about assuming some
"theological position" before coming to read Scripture he himself assumes one in
the way he approaches his analysis. Francis Fiorenza, in his article "The Crisis of
Scriptural Authority", observes the assumptions about God's agency that animate
this aspect of Kelsey's writing:

> The functional interpretation of scriptural authority has the problem that it begs the
> question. By explicating the normativeness of the Scriptures on the basis of a *de facto*
> authority, it does not sufficiently spell out the *de jure* authority. Kelsey's original proposal
> argues … that the authority of the Scriptures depends upon its functional role, that is,
> upon the claim that this is the way that Scriptures function in the Christian community
> as such … The *de facto* use is the function. The *de jure* use is **the relation of God to
> Scripture.** The *de jure* is not grounded in God's revelatory self-presence but rather in God
> as sanctifier and transformer of human identity.[27]

Fiorenza's criticism points to the suggestion that Kelsey cannot proceed with a
de facto description of the function of Scripture without assuming some kind of *de
jure* relationship between God and Scripture. There is an inherent tension within
Kelsey's work at this point.

We highlighted the *formal* analogy between this tension in Kelsey with Frei's
early work above. In this there is also, then, a *material* tension that they share.
We noted in Chapter 3 how Frei had difficulty in accounting for the agency which
causes the transition between the meaning being ingredient in, and emerging from,
the text. This is similar to Kelsey's silence on the shape and relationship of human
and divine agency in the reader as he or she "uses" the text. In both portrayals there
is no concerted attempt to account for the material shape of the divine agency which
links the reader and text. We will see below that functionalist hermeneuticians
instinctively recognize this deficiency and supplement Kelsey's purely functionalist

---

[26]   Kelsey, *Uses*, pp. 215-6.
[27]   Francis Schüssler Fiorenza, "The Crisis of Scriptural Authority" in *Theology at the
End of Modernity* (Philadelphia, 1991), p. 359. Bold emphasis mine.

account with various material descriptions of that agency. This often happens by way of minimalist theological constructions, in affirming the Spirit's activity in the church, (Hans Frei's later work, Stephen Fowl) as well as non-dogmatic constructs, by acknowledging some kind of anonymous transcendent activity present in all human culture and religions (Werner Jeanrond and James K. A. Smith).

So far we have discussed six of the seven approaches Kelsey surveys in Part I of *Uses*. The seventh approach is that of Karl Barth. Kelsey's reading of Barth is particularly one-sided as a result of his preoccupation with the human agent in the construal and use of Scripture. In Chapter 5 we will discuss Barth's hermeneutic as one of the definitive examples of a type three approach. There we will highlight how Barth presents divine action as that which is prior and determinative in biblical hermeneutics. This stands in absolute contrast to the assumption behind Kelsey's analyses; that the reading of Scripture is determined by its "use" by a human agent. Thus the triangle typology shows how, in this case, the representation of Barth's thought is severely distorted.

So: whereas Kelsey sees the groups in *Uses* as two distinct groups of three with Karl Barth's approach (the seventh) being simply a transition from the one group to the other, our analysis sees Kelsey's grouping differently. First, there is a strong degree of similarity between the two groups of three: we locate all six of them in my type one. Second, Kelsey exemplifies an alternative approach as the first example of our type two. Finally, Barth is properly viewed as an alternative to *both* types one and two, as the first example of our type three.

Kelsey's analysis of type one approaches shares an important common feature with them: he, like they, discuss the act of reading primarily in individualistic terms. The development of type two approaches subsequently accommodated Kelsey's arguments and supplemented them, emphasizing the community or collectivist uses of scripture. Very quickly, then, discussions became animated not only by the function or use of Scripture in the community as the most logical means to correct the hegemony of modern type one approaches but also as a corrective to the similar problems in the modern construal of the self-sufficient *individual*.[28]

The focus on the function of Scripture in its use by the community came to be the arena of common ground for the now familiar debate between the so called "postliberal" or "Yale school" and the "Chicago school" of theology. Certainly there are now many who do not see themselves as committed to either of these two schools, yet any who wrestle with the relevant issues involved in the reading of Scripture inevitably find formation and helpful conversation partners in the interaction with and between them.

Members of the postliberal group traditionally have had greater contact and interaction with theologians and groups who we would think of as more conservative. There have been ongoing and substantial engagements between American Evangelicals and the postliberals, for example.[29] The chief reason for this is that the postliberal approach has tended to try to think either "from the Church" in the

---

[28]   This is also illustrated in the shift from Kant to Habermas.

[29]   See *The Nature of Confession* edited by Timothy R. Philips and Dennis Okholm (Downer's Grove, 1996).

case of Lindbeck, or "from the Bible" in the case of Frei's early work. Thus their work is more palatable to Evangelicals and others who have a stronger appetite for maintaining the distinction between the Church and the "world", giving preference to the former in setting up categories for theological thought and language and also in their strong sense of the authority of Scripture. Postliberal thinkers are also more sympathetic to the employment of dogmatic kinds of language and expressions, although they themselves have been reticent in producing dogmatic work in writing. The Chicago school, on the other hand, has attempted to work out the implications of a collectivist functionalism by way of general anthropological categories and makes every effort to set aside particularistic kinds of assumptions about the church or theological language. This makes its work more amenable to those in more liberal theological contexts.

The individuals we survey in this chapter are all indebted in different ways to this debate. Thus in this chapter we will discuss Hans Frei (his later work), Werner Jeanrond who seeks to develop his hermeneutic with the help of the work of David Tracy, and Stephen Fowl who has been influenced by both.

The Later Hans Frei: The Emergence of Meaning in the Tradition

Hans Frei stands as a particularly illustrative figure in this survey in that the trajectory of his work took him from type one to a moderate position in type two. This shift should not be thought of as either sudden or as an abandonment of one position for another. Rather, Frei increasingly became aware of questions which were not answered by his early defense of the integrity of the text. His later position can be read as an attempt to maintain the integrity of the text and also account for the additional issues that arise when one is confronted by the problem of the extratextual agency involved in the emergence of meaning from the text to the reader. We saw Frei's own awareness of this problem in his comments to the Barth society in the last chapter.

Frei's exploration of the role that tradition and the community play in the construal of the *sensus literalis* of Scripture is the context for the development of his thinking on this question. He was also influenced by his constructive working relationships with George Lindbeck and David Kelsey.[30] As we saw in the last chapter, he had choices to account for this agency other than the reading community—his discussion of the role of the Holy Spirit in Calvin's hermeneutic, for example. Frei discusses this sympathetically but chose not to explore it further.[31] He also could have reexamined the role of the human author in relation to the divine author, as Vanhoozer had subsequently done. Frei would have been hesitant about this option in that it bears too strong a resemblance to the modes of thinking which led to the problems associated with getting "behind the text."

---

[30] Lindbeck normally gets most of the "credit" for influencing Frei, but Kelsey's impact should not be underestimated.

[31] For an exemplary postliberal exploration in this direction see Kathryn Greene-McCreight, "We are Companions of the Patriarchs," in *Theology and Scriptural Imagination* (Oxford, 1998).

The reasons why he did not explicitly pursue the former option are not clear. It may, in part, be attributable to its overt theological character. Frei was uncomfortable with thinking of himself as a theologian: he saw himself more as a historian. This theological reticence is one reason why Frei never fully resolved the problem of the emergence of meaning. Theology aside, he is at a loss to systematically relate the agency of the human text and readers with divine agency. In other words, his reticence to explore the problem in *material* theological terms resulted in a situation where he limited himself to attempt to see a way *formally* or "systematically" to negotiate the human and divine agency in the production of the meaning of the text of Scripture. We will not pursue the point here, but suggest that it may, in the end, be that the only way to "systematically" discuss the relationship of human and divine speech action in Scripture is not by way of formal or methodological considerations, but by means of material and dogmatic categories.

Despite Frei's theological reticence, he demonstrates the inescapability of theological categories. This will be seen both in his criticisms of his earlier work and also in his development of the role of the community of readers in the emergence of meaning. As he proceeds theological comments hinting at the nature of divine agency in the determination of the *sensus literalis* also appear. Thus in the same way that we saw Vanhoozer's movement within the triangle to a position more balanced between type one and three inevitably drew him closer to issues related to type two; Frei's movement from type one to type two necessarily brings him nearer to the issue of divine agency in type three.

Formerly he cast the "literal" meaning as being exclusively derivative from the linguistic patterns in the text itself. In the early 1980s we see his attention shift to account for the agency of the community in the emergence of that meaning. One of the earliest indications of this shift is from a presentation he gave in 1982 entitled "Theology and the Interpretation of Narrative: Some Hermeneutical Considerations."[32] In it Frei explores two ways of doing theology, the *Wissenschaft* model, inherited from the German University system, and a second way—"the self description of Christianity as a religion."[33] His preference is for the second "postliberal" model.

He goes on to discuss three ways of thinking about how to account for the *sensus literalis* of Scripture and relates them to this second way of doing theology. The second of the three ways is characterized by trading on the "principled difference" between the sense and the reference of a text. He responds to this approach from the standpoint of the postliberal model of theology:

> Seen one way, namely, from a vantage point of a *principled* difference between the linguistic "meaning" of narratives and their translinguistic "reference," hermeneutical inquiry is—in the second [postliberal] way of doing theology—confined to description and conceptual use of the narratives, and it eschews going further to the point of indicating the manner of their true reference.[34]

---

[32] Hans Frei, "Theology and the Interpretation of Narrative" in *Theology & Narrative* (New York, 1993), pp. 94-116.

[33] Frei, "Interpretation of Narrative," p. 96.

[34] Frei, "Interpretation of Narrative," p. 103.

Frei seems to be affirming the meaning/reference distinction as he employed it in *Identity* where he insisted that our reading initially confine itself to issues of meaning apart from reference. However the "principled difference" between meaning and reference which was assumed in *Identity* is now severely qualified. He goes on:

> But for this [second, postliberal] way of doing theology this "principled difference" is precisely one of those philosophical constructs or conventions that may have to be subordinated and may not apply in an ordinary way but only ambiguously when it comes in contact with the self-description of the Christian religion.[35]

Frei is engaged in a moment of self-deconstruction. He acknowledges that the meaning/truth distinction he employed it in the early writings is itself a construct and is only variously related to the actual expression and embodiment of the particularities of the Christian religion in its reading of Scripture. In other words, the distinction between meaning and truth may not be the most appropriate way for describing the way the Christian community reads Scripture. There is also implicit here the admission that the Christian reading of Scripture is both unique and that the employment of *any* general hermeneutical schema will be inadequate to account for this uniqueness. He continues,

> On that reading [the second way of doing theology] the question of "reference" is **included** in hermeneutical-theological inquiry because it is solved descriptively in the case of *this* narrative … The linguistic account, that is, the narrative itself, renders the reality narratively … Whatever may be true of other instances of linguistic or narrative worlds and what they refer to, in this case the depicted story renders reality in such a way that it obviates the translinguistic reference questions as a separate question.[36]

"Reality," *which includes both meaning and reference*, is, then, rendered by the reading of the story in this second way of doing theology. In the particularity of the Christian reading of the Bible "truth" is also, then, ingredient *in* the literal reading as it is read by the Christian community. Frei responds here to the problem of accounting for the extratextual agency that renders the meaning to the reader by: first, relativizing the strict meaning/truth distinction which he employed with such vigor in his earlier writing. Second, he now begins to account for the role of the practices of the Christian tradition and community in the rendering of that which resides in the text, including both "meaning" *and* "truth." "[T]he *sensus literalis* [he writes] is the way the text has generally been used in the community. It is the sense of the text in its sociolinguistic context—liturgical, polemical, and so on."[37]

These ideas find an even greater emphasis in the more widely known and cited paper given a year later entitled "The 'Literal Reading' of Biblical Narrative in the Christian Tradition: Does it Stretch or Will it Break?"[38] In the first section of this

---

[35] Frei, "Interpretation of Narrative," p. 103.

[36] Frei, "Interpretation of Narrative," pp. 103-4. Bold emphasis mine.

[37] Frei, "Interpretation of Narrative," p. 104.

[38] Hans Frei, "The 'Literal Reading' of Biblical Narrative in the Christian Tradition: Does it Stretch or Will it Break?" in *The Bible and the Narrative Tradition* (New York, 1986) pp. 36-77. It is also included in *Theology & Narrative*, pp. 117-52.

paper[39] Frei describes the process by which the literal meaning came to be primary in the Christian religious tradition. First, the Christian tradition, within the Hebrew matrix in which it evolved, appropriated features of that matrix by reorienting them, deriving their meaning "directly from (or [in reference] to) its sacred story, the life, teachings, death, and resurrection of Jesus the Messiah."[40] "Second, it was largely by reason of the centrality of the story of Jesus that the Christian interpretation in the West gradually assigned clear primacy to the literal sense in the reading of Scripture."[41]

Shortly thereafter follows a comment which has resulted in alarm and confusion about Frei's own thought regarding the role tradition in determining the meaning of Scripture. He suggests that

> We have noted that the literal reading of the gospel stories was the crucial instance of this consensus in the early church. What is striking about this is that the "literal" reading in this fashion became the normative or "plain" reading of the texts. There is no a priori reason why the "plain" reading could not have been "spiritual" in contrast to "literal," and certainly the temptation was strong. The identification of the plain with the literal sense was not a logically necessary development, but it did begin with the early Christian community and was perhaps unique to Christianity.[42]

Frei's interpreters often point to this passage and suggest that he has given the community of readers the *sole* agency and responsibility for determining the reading of texts.[43] However this reading of Frei should be qualified. For one, the passage above begins with the *second* sentence of the paragraph. The first sentence reads "Interpretive traditions of religious communities tend to reach a consensus on certain central texts."[44]

This locates Frei's argument within a larger context that determines the implications of his argument. The way Frei is often read discounts this context. Thus he is read to be suggesting that *within the particular Christian tradition* the literal reading, which became the primary reading, could have been something else; a spiritual reading; that the *Christian* tradition could have read this text in another way than that which gives preference to the literal. This is not what he is saying. His argument should be read as follows.

Religious communities tend to arrive at various degrees of consensus regarding how their religious texts should and should not be read. There is no logically necessary reason for religious communities to read their texts literally; in fact, many do otherwise, even reading the same texts that comprise Christian Scriptures in other

---

[39]   Frei, "Literal Reading," pp. 39 ff.

[40]   Frei, "Literal Meaning," p. 39.

[41]   Frei, "Literal Meaning," p. 39.

[42]   Frei, "Literal Meaning," p. 41.

[43]   I have in mind here primarily the way many American Evangelicals have read this shift in Frei's thinking, including Carl F. H. Henry, "Narrative Theology, An Evangelical Appraisal,"; Andreas Kostenberger, "Aesthetic Theology: Blessing or Curse?,"; Alistair McGrath, "An Evangelical Evaluation of Postliberalism," and *A Passion for Truth* (Downer's Grove, 1996) and Kevin Vanhoozer. See discussion in chapter 1 on Vanhoozer.

[44]   Frei, "Literal Reading," p. 41.

ways. The strong identification of the literal sense as the primary and plain sense is unique to Christianity among religions. Nevertheless, because of the complexity of the relationship of the Hebrew scriptures and the New Testament (as well as other unnamed reasons) the "temptation" for Christians to read their Scriptures other than literally was (and still is) strong. Despite this, to read the texts of the Christian Scriptures in another way other than by giving primacy to the literal reading is to read them in a religious mode other than Christian.[45]

In other words, Frei is suggesting that it is logically possible for religions to arrive at consensus for reading their Scripture in various ways; both literal and non-literal. It is also logically possible for the Christian Scriptures to be read in ways other than the literal. This, however, is not a Christian reading but that of some other religion. Further, this argument says something about readers but does not assert anything positively or negatively about texts per se. The Christian reading, as we noted, for Frei, is derivative of the centrality (and literality) of Jesus' life, death, and resurrection. According to Frei, it would then be little more than an exercise in creative anachronism to suggest (as many suggest that Frei is arguing here) that the *Christian* reading of Scripture *could have* resolved itself in favor of some other way of reading rather than the way that it did.

This issue of the role of the *text* is never raised by Frei in this article, but the absence of such an argument should not be assumed to mean that there would not be a place to make it or that it no longer had any place in his hermeneutics. He did suggest a continuing place for the directive role of the text in "Interpretation of Narrative" written a year or so before and, we will see below, makes the same points in *Types of Theology* written a few years later.

With these qualifications in place we can better perceive Frei's critical commentary on his early work in "Literal Reading."[46] He describes his earlier distinction between meaning and truth and notes the strong resemblance to "Anglo-American 'New Criticism'". He now acknowledges that this idea trades on the idea that "truth" is not a universally accessible category and should be set aside for the benefit of "meaning" which *is*, in some sense, generally accessible.[47] Frei admits that this construct, "even though less high-powered, general theory it remains."[48] He then goes on to outline the problems he now sees with his earlier work. We will work through this as it is significant for understanding Frei's later thought.

He describes two weaknesses of his earlier approach. "First, the claim to the self-subsistence or self-referentiality of the text apart from any true world is as artificial as it may (perhaps!) be logically advantageous." This is similar to the self critical remarks he made in "Interpretation of Narrative" on the inadequacy of employing a "principled difference" between meaning and truth. He goes on:

> Second, it is similarly artificial and dubious to claim a purely external relation of text and reading, which in effect sets aside the mutual implication of interpretation and textual

---

[45] See the discussion that immediately follows the lengthy quote above. Frei, "Literal Reading," pp. 42-3.

[46] Frei, "Literal Reading," pp. 61-8.

[47] Frei, "Literal Reading," p. 63.

[48] Frei, "Literal Reading," p. 64.

meaning … In short, the less high-powered general theory that upholds the literal or realistic reading of the Gospels may be just as perilously perched as its more majestic and pretentious hermeneutical cousin.[49]

This second weakness of his early position has a direct bearing on the location of his later work in our typology. Frei believes it necessary to critique his early commitment to the separation of meaning and truth but, in the same move, also criticizes the more broadly held hermeneutical polarity between text and reader. So, even here, in the article in which he is supposed to be most dismissive of any role for the text in determining meaning in favor of the reader, to read him as doing so one must continue to employ some form of the very distinction between reader and text he wishes to eschew. Further, as we will see below, the thrust of his argument in "Literal Reading" is to put the agency of the reader under *closer* scrutiny and *greater* chastening than he felt he had before.

One of the advantages of the typological triangle is that it assumes a constructive and inextricable relationship between human and divine agency; between text and reader. We can represent Frei's later position fairly, then, as moving into the area between types one and two and that his preoccupation with the community and tradition of readers in the later works would justify our putting him just on the type two side of the divide.

We see that he also moves up from near the base of the triangle toward type three. This is so in that he not only begins to carve out a more substantial role for the reading community but also comes to recognize the inherently theological nature of reading Scripture. We return to his line of argument in "Literal Reading" as he describes an even "greater problem" with his early writings:

> Endowing the text with the stature of complete and authoritative embodiment of "truth" in "meaning," so that it is purely and objectively self-referential, is a literary equivalent of the Christian dogma of Jesus Christ as incarnate Son of God, the divine Word that is one with the bodied person it assumes. Here is a general theory about texts of which the paradigm case is not only in the first instance not textual but, more important, is itself the *basis* rather than merely an *instance* of the range as well as cohesion of meaning and truth in terms of which it is articulated.[50]

The idea of the perfect self-referential unity of meaning and truth in the text assumes a paradigm instance of that unity. That instance, Frei suggests, is, in the first place, neither available in a particular textual example, nor is it recognizable as some kind of general class of texts. Rather, this is the literary equivalent to the incarnation of God, who is a person and not a text, and is a particular ascriptive subject, and not a mythical general human paradigm. He immediately goes on to describe the unique difficulty in attempting to formally construct a general hermeneutic on this basis[51], that

---

[49] Frei, "Literal Reading," p. 64.

[50] Frei, "Literal Reading," pp. 64-5

[51] We will see in chapter 5 that James K. A. Smith attempts to use the incarnation as a "principle" in just this way.

[I]f the *truth* of such a dogma as that of the incarnation is to be affirmed, it has to be done by faith rather than rational demonstration ... [also,] if the dogma is to be held consistently, its very *meaning*, that is, its logical [and] ontological conceivability, is a matter of faith and therefore of reason strictly in the mode of faith seeking understanding.[52]

The greater problem with his earlier approach then, has two aspects: first, that it cannot assume the self-referential integrity of meaning and truth in the text as a general formal textual category; second, that it cannot assume that one can assume a purely descriptive (and not explanatory) stance *as a reader* with the text in that scenario. The truth/meaning integrity of the text in that case *demands* the assumption of some explanatory stance, or truth stance by the reader:

> The implicit rule of religious use or "rule of faith" under which [this kind of reading] will be done is that the conceivability of the unity of the two categories in personal ascription ... is dependent on the *fact* of that unity. Conversely, then, it has to be denied that the fact is logically dependent on the conceivability of the categories' unification. All descriptive endeavors ... will bread down or else ... remain incomplete.[53]

Here is a full chastening of his earlier work in that he now recognizes that the assumption that a text is inherently self-referential and contains a unity of truth and meaning requires an overt faith stance by the reader. Thus his earlier demand that the reading of Scripture initially should assume only a descriptive, and not explanatory, posture is unrealistic, at least in the case of Scripture. This is a *greater chastening* of the agency of the reader in his hermeneutic insofar as he now is more cognizant of the inescapability of reading from a stance which, as part of its creaturely limitations, *must* employ *both* descriptive *and* explanatory schemes. Schemes that must be thought of as "adequate" but still limited and qualified. He goes on,

> The implication of this reserve is that the full, *positive explanation* of the rule's rational status ... will have to await another condition than our present finitude. For now, the faith articulated in the dogma is ... indeed not irrational, "paradoxical" or "fideistic," but rather rational yet fragmentary.[54]

These are two things which Frei sees as lost on New Critics:

> The irony of New Criticism ... is to have taken this specific case and rule and to have turned them instead into a general theory of meaning, literature, and even culture, in their own right. Detached from the original that is the actual, indispensable ground and subject matter of its meaning, the specific rule is turned about instead into its very opposite, a

---

[52] Hans Frei, "Literal Reading," p. 65. I added the emphasis on "truth" to lend clarity to his argument.

[53] Hans Frei, "Literal Reading," p. 65.

[54] Hans Frei, "Literal Reading," p. 65. Gary Comstock, in an article that is influential, but a serious misreading, of Frei, "Truth or Meaning: Ricoeur Versus Frei on Biblical Narrative", *Journal of Religion,* v. 66, April, 1986, pp. 117-40 accuses Frei of viewing the employment of truth schemes as being "all or nothing". In light of the discussion above it is clear that this is a serious misreading of Frei.

scheme embracing a whole class of general meaning constructs, from a Christian culture ... to genres of literature. [Texts] are all understood "incarnationally" or "sacramentally."[55]

We will see in Chapter 5 that this is the very way that James K. A. Smith will approach this question. Frei goes on to assert that this is an untenable position from a theological standpoint for Christians:

> As a result, the original of this process of derivation, the doctrine of the incarnation of the Word of God in the person and destiny of Jesus of Nazareth, has now become an optional member within the general class, in which those who subscribe to the class may or may not wish to believe.[56]

The thrust of Frei's argument in "Literal Reading," then, is not the grand endorsement of the determinative role of the reader as it is sometimes portrayed. He is actually chastening the attitude and stance of the reader, including the heavy handedness of his own early views. He is now very critical of what he sees as his own earlier willingness to take an ad hoc rule regarding the ideal ingredient relationship between meaning and truth in texts and using it as a general formal schema that idealizes the stance of reader solely in terms of meaning. He also sees that one result of such a move is that it takes the particular behind such an assumption, the incarnation of God in Christ, strips it of its particularity, transforms it into a formal abstract schema, and then turns around and tries to reproduce the particular within the general. At best this means the dog is chasing its own tail, at worst the snake is consuming itself.

The phenomenon of turning the "rule" into the "schema" and the theological difficulties in such a move is not a problem limited only to the New Critics or to Frei's early work. We saw Kevin Vanhoozer (as well as Francis Watson) argue for a general literary category that is derivative of the creational status of language, or the self-relatedness of God in the economic Trinity, and the incarnation. We will also see James K. A. Smith, in Chapter 5, make a strong argument for understanding all human language as proceeding under a general formal schema of first, creation, and then, incarnation. These approaches make similar moves and trade on similar distinctions as those about whom Frei is critical. In each case, the problem remains of how the particular instance of God's action can be abstractly rendered to construct a non-particular general schema under which the particular then somehow appears. Material theological problems arise where this is attempted. Thus the particularity and uniqueness of Scripture is difficult to discern in Vanhoozer's case and the uniqueness, fullness, and exclusiveness of the revelation of God in Jesus Christ in Smith's. These particular and substantial theological terms, in each become, in Frei's words, "optional." Frei's own well known variation of the cart before the horse metaphor regarding his own work is relevant here:

> There may or may not be a class called "realistic narrative," but to take it as a general category of which the synoptic Gospel narratives and their partial second-order

---

[55] Hans Frei, "Literal Reading," p. 66.
[56] Hans Frei, "Literal Reading," p. 66.

redescription in the doctrine of the Incarnation are a dependent instance is first to put the cart before the horse and then cut the lines and claim that the vehicle is self-propelled.[57]

Our reading of Frei's article "Literal Reading" is at variance with the way it is often read; as abandoning the text for the community. We see as a further justification of this how Frei continues to struggle to maintain a properly constructive role for the text even in the later writings. Frei's later work is, nevertheless, admittedly preoccupied with the agential role of the tradition even as he also increasingly discusses the role of divine agency. Frei does finally begin to see that it is only in the consideration of the negotiation of divine and human agency that the problem of the extratextual agency which produces the emergence of the meaning of the text of Scripture is resolved. So: compared to other religions which have sacred texts at their center, these problems are uniquely surmounted in the Christian reading of Scripture. Christianity alone is able to overcome these problems because of the Incarnation of Christ who *is* the Word of God: "The reality is given linguistically; it is linguistic for us. It is as *Word* that God's presence is incarnate, and that Word is *incarnate* and not merely transcendent."[58] The next step for Barth, which Frei does not take, is to then describe how Scripture is a witness to the incarnate Word (and neither its extension or one among a generic class of extensions in an "incarnation principle).

We go on now to see how Frei continues to affirm the place for the text in his posthumously published *Types of Theology*. Here he reaffirms one of the most significant and salvageable aspects of his earliest work in *Identity*; the "ascriptive" identity of Jesus as the literal meaning of the Gospels. He writes,

> 'Literal sense' here applies primarily to the identification of Jesus as the *ascriptive* subject of the descriptions or stories told about and in relation to him ... All other senses of the quite diverse and changing notion 'literal' are secondary to this (to my mind, basic ascriptive Christological) sense of 'literal,' that the subject matter of these stories is not something or someone else, and that the rest of the canon must in some way or ways, looser or tighter, be related to this subject matter or at least not in contradiction to it. This is the minimal agreement of how 'literal' reading has generally been understood in the Western Christian tradition.[59]

Most of this sounds familiar. The new qualifications are that the literal reading is now acknowledged to be more complex than one single univocal meaning. This relieves the pressure on the text for rendering the one singular literal meaning beyond itself and is able to better accommodate the agency of the church in the reading. The various readings are subsequently ruled and maintained by the "consensus" and the "minimal agreement…in the Western Christian tradition." Frei continues to discuss this issue throughout *Types* in relation to his earlier affirmation of the integrity of the text. Thus it is still the case that "The text means what it says" and that

---

[57] Hans Frei, "Literal Reading," p. 66.
[58] Frei, "Interpretation of Narrative," p. 104.
[59] Frei, *Types*, p. 5.

[T]he reader's redescription is just that, a redescription and not the discovery of the text as symbolic representation of something else more profound. But in the *process* of redescription we can—and indeed cannot do other than—employ our own thought structures, experiences, conceptual schemes; there is neither an explicit mode for showing how to *correlate* these things with the job of redescription, nor is there a fundamental conflict between them. Without knowing success or lack of it in any given case beforehand, it is an article of faith that it *can* be done; it *is* done.[60]

He is still struggling with the emergence question. Frei has, however, achieved some clarity about the nature of the problem. He now insists that this transition does, in fact, occur and that the trust in this actuality is, like the unity of truth and meaning in "Literal Reading," "an article of faith." He now also acknowledges that the problem of extratextual agency of reading is related to the relationship of human and divine agents even if he still believes that we are inevitably agnostic about the material nature of their interaction.

Frei wanted to retain a determinative role for the text. We see this again in his final attempt at a balancing act between the roles of text and community in *Types* as he outlines "three rules" for determining the "literal" meaning of the Bible. He offers these as "informal rules" which are applied in various ad hoc ways depending on the context.[61] It would be mistaken to attribute to Frei's ordering of them to imply importance or authoritative status. Any, all or some combination of them would be appropriate depending on the situation.

> The first rule is that … the literal meaning of the text is precisely that meaning which finds the greatest degree of agreement in the use of the text in the religious community. If there is agreement in that use, then take that to be the literal sense … the greatest degree of agreement on the applicability of the literal sense…was in regard to the person of Jesus in the texts … So the first sense of the literal reading stems from the use of the text in the Church.[62]

In his early work the literal meaning was defined primarily in terms of a quality of the text itself which impresses itself on the reader. Now, the *agency* for the literal meaning is shared between text and tradition. Some have continued to suggest that this shows that Frei took the "linguistic turn" at this point in his career and abandoned the role for the text in any determination for the literal meaning.[63] However, as we have already shown above, Frei's earlier emphasis on the meaning being an inherent quality of the text is not abandoned or lost in his later work but extended and qualified. In this list of three rules in *Types* the role for the text is brought more clearly to bear in the second and third rules.[64]

---

[60]   Frei, *Types*, p. 44.

[61]   Frei, *Types*, p. 14.

[62]   Frei, *Types*, p. 15.

[63]   So Wolterstorff, Vanhoozer, McGrath, and Gerard Loughlin, "Following to the Letter: The Literal Use of Scripture," *Literature and Theology* 9:4 (December 1995), pp. 370-82.

[64]   These last two rules are articulated in almost exactly the same way as they were in Frei's 1982 Haverford College Lecture, published as "Theology and the Interpretation of Narrative: Some Hermeneutical Considerations" *Theology and Narrative*, pp. 94-116. The

The second rule ... is that it is the fit enactment of the intention to say what comes to be in the text ... there's an admission by and large that texts are written by authors, human, or divine ... . But what is interesting is that the intention and its enactment are thought of as one continuous process—one intelligent activity, not two—so that you cannot for this purpose go behind the written text to ask separately about what the author meant or what he or she was really trying to say. You had better take it that the author said what he or she was trying to say.[65]

And

The third rule has to do with the descriptive fit between the words and the subject matter, and thereby hangs a very long story[66]... The literal sense, in my mind, is one that asserts not only the coincidence between sense and subject matter, but may even...go further and suggest that we may be asking a misplaced question when we make a sharp distinction between sense and subject matter.[67]

It is clear from both the second and third rules that Frei still believes in a determinative role for the text itself in rendering the literal meaning. This also confirms that he is not "abandoning" his early position, but is, rather, attempting to preserve those early insights while pursuing the pressing questions about the "emergence" of meaning which caused him to look at the role of the interpretive tradition of the Church, and to the accompaniment of divine agency. George Hunsinger can, then, be read as slightly overstating the nature of this shift in Frei's latter works when he suggests that

In *Types of Christian Theology* Frei presupposes and extends the method he adopted in the "literal reading" essay. That is, he again stresses the *sensus literalis* as a communal consensus **rather than** as a literary structure, allowing the relation between the two to remain implicit though vague.[68]

This, again, puts too much weight on one way of reading the "literal reading" essay. Also, the "rather than" can be read to imply some degree of separation or even opposition between readers and texts and of Frei's adoption of one over against the other; as if in Frei's mind this was an either/or dilemma. Frei's position is more nuanced. He is trying to do justice to both aspects; separating them at times for the sake of descriptive and conceptual clarity while still viewing them as functioning

---

first rule also has an emphasis in this lecture so there are lines of continuity in Frei's later thought that locate the emphasis on the socio-linguistic tradition in *Literal Reading* as the new facet, not the new position.

[65] Frei, *Types*, p. 16. Kevin Vanhoozer, "The Spirit of Understanding: Special Revelation and General Hermeneutics", *Disciplining Hermeneutics* (Grand Rapids, 1997), pp. 145-6.

[66] This "very long story" might be a reference to Frei's *The Eclipse of Biblical Narrative*

[67] Frei, *Types*, p. 16.

[68] George Hunsinger, "Afterword" in *Theology and Narrative*, p. 263, bold emphasis mine. Hunsinger, here, imposes something of an either-or on Frei's work which we saw Vanhoozer do, as well, above. Hunsinger, however, is much nearer to the mark than most other readers, including Vanhoozer.

together in some sort of constructive and organic harmony. How we would construe their relationship depends on the interpretive situation. Frei was struggling mightily to work out a way of faithfully characterizing this relationship of text and community and so Hunsinger is nevertheless correct to see this as "vague." This vagueness is attributable to the residual problem of agency with regard to the rendering of meaning in Scripture to the reader and community, and Frei's reluctance to address it from a more overtly material theological perspective. Frei does, however, recover for a moment from the typical postliberal theological reticence and addresses this issue with greater dogmatic clarity when he writes,

> What is written is the Word of God. The divine touch on it is not extravagance, by which the written word might be transformed into that about which it is written. Christians do have to speak of the referent of the text. They have to speak historically and ontologically, but in each case, it must be the notion of truth or reference, that is re-shaped extravagantly, not the reading of the literal text. Any notion of truth that disallows the condescension of truth to the depiction in the text, to its own self-identification, with, let us say, the four-fold story of Jesus of Nazareth taken as an ordinary story, has itself to be viewed with profound skepticism by a Christian interpreter.[69]

And later concludes:

> I plead then for the primacy of the literal sense and, it seems to me, its puzzling but firm relationship to a truth toward which we cannot thrust. The *modus significandi* will never allow us to say what the *res significata* is. Nonetheless, we can affirm that in the Christian confession of divine grace, the truth is such that the text is sufficient. There is a fit due to the mystery of grace between truth and text. But that, of course, is a very delicate and very constant operation to find that fit between textuality and truth.[70]

Truth, then, is that "toward which we cannot thrust." Any claim about the overbearing role of the community in the determination of the *sensus literalis* in Frei's later works need to be further qualified by this acknowledgment. The truth of the text, for Frei, is that which condescends to the text and administrates "to its own self-identification." This happens as a matter of the course of "divine grace"; "the mystery of grace between truth and text." This is probably as overt a theological indication that we get from Frei. It is still vague. Nevertheless, Hunsinger's fears about Frei's usurpance of the determination of the text's meaning and truth by the activity of the church should be (at least partially) alleviated.

Summarizing, in *Eclipse* and *Identity* meaning and truth are ingredient forces within the text itself. In *Theology & Narrative* and *Types* Frei adds an emphasis on the role of the Church's traditional reading in co-determining the meaning. Nevertheless, "truth" is still not directly attributable to human agency but to gracious divine action which may indirectly assert itself via text, tradition and community.

The chronological trajectory of Frei's work, then, travels the axis at the base of the triangle I have described; from being firmly located in the lower corner of type one with those who emphasize *what Scripture says* or *contains* to just across the

---

[69]   Frei, "Conflicts in Interpretation," *Theology and Narrative*, pp. 163-4.

[70]   Frei, "Conflicts in Interpretation," *Theology and Narrative*, p. 166.

border line between type one and type two which emphasizes *what reader(s) do* as the initial or primary access point or emphasis. We also saw that overtly theological discussions pertaining to divine agency also naturally arose. Thus his trajectory not only moves from the left corner toward the right corner but also begins to rise up away from the bottom axis (the preoccupation with human agency) toward the top axis (accounting for divine agency). All of the figures in our survey, so far, have made this gesture toward divine agency in the course of their development. This indicates a common point of reference and the collective gravity of this issue for biblical hermeneutics as the influence of the Enlightenment epistemological tendencies which stress immanent terms of inquiry begins to eclipse and fade.

Werner Jeanrond: Reviving the Critical Interpreter

Werner Jeanrond's book *Text and Interpretation as Categories of Theological Thinking*[71] is a classic example of a type two attempt to revive the critical character of Enlightenment epistemological commitments for biblical hermeneutics. The title of the book itself also conveys the perception and definition of the range of issues that most modern biblical hermeneuticians see as encompassing: residing exhaustively between the immanent human agency constituent in the text and in the reading. Thus his "general theory" of reading is set up as the dialectic between "text, text genre, and text style" and "reading, reading genre, and reading style"[72]

His theory is set up in critical conversation with the work of Gadamer, Habermas and Ricoeur. His main criticism of Gadamer is that he leaves us in a position where we do not have an adequately critical mechanism by which to ferret out wrong interpretations. Gadamer's concept of understanding is inadequate in that it "is a process and not an action of the understanding subject. Understanding happens to us rather than through us." He appeals to Habermas to counter this perceived weakness, arguing that

> In order to achieve intelligent results from understanding, that is to say results for which one can take responsibility, nothing short of endless criticism is necessary in countering this fallibility … Every case of textual understanding which lays claim to public validity must be revisable and surely that also means verifiable. There is therefore constant need of a methodological component. It is not the function of this methodological component to produce truth but to secure critically the process of its disclosure.[73]

This methodological component Jeanrond calls "interpretation" which is meant to be all encompassing, pervasively critical, and transcendent of "understanding."[74] The critical component is essential for Jeanrond in that

---

[71] Werner G. Jeanrond, *Text and Interpretation as Categories of Theological Thinking* (Dublin, 1988).

[72] Jeanrond, *Text and Interpretation*, pp. xvii – xviii.

[73] Jeanrond, *Text and Interpretation*, pp. 34-5.

[74] Jeanrond, *Text and Interpretation*, pp. 35-7.

> Without such enlightenment…theological text reception would have to remain uncritical and that in turn would signify that theology as a whole would deal with texts on a dubious basis. And as a result it could never move forward to patterns of activity which would be publicly transparent and capable of standing up to critical reflection.[75]

The critical mode that Jeanrond advocates is strikingly similar to Kant's in that antecedent judgments should be suspended; that the influence of judgments, especially theological judgments, as well as other agents on the investigation is suspect. Despite his earnest efforts at approaching these issues without the encumbering effects of theology[76] the stance he nevertheless assumes with respect to divine agency is apparent at key points in his analysis. To the extent we can demonstrate how constructive theological issues, particularly those involving divine agency, accompany his analysis our typological framework receives greater affirmation as a tool for the more exhaustively accounting for the complexity of reading Scripture, as well as its potential as a tool for the comparison of differing approaches to reading.

Jeanrond sketches out his project in Chapter 1. There are several hints, here, of theological assumptions he makes regarding divine action. For example, on page 2 he asserts that "The historical revelation of God in Jesus Christ has taken on text character to the extent that human beings have linguistically borne witness to it and handed it down."[77] This already suggests a constructive theological position regarding God's agency and its relationship to the text of Scripture subsequent to God's act in Christ: God's revelatory agency in Jesus Christ has been wholly translated into a textual tradition and the subsequent agency invested in this textual tradition is purely defined in immanent categories of human agency in the matrix between the incarnational experience transmitted in the text and the tradition of reading that recreates that experience in the present.

This illuminates Jeanrond's warning that "To refuse to consider the primacy of textual understanding would mean to expose oneself right from the beginning to the possibility of denying the importance of that which constitutes the sustaining sources of Christian theological thought, namely the texts."[78] And, that "One must therefore hold on to the insight that Christian theology, in its concrete questioning, receives from texts inspirations for reflective action.[79]"

Here "text" functions as a metaphor. "Texts," sustain and inspire Christian theology. They provoke and challenge their readers. This metaphorical language implies notions of agency and indicates dogmatic assumptions about that agency. There are also theological judgments at work in these statements; particularly judgments about God's agency and action as it relates to human agency. Who or what is initiating and maintaining this sustaining and inspiring action? Who provokes and challenges? God? The biblical authors? The Christian tradition? The present community of faith? Some combination of these?

---

[75] Jeanrond, *Text and Interpretation*, p. 5.

[76] Jeanrond, *Text and Interpretation*, p. xvi.

[77] Jeanrond, *Text and Interpretation*, p. 2.

[78] Jeanrond, *Text and Interpretation*, p. 3.

[79] Jeanrond, *Text and Interpretation*, p. 3.

We can begin to answer these question in regard to Jeanrond's work and illuminate his position on the relationship of human and divine action in his thinking on what constitutes "fundamental theology." His definition follows that of Helmut Peukert whom he quotes:

> [A] fundamental theology which is developed as a theory of communicative action through the paradox of anamnetic solidarity is faced with the task of developing a hermeneutics of the history of religion in connection with a theory of the development of human consciousness and action as a whole.[80]

Jeanrond sees *Text and Interpretation* as making good on this suggestion by Peukert. Fundamental theology is, for Jeanrond, the establishment of a framework by which to understand the nature of human communicative actions *prior to* the consideration of the particular form those actions take in text production, tradition and reception, including and especially *theological* interpretation.[81] His suggestion that we should look to "the history of religion ... with a theory of the development of human consciousness and action *as a whole*" gives us another clue to the shape of those judgments.

Jeanrond assumes that whatever agency constitutes the provocation and inspiration of the texts of Scripture will only be effectively indicated in a study of the *whole* of human consciousness and action. This functions as an antecedent judgment in that it rules out taking the initial or decisive indication from the communicative actions of any *particular* group or action. By extension, the implications for the possibility of divine action are that the divine would also be restricted from taking specific and uniquely definitive action towards and within a particular human community, but would be assumed initially to act equally and universally in all human religious communities.

As Jeanrond proceeds, discussing and contrasting his approach with other figures, he singles out Gadamer to contrast with his own. He summarizes what he sees as Gadamer's view of tradition and offers a rather harsh estimation of its result: that it represents little more than a manipulation, that,

> [T]he understating person becomes a plaything of the process of tradition, which in its handing on mediates itself with an authority that has to be affirmed. In this process of understanding therefore the options are either to participate consciously in it or descend into unawareness.[82]

---

[80] Jeanrond, *Text and Interpretations,* p. 4 quoting Helmut Peukert, *Science, Action and Fundamental Theology: Toward a Theology of Communicative Action* (Cambridge, 1984), p. 215.

[81] "[T]he significant works on theological hermeneutics which have been produced in the last few decades are not to be overlooked. However, it is our aim in the first place to search for a *universal* theory of the process of interpretation which precedes and grounds them all and which puts us in a position for the first time, to determine the place and value of *concrete* theological-hermeneutical perspectives ...", Jeanrond, *Text and Interpretation*, p. 8.

[82] Jeanrond, *Text and Interpretation*, p. 30.

The implications for divine agency in this claim is straightforward: either God's agency *is* active with tradition, making God culpable for being heavy handed and treating us as playthings, or God is *not* acting with tradition and humans are fully responsible for the distortions inherent within it. An alternative position to these two, that God's action is present in tradition and is so both appropriately and helpfully, and how this would ever be affirmable, is not an option. God's action is, then, in Jeanrond's system, wholly contingent upon the critical evaluations and affirmation of present human action and does not act in accordance with any traditional influence that may carry sway in our thinking and acting; a sentiment which resonates strongly with the modern bias against antecedent operational judgments.

We see this confirmed as he advocates the work of Paul Ricoeur. Jeanrond develops the critical component of his system by means of Ricoeur's notion of "distanciation." He quotes Ricoeur who argues that

> [T]here are problems of interpretation because there are *texts, written* texts, the autonomy of which ... creates specific problems; these problems are usually solved in spoken language by the kind of exchange or intercourse which we call dialogue or conversation. With the written texts, the discourse must speak by itself.[83]

Jeanrond asserts that the autonomy of the written text is a byproduct of its distanciation and creates a situation where the "possibility of correction is... absent."[84] He has in mind here the correction an author could provide in an actual face to face encounter with a reader. Human authors are normally absent and so cannot provide correction like a speaker at a conference could. There is a positive side to this distanciation, however, as

> In language as written the reference of a text is freed in a threefold manner ... the relatedness of a text is now independent of the author who has expressed it, independent also of the possible context on which the text was produced and of the circle of addressees to whom it may have been aimed. It is only in the act of reading that the relatedness of the text is re-created and this happens by and with reference to the reader and his/her world horizons ... . In the act of reading then, the distanciation of the text is not negated but rather acknowledged and made fruitful to the extent that the text now receives new references to a new world, namely that of the reader.[85]

We are, then, cut off from whatever authorial action comprised the composition of the text. Jeanrond emphasizes that this cutting off is actually freeing; a fruitful condition. This gives us two indications about where to locate Jeanrond on the triangle. First, whatever *human* agency is invested in the text itself is strictly imprisoned within it; we do not have access to that authorial agency. Thus the text becomes an inert tool that is only subsequently animated by the agency of the reader(s). This locates him in the extreme position of type two in the very far bottom right corner.

---

[83]   Jeanrond, *Text and Interpretation*, p. 44 quoting Paul Ricoeur, "Metaphor and the Main Problem of Hermeneutics" p. 138 in *The Philosophy of Paul Ricoeur: An Anthology of His Work* (Boston, 1978).

[84]   Jeanrond, *Text and Interpretation*, p. 45.

[85]   Jeanrond, *Text and Interpretation*, p. 48.

The distanciation of the human author from the present reading of the text is also a distanciation of divine agency. Jeanrond's proposal exclusively locates the source of the action which produces present meaning as originating in the critical action of the present reader. Jeanrond believes the ideal reader to be cut off and distanciated from the influence of *any* compositional agency in Scripture; human or divine.[86] The present reader is isolated from any assistance of authoring agency of Scripture and is left alone to provide the impetus to produce the meaning of the text of Scripture in the present. "This new appropriation becomes a new event of the text independent of the author, etc."[87]

Jeanrond does not, however, wish to appear too exacting in this.[88] Nevertheless, the text's role continues to be limited to the role of instruments waiting for the prompting and animation of the reader: "Texts are carriers of sense."[89] In the end the role of the text tends to be reactive or passive in Jeanrond's proposal.[90] The text is a flexible form in which we pour our many various readings. The text accommodates some interpretations better than others and is relatively fluid—its only confinement being the form of our present context.

Jeanrond's view of the text as something of a wax nose is also clearly indicated in his later book *Theological Hermeneutics: Development and Significance*.[91]

> Some hermeneuts [he writes] liken the interaction between reader and text to the conversation between two persons. Yet this image does not capture the full nature of reading. Reading is not a conversation between two equal partners who possess equal ability of acting and reacting. Rather, the text is a somewhat weaker partner which, for instance, is unable to defend itself against violations of its integrity by ideological readers. At best the text is empowered by a reader to unfold its meaning during the act of reading.[92]

He also continues to advocate for an exacting critical pre-theological sifting of the terms of reading. He sees this as the best way to prevent theological readings from becoming oppressive.[93] Thus "theology" must always be qualified by the prior critical moment of the "hermeneutical." He writes:

> [T]he critical point in any treatment of theological hermeneutics is whether one favors a *theological* hermeneutics or a *hermeneutical* theology. The first claims that all texts have a

---

[86] Jeanrond also indicates that Scripture itself, in its composition, is already conditioned by distanciation from divine action in that the "biblical texts are of course themselves interpretations of the process of divine manifestation." Jeanrond, *Text and Interpretation*, p. 102, also pp. 118 ff.

[87] Jeanrond, *Text and Interpretation*, p. 50.

[88] Jeanrond, *Text and Interpretation*, pp. 62-72 and Chapter II.

[89] Jeanrond, *Text and Interpretation*, p. 81.

[90] "Metaphorically speaking, the text is rather in the nature of a path to be trodden by the reader." Jeanrond, *Text and Interpretation*, p. 88.

[91] Werner G. Jeanrond, *Theological Hermeneutics: Development and Significance* (New York, 1991).

[92] Jeanrond, *Theological*, p. 7.

[93] Jeanrond, *Theological*, p. 8.

theological dimension, at least implicitly. The second claims that theology is by its nature a hermeneutical exercise since it deals with a tradition mediated in no small measure by written texts and their interpretation. In this book we shall follow the second path and investigate the hermeneutical nature of theology and its implications for the Christian movement's self-understanding. Only then, on the basis of such a properly examined hermeneutical method, may we be equipped to venture into the related, but much larger question of *theological* hermeneutics.[94]

The possibility of a regional hermeneutic for Scripture shaped in any way by theological judgments is excluded. He also indicates another characteristic of the restriction to immanent categories in that he continues to understand the hermeneutical problem to be exhaustively defined in the tension between "text" and "reader."[95]

He summarizes, appealing to a phenomenological framing of hermeneutics, which accepts the limits of Kantian epistemology. He writes,

> A phenomenological description of the act of reading seems to be called for in the context of theological interpretation in order to retrieve the general dimensions of reading before allowing the particularly theological imagination to enter the process of text-interpretation. Such a phenomenological treatment of reading then may free theological interpreters to realize anew their dependence on ordinary means of human communication.[96]

We saw above that Jeanrond's notions of divine action preclude the particular action of God in speaking within a particular tradition or religion. His insistence on focusing on the general dimensions of reading in *Theological Hermeneutics* is dogmatically consistent with that view. Even though he continually advocates a theologically neutral approach and claims to be proceeding himself within such, "before allowing the particularly theological imagination to enter the process" there continue here, as before, to be indications otherwise. This tension surfaces in his discussion of Karl Barth. His description of Barth's hermeneutic, particularly in his differences with Bultmann, is perceptive at certain points. He begins,

> It is essential for us to appreciate that the hermeneutical question for Barth does not arise originally from a conscious methodological concern, i.e. how to devise an appropriate theory of text-understanding. Rather, the hermeneutical question entails for him the ultimate material question of theology, namely: who is God and who am I?[97]

The only qualification I would make of this characterization is that Barth's "question" is only the first half of the question and the latter half "who am I?" is, following the analysis of David Kelsey, something of an imposition. He goes on to distinguish between Barth and Bultmann.

> Bultmann tried to analyse the process of human understanding first. In the sense that we can say that while Barth's hermeneutics is material, Bultmann's is formal. Barth rejected the imposition, as he saw it, of any formal hermeneutical principles in the human appreciation

---

94 Jeanrond, *Theological*, p. 9.
95 Jeanrond, *Theological*, p. 78.
96 Jeanrond, *Theological*, p. 94.
97 Jeanrond, *Theological*, p. 128.

of God's revelation. Bultmann rejected the material imposition, as he saw it, of a particular theological dogmatics on every effort to begin the process of understanding.[98]

This is essentially correct. It should be noted, however, that this description of their relationship trades on the possible distinction between the material and the formal dimensions of hermeneutics. Bultmann's own followers (including Fuchs and Ebeling, whom Jeanrond later discusses), came to realize that a more exact form of this distinction is ultimately untenable. Jeanrond never addresses this problem and goes on to express his criticism of Barth's hermeneutic assuming this formal/ material duality:

> [T]exts can only begin to witness to something when they are read. Therefore we have to ask how we can control Barth's own interpretive experience if not by participating in the process of text-interpretation itself? But such a participation must be protected against possible ideological distortions as well as against any kind of dogmatic pre-determination of new acts of reading. It seems to me that there is no possibility of a shortcut to the meaning or sense of the biblical texts. Texts need to be interpreted in order to be understood. Hence, in order to see whether or not Barth's universalization of his own hermeneutical experience is legitimate we must go the long way through the text themselves. There can be no critical macro-hermeneutics without critical micro-hermeneutics! Without such a continuous test Barth's criterion for biblical interpretation, i.e. God's self-revelation in Jesus Christ, remains indeed mere positivism.[99]

His criticism of Barth has an ironic twist. He is overly concerned with Barth's positivism and imposition of a certain kind of reading under certain dogmatic assumptions about God and God's revelation. His response is to ask how it is that we can control Barth's reading; how it is that we can "protect" the process. It would seem that, in this case, the response to Barth's restrictions is to impose different ones. And the restrictions Jeanrond would impose have just as clearly a dogmatic shape as Barth.

Thus: Jeanrond's characterization of the dilemma facing present readers is only true and preferable to Barth's if the principle of distanciation is applied to both the human author *and* the divine author of Scripture. In the absence of any other agent to initiate the interaction between text and reader the reader assumes sole responsibility. But this sidesteps Barth's primary hermeneutical point, that God acts, and acts in a way that is prior to and encompasses our own action. The denial of Barth's positivism is a negativism, but is no less assertive or constructive from a theological perspective.

In the end, Jeanrond's protest against Barth, that the reading "must be protected against ... any kind of dogmatic predetermination," begins to sound hollow. This comes even more to the fore when we finally arrive at the heart of his differences with Barth.

---

[98] Jeanrond, *Theological*, p. 130.
[99] Jeanrond, *Theological*, p. 135.

[W]ith Bultmann we too must ask Barth why an open discussion of the presuppositions of any approach to texts would need to be seen as *determining* our understanding of these texts. Of course all interpretive efforts are *conditioned*. But there is a big difference between conditions and determinations! As long as our discussion of the interpretive conditions is a truly open discussion, one fails to see why God's Spirit should not be able to lead us towards an always deeper appreciation of the truth of the Bible precisely through such discussion ... The radical distinction between God and the world in Barth's thinking has made it impossible for Barth to address the double need of theological hermeneutics ...[100]

The invoking of God's Spirit at this point is puzzling. The critical moment of perceiving the hermeneutical conditions is, he told us before, *not* theological, and should be pre-dogmatic. Once the rhetoric is pierced, Jeanrond's issue with Barth is in terms of the latter's (perceived) "radical distinction between God and world." It is clear, then, that his primary point of contention with Barth is, at its core, both theological and dogmatic. Jeanrond's view of God demands that God's *present* activity be given absolute priority in the reading. God's past action, either in the text or in the interpretive tradition, is denied any purchase. Further, he insists that God's action not only be recognized as present, as we saw above, but also as presenting equally in the whole of human cultures and religions. God is not free to act uniquely, or exclusively in any one.[101]

In light of the obvious dogmatic categories under which his view of divine action proceeds, it becomes increasingly awkward to assert, as he does, that these are simply "general conditions" and are not "determinations." Jeanrond's chastisement of Barth as being "neo-orthodox" in the end fails to come to terms with the fact that he himself has a standard of orthodoxy which both determines his hermeneutic and is a rule of faith by which he measures Barth and finds him wanting.

Our analysis of Jeanrond illustrates how he is a classic example of type two as indicated in his preference of the synchronic action of the interpreter as the determiner of the meaning of Scripture over and above the human action constituting the text, or in the divine action constituent to either the text or reader. His location on our triangle is in the extreme bottom right corner of type two. He gives absolute preference for the action of contemporary synchronic readers in the production of meaning. We indicate his position below in relation to the other type two thinkers we discuss:

---

[100] Jeanrond, *Theological*, p. 137. Emphasis his.
[101] Jeanrond, *Theological*, p. 177.

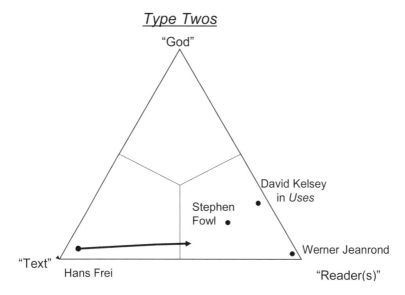

Fig 4.1 Mapping Type Twos

Jeanrond is also an instructive example for the testing of our typology in that he is someone who believes it is possible to do a phenomenological ontology of human communicative action prior to and apart from assuming any constructive operative antecedent judgments regarding God's transcendent action.[102] Yet when we carefully examine his framework we can clearly see the presence of strong theological bias. By now it should go without needing saying that this is not a criticism, but is inevitable.

Stephen Fowl: The Community's Underdetermined Engagement with Scripture

Stephen Fowl, in his influential book *Engaging Scripture: A Model for Theological Interpretation*,[103] engenders another variation of a type two approach. He frames three ways of reading: "determinate," "indeterminate," and "underdeterminate". Type

---

[102] He characterizes David Tracy's hermeneutic, which he sees as sympathetically related to his own, as follows: "Tracy understands this model of interpretation as a universal heuristic model, which can 'guide the concrete programmes of concrete and particular differing theologies'. The interpretation model is not, accordingly, itself theological interpretation but rather the theory of such an undertaking." Jeanrond, *Text and Interpretation,* p. 132. He quotes David Tracy, "Project 'X': Retrospect and Prospect", *Concilium* 170 (1983), p. 32.

[103] Stephen Fowl, *Engaging Scripture* (Oxford, 1998). See bibliography for other relevant writings by Fowl.

one approaches in our typology are members of what Fowl calls the "determinate view."[104] He suggests that

> In the end, this view of determinate biblical interpretation seeks to secure stability and coherence for Christian faith, worship, and practice, by ascribing a particular, stable and coherent property to the Bible (i.e. meaning) .... This view, however, is theoretically mistaken in thinking of meanings as properties of texts, and theologically mistaken in locating the bases of coherent and faithful Christian faith and practice in the text of the Bible interpreted in isolation from Christian doctrines and ecclesial practices.[105]

In this are hints at the way that he will underwrite his own approach; that the reading of Scripture should be discerningly located within the ecclesial practices of Christian communities. He is aware of the danger of submitting the reading of Scripture to the whims of human agency, however, as seen in his description of the second alternative he wishes to avoid: the "anti-determinate" approach.

> [A]nti-determinate interpretation ... avoids the quest for mastery over the text in the name of a determinate theory of meaning. It warns against the temptation to see established interpretations as the "natural" ones. It renders interpretation provisional and urges a sort of humility ... It is pretentious, however, in suggesting that the history of biblical interpretation must be seen within the pervasive scope of the metaphysics of presence and that, thereby, there is a moral demand to resist this by reading deconstructively ... To avoid this problem, any alternative to deconstruction will have to recognize both the provisionality and plurality of biblical interpretation, and be self-reflexively critical of Christian practice, without practicing deconstruction.[106]

He clearly wants to avoid what he sees as the chaos and whimsy of pure deconstructionist readings. *Engaging* is his attempt to both describe and demonstrate his alternative to over- and anti-determined reading; the "underdetermined" reading. This approach is influenced by the postliberal view of the ad hoc employment of truth schemas.

> Given the diverse and particular ways Christians need to interpret and perform specific scriptural texts, an underdetermined account of scriptural interpretation will allow Christians to articulate this diversity without having to fit it all under a single determinate theory of interpretation.[107]

He also wants to avoid reducing the reading of Scripture in some facile way to any one of its component aspects. He writes: "Rather I wish to argue that theological convictions, ecclesial practices, and communal and social concerns should *shape and be shaped by* biblical interpretation."[108]

Within these broadly defined intentions we see some of the particular emphases in his work as resonating with Kelsey's analysis in *Uses* while refining it. Kelsey

---

[104] Fowl, *Engaging*, pp. 33-4.
[105] Fowl, *Engaging*, p. 40.
[106] Fowl, *Engaging*, pp. 54-5.
[107] Fowl, *Engaging*, p. 59.
[108] Fowl, *Engaging*, p. 60.

sought to shift the attention from debating between different notions of textual essence to discerning the nature of the reader's use of scripture: Fowl wants to shift it to the reading practices of the community. Fowl nuances Kelsey's approach by highlighting the communal, relational aspect of the reading. Fowl expands the discussion to describe the myriad of ways that the Church's self-perception can and should be challenged in the course of her engagement with Scripture. He writes that

> Even though a community and its members must ultimately be responsible for their own interpretive practices, their self-critical scrutiny may be directed and inspired by particular members within that specific Christian community, members of different Christian communities, or those outside any Christian community. It is impossible to predict precisely where such prophetic insight might come … my claim is that is must be attended to vigilantly because one cannot know exactly how to evaluate it in advance.[109]

We see again a nod to the postliberal emphasis on not deciding on the framework prior to the actual act of reading or doing theology. Fowl also is careful to locate the church's reading activity in relation to challenges that may confront that way of reading from outside. This is similar to Watson's discussion in *Text, Church and World* as we saw in Chapter 2. However, his location and discussion of "text" is even more qualifying than Watson in terms of the predominant role of the agency of the reading community. Thus if they are to avoid the "tendencies to read scripture to underwrite their sin, then they must attend to themselves. That is, they must primarily be concerned with their own common life, with the role of scripture in that common life, and with the voices of those both inside and outside the community which offer words of prophetic critique of the community and its interpretive practices."[110]

The "prophetic critique" has a priority in his hermeneutic and, we will see, Fowl tends to emphasize this and neglect others; questions on this will emerge. Additionally, the divine action that this arrangement is that in which the present work of God in the prophetic challenges to the church is highlighted and, in turn, divine action in either the text or in the received tradition, is subordinated. Fowl is aware of the nature of these beliefs and the role they play in his portrayal:

> Given that Christians also recognize that God's actions can be surprising and that the path leading to the ultimate consummation of God's will for the world may well be filled with twists and turns unanticipated by humans, and which may require unconventional interpretive strategies, it does not seem too difficult to give an account of God's activity related in scripture that will be consistent with notions of God's unified will. Of course, this claim cannot simply be extracted from scripture. Rather it presumes a doctrine of God (which is itself shaped by Scripture) and God's providence, and is confirmed by the presence of a contemporary community which both testifies to God's continuing action in its midst and presents itself as the continuation of God's actions.[111]

---

[109] Fowl, *Engaging*, p. 82.
[110] Fowl, *Engaging*, p. 85.
[111] Fowl, *Engaging*, p. 20.

He also acknowledges that his emphasis is on the synchronic action of God in the present work of the Spirit:

> I am ... more concerned with what might be said, in a temporally more immediate way, about the role of the Spirit in interpretation. While specific decisions and resolutions of disputes within the church should be open to revision, Christian communities, like everyone else, must also make decisions and resolve disputes without the benefit of retrospective judgments. Can Christians in the midst of interpretive and practical disputes recognize, account for, and interpret the Spirit's work in more immediate ways? To answer these questions, we should look to Acts 10-15 ... In examining this passage, I wish to show that there are habits, practices, and dispositions narratively displayed here that are crucial for contemporary Christian communities as they struggle to read and embody scripture in the Spirit.[112]

On the one hand he suggests that we "must make decisions and resolve disputes without the benefit of retrospective judgments." This, again, minimizes or subordinates the divine action in the judgments of the received tradition. It also resonates with the Enlightenment bias against antecedent judgments. On the other hand, in appealing to the Acts passage he suggests that there are formal characteristics that are "narratively displayed." As he looks to this passage he will distill "formal" patterns, abstracting them from their material bases and context. He continues, affirming only a *formal* authority for the pattern of actions the church undertook in Acts regarding the inclusion of the Gentiles into the church:

> For my purposes, the prescriptive (and no doubt idealized) picture found in these chapters is more important than their historical accuracy. Even if the actual making and enacting of decisions regarding Gentile inclusion in the earliest Christian communities was much more rough and tumble than Acts relates, the importance for contemporary Christians of how these decisions *should* have been worked out remains.[113]

The manner in which this decision was resolved, as represented in Acts, is a definitive formal paradigm for how the present community should approach disputes within the church. He sees the important thing here to be the method that the church models: a method that can, and should, be abstracted from the particularities of the issue that the church faced and can then, in turn, be applied to any new situation that the church may encounter.[114]

This is a key to his argument which, again, locates him in type two. The present work of the Spirit guides us, "provides the lenses" [115] to read Scripture. Scripture itself does not; neither does tradition. He quotes Luke Timothy Johnson affirmingly at this point, who writes,

> What is remarkable, however, is that the text is confirmed by the narrative, not the narrative by the Scripture. As Peter had come to a new understanding of Jesus' words because of the

---

[112] Fowl, *Engaging*, p. 103.
[113] Fowl, *Engaging*, p. 104.
[114] Fowl, *Engaging*, p. 113.
[115] Fowl, *Engaging*, p. 114.

gift of the Spirit, so here the Old Testament is illuminated and interpreted by the narrative of God's activity in the present.[116]

He does not want to completely idealize this reading process, however, and does admit some role for the received patterns of interpretation. There are further qualifications that come with this. He writes,

Understanding and interpreting the Spirit's movement is a matter of communal debate and discernment over time. This debate and discernment is itself often shaped both by prior interpretations of Scripture and by traditions of practice and belief. This means that in practice it is probably difficult, if not impossible, to separate and determine clearly whether a community's scriptural interpretation is prior to or dependent upon a community's experience of the Spirit.[117]

The qualification, here, is probably intended to limit the potential damage imposed by all too quick assumptions about the relationship of the Sprit with the present actions of the Church. However, the net effect may be the opposite. Throughout the book, to this point, his emphasis is on present divine action. Now, that action itself is qualified in relation to the "communal debate and discernment over time." The net result of this may not be the intended reigning in of impulsive communities but the further subordination of divine action to human and thus, in the long run, investing human judgments with more decisiveness, not less. He also, here, gives a passing nod to the inevitable influence of tradition and scripture in the matrix of the present community but it is unclear whether the influence they exert can ever be specifically affirmed (an odd outcome for a Catholic) or whether they are only hampering the reading.

He offers a succinct adage that captures the gist of his approach:

[I]f Christians are to follow the examples found in Acts 10-15 and read scripture with the Spirit, that is, as the Spirit reads, then it will be essential to learn to read the Spirit, to discern what the Spirit is doing.[118]

The example of the church's decision making in Acts is presented as the formal paradigm for how the church should now read. How this reduces to only a *formal* authoritative paradigm in Fowl's account now becomes clearer. For example, whatever *material* authority that prior decisions the church has made are further relativized:

[S]imply repeating what has been done before will not insure fidelity. Changing historical circumstances will change the significance, meaning, and effects of traditional words and practices whether we like it or not. Christians have no choice but to struggle, argue, and debate with one another over how best to extend our faith, worship, and practice in the present and into the future while remaining true to our past. In this struggle, testimony

[116] Luke Timothy Johnson, *Scripture and Discernment*, (Nashville, 1996), p. 105.
[117] Fowl, *Engaging*, p. 114.
[118] Fowl, *Engaging*, p. 115.

about the Spirit's work in the lives of others muse become as central to contemporary Christians as it was to the characters in Acts.[119]

He goes on to suggest how this discernment occurs.

[O]ur prospects for interpreting the Spirit are closely linked to our proficiency at testifying to the Spirit's work, particularly the Spirit's work in the lives of others. Such testimony depends on the forming and sustaining of friendships in which our lives are opened to others in ways that display the Spirit's working.[120]

The paradigm in Acts is that the Church recognized the work of the Spirit in the lives of Gentiles and changed their reading of Scripture to accommodate that. This becomes a model that we also can follow. With respect to divine agency this assumes two things; that the Spirit's work in Acts in some sense pre-empts Scripture, and that the preemptive model is one we are as justified in enacting as the church in Acts was. Although it will not detain us here, both of these assumptions are not beyond challenge.

What are the consequences if this is only a *formal* prescription for how we can evaluate issues confronting the church community? Is this simply a paradigm for us to follow? What of the *material* decision made then? Or here and now? Could we envision the inclusion of Gentiles to be challenged in the future if it is suggested that the Spirit is leading the community to do so? If not, why not? The issue I am trying to press in this line of questions has two aspects, both of which ultimately resolve themselves in terms of the relationship of divine and human agency and action in the composition and reading of Scripture.

First, what, if any, is the relationship between the formal and material aspects of the sequence in Acts? Second, where, in Fowl's account, does he ascribe the uniqueness of Scripture? Are Christ's actions formal and repeatable? Are God's? Are Paul's? And what, again, is the relationship between the formal and material aspects of these actions? Should we repeat the formal but not the material? All of these questions have overt and particular theological bearings; particularly with respect to the relationship of human and divine action. These questions may have answers but they are not addressed in *Engaging Scripture*. We go on to examine one final feature of Fowl's work.

Throughout *Engaging Scripture* Fowl is nearly exclusively concerned with "prophetically challenging readings"; that is, readings that differ from the status quo.[121]

In this relentless focus of attention there continues to be a bias against any traditional or "settled" readings. Fowl's book seems to only envision and account for "counter-conventional" interpretations. However, in the end, what amount of our reading can properly be characterized as such? What of our readings that *confirm* and *reaffirm* conventional readings? There is no attention in Fowl's account for this. The dogged preoccupation with counter convention has a rhetorical effect as

[119] Fowl, *Engaging*, p. 117.
[120] Fowl, *Engaging*, p. 119.
[121] Fowl, *Engaging*, p. 157.

well as a synergistic relationship to the particular theological bias that animates his proposal. Thus, as we saw, his qualifications of text and divine action join with his singular attention to challenging readings to give his proposal a fundamentally and pervasively revolutionary flavor. Revolution without armistice, however, is anarchy.

We can clearly locate Fowl's location on our typology in the bottom right corner of type two. His emphasis on the priority of synchronic human action as a means of determining what the Spirit is doing establishes the preference of human agency which locates him near the bottom axis. His qualification of the role of scripture as being the object of the action of our reading through the lens of our present experience of the Spirit also indicates a placement to the far right. His location is, in the end, very near to Kelsey's, although Fowl is somewhat more cognizant of some of the overtly theological issues that pertain to his approach.

Fowl once wrote a sympathetic introduction to the canonical interpretation approach of Brevard Childs. In it he suggested that

> Childs … is quite open about the preunderstanding he brings to the OT … Childs, however, does not attempt to present a systematic justification of his preunderstanding … one wonders if Childs' critics might find it more satisfying if he justified the elements of his preunderstanding in a more systematic way. If nothing else, it would allow scholars with different preunderstandings to have a more fruitful dialogue with Childs.[122]

Fowl gives good advice to Childs. Others have made similar observations about Childs' work. We have seen above that there are substantial views pertaining to divine action and its relationship to human action that underwrite Fowl's account. Heeding his own advice would be a helpful next step for others to engage with his work on the full range of issues involved in the Christian reading of Scripture. Our typology is intended to be one such framework within which that negotiation and conversation can take place.

The Implications of Type Two: Benefits and Detriments

We are now in a position to consider the results of our brief survey of type two approaches. There are, as in type one, two benefits or strengths and two weaknesses that we will discuss for type two approaches to reading Scripture. The first strength, as well as the first weakness, is methodological; the second, in each case, again, are theological.

First, the strength of type two, in methodological terms, is that the nature of the situatedness of the reader is recognized and given more exhaustive attention. Type two approaches—hermeneuticians, phenomenologists and theologians—have exerted vast amounts of resources in describing and defining the nature of human agency that accompanies the reader in the engagement with texts. At no point in human history has a literate culture been more aware of the many varied motivations

---

[122] Stephen Fowl, "The Canonical Approach of Brevard Childs" *The Expository Times* Vo. 96 No. 6, March, 1985, p. 175.

and propensities that readers employ. The creative potential and the violent and oppressive nature of the human reader are familiar topics in the hermeneutical debates and the great sensitivity to the nature of these issues is of great value for the Christian interpretation of Scripture. These developments remind readers of Scripture of the importance of carefully handling the necessary questions related to presuppositions and manipulation.

The second, theological, benefit has a clear relationship to the methodological. This is seen in those representatives of type two who are cognizant of and attendant to the violent and sinful tendencies in the reader towards the text. Thus type two approaches are more liable than type one to recognize the inherent limitations of certain historical critical procedures, and helpfully uncover and redress the politically and theologically biased underpinnings of exegesis that purportedly proceed under the Modern banner of neutrality. However, this sensitivity has an analogously critical expression to that of type one. Just as type ones often criticize each other for not accounting for the "evidence" of the text, so type two approaches will not only be critical of type ones for being politically invested in distorting and oppressive ways of thinking but are quick to accuse each other in those same terms.

Nevertheless, the commitment of type two approaches to submit the reading action to the fullest possible attention and scrutiny remains a theological strength, particularly in holding each other as well as type ones accountable for their limitations and contingencies. From a *theological* standpoint type two approaches, then, perceive themselves to be committed, albeit in often times conflicting manners, to the accounting of the created, sinful and fallen, and redemptive conditions of the reader. This theological strength remains despite their differences.

There are, conversely, two detrimental aspects of type two. The weaknesses of type two approaches are an expression of their strengths gone to extremes. Thus the extreme positioning of representatives of type two in the far bottom right corner of the triangle demonstrates their isolation from the formal and material strengths of types one and three. This isolation results in the diminishment of the necessary accountability that these types present. This most often results in extreme type two approaches in the propensity to distinguish and abstract the natural relationship of divine and human agency in reading Scripture. The human agency of the reader ends up assuming greater responsibility in their proposals than is appropriate.

The *methodological* detriment occurs when the focus on the present action of the reader becomes the singular defining determination in the reading. This bias is demonstrated in the extreme type two approach when the perception of the problems of reading are viewed within a hermetically enclosed hermeneutical circle. This circle is one which is animated by the action of the reader and is impervious to the interruption or disruption by divine agency transcendent of the circle.

The first *methodological* detriment of type two tends, then, to neglect the corollary issues represented to the reading by type one in the abstraction of the reader from the agency of the author in the text. The second, *theological,* detriment of type two also relates to this abstraction but does so as it is an abstraction from the correlate issue represented by type three; divine action. This abstraction is a neglect, denial or removal of the reading of Scripture from the divine action that underwrites and accompanies the reading of the text. This includes both the accompaniment of the

Spirit in guiding the diachronic tradition and in leading the synchronic church in the reading and appropriation of Scripture.

This is reflected in the investment in synchronic human agency to account for the reading with a subordination of divine agency. The difficulty with this view is the problem of subordinating God to humanity, and the implications of what that does or does not mean for one's view of theology proper. Karl Barth's Romans commentary was a cannon shot across the bow of the ship of modern theology which had accepted the Enlightenment's epistemological terms, as we outlined them in Chapter 1, and, in his view, was restricting God by this very subordination. Also, similar to one of the detriments of type one, the extreme of type two also are prone to an overestimation of reason's capacity for objectification and an overinvestment in the ability of human investigation to proceed with objectivity and comprehensiveness regarding its own action. This results in a similar abstraction of human agency apart from a full consideration of its location within the purview of divine action.

In theological terms this abstraction, like type one, runs the danger of pressing human inquiry into service beyond its limited created capacity to perform. These are both progeny of the Enlightenment epistemological restrictions we discussed in Chapter 1. The more extreme forms of type two will assume, along with Kant and extreme type ones, that the more objective and ethically responsible reading of Scripture will be initiated and maintained by the synchronic self-sufficient reader(s) apart from the corrupting influence of any diachronic tradition or agency, human or divine.

The temptation of type two can be simply represented by the story of the building of the Tower of Babel. The assumption is that God can be reached by our efforts, regardless of God's distance. The reading of the text, the determination of its meaning, and the transformative force of its truth are the primary or sole responsibility of the reader or reading community to perform. The danger of abstracting this action from God's gracious accompaniment in both synchronic and diachronic terms is analogous to the results of the Babel story. If we construe the task of reading as one where we are left alone to initiate and guide the reading then each of our individual or collective hermeneutical circles remain closed and isolated. The distinctive language of our communities and our selves lacks any extra-systemic determination or direction. Our speech action eventually dissembles and dissolves into chaos and incoherence.

Chapter 5

Type Three: Prioritizing Divine Agency: God's Agency In, With, and Under Scripture and its Reading

This third and final type occupies the top corner of our triangle. First, type threes see the initial, primary, or decisive issues in reading Scripture as being derivative of some aspect of the question "What is God saying or doing?" Second, in answering this question, they give priority to some dimension of divine activity. Accompanying this is a subordination of the roles of the human agency present in both the text (type one) and the reading (type two). The location of type three within the triangle is determined by how they handle each of the issues they share with the other two types. In other words, how they negotiate the problem of the reader and the text by way of their orientation *from* the priority of divine agency.

Approaches that belong to this third type are normally viewed from a modern perspective as participating in a separate and subsequent activity to the work of types one and two. The consideration of what God "is saying," is viewed as the "application" of the methodologically prior and more important act of exegesis (for type ones) or of discerning the theological shape of the context within which one is reading and addressing (for type twos). Authors we will survey as representatives of the third type are Karl Barth, Nicholas Wolterstorff, and James K. A. Smith.[1]

Karl Barth: God's Word as God's Act

Our analysis of Barth will rely primarily on Chapter 3 in the *Church Dogmatics* on "Holy Scripture."[2] We will also look at relevant sections in his *Göttingen*

---

[1] Other representatives of this type include G. C. Berkouwer, see *Holy Scripture* (Grand Rapids, 1975); also Donald Bloesch, *Holy Scripture* (Downer's Grove, 1994), Jean-Luc Marion and Hans Urs von Balthasar.

[2] Karl Barth, *Church Dogmatics* – hereafter *CD* - (14 volumes, Edinburgh: T and T Clark, 1956-1975), *1.2*, pp. 457-740. On Barth's hermeneutics also see Mary Kathleen Cunningham, *What is Theological Exegesis?* (Valley Forge, 1995); David F. Ford, "Barth's Interpretation of the Bible," in *Karl Barth: Studies of His Theological Method*, edited by S. W. Sykes, pp. 55-87 (Oxford, 1979); George Hunsinger, *How to Read Karl Barth* (Oxford, 1991); Bruce McCormack, "The Significance of Karl Barth's Theological Exegesis of Phillipians", in *Karl Barth's Epistle to the Philippians* (Louisville, 2002); Paul Minear, "Barth's Commentary on the Romans, 1922-1972, or Karl Barth vs. the Exegetes," in *Footnote to a Theology* (Canada,

Dogmatics[3] and select passages from other writings. The thing that designates Barth as a (if not "the") prototypical type three is that he orients his view of Scripture intentionally and persistently from the standpoint of God's free and gracious prior action:[4]

> There is only one Word of God and that is the eternal Word of the Father which for our reconciliation became flesh like us and has now returned to the Father, to be present to His Church by the Holy Spirit. In Holy Scripture too, in the human word of His witnesses, it is a matter of this Word and its presence. That means that in this equation it is a matter of the miracle of the divine Majesty in its condescension and mercy ... In this equation we have to do with the free grace and gracious freedom of God.[5]

Barth specifically orients this by way of the confessional logic of the Incarnation, death and resurrection, ascension, and, most importantly, heavenly session of Jesus Christ. So: the only proper way to construe the Bible is in the sequence of thinking that begins with the "Word of the Father" which, as Jesus Christ, is now present at the right hand of the Father, sharing His presence with His Church by way of the Holy Spirit.

This immediately calls to mind our discussion of Frei's book *Identity* and the problems he encountered. Here: Frei, as appreciative and indebted as he was to Barth, missed the key point. For Barth, reading the Bible is only to be properly framed by the acknowledgment that it is an expression of the ascended Christ sharing His presence. "Presence" is, in this sense, and exclusively for the Bible as God's Word, necessarily prior to and broader than "identity." Christ's presence is the milieu in which we read and receive and share His identity. So:

> It is when we are clear that in all our exposition we can only think and explain this event, that we are equally clear that for our part we can never do more than think and explain it. All the possible denials and dissolutions of this present into all kinds of pasts and futures have their source in the fact that this present is not respected as the divine present. It is thought that we can and should turn everything upside down and treat this present as a created human present which we can seize and control.[6]

The arrays of issues that accompany the dogmatic question of the nature and reading of Scripture are all consistently worked out by Barth with this priority in place. For example: the authority of Scripture. Holy Scripture "has" authority over any other writings. Scripture also "is itself the Word of God." "[T]he "has" and "is"

1974); James Wharton, "Karl Barth as Exegete and His Influence on Biblical Interpretation" *Union Seminary Quarterly Review* 28/1 (Fall, 1972): 5-13.

[3]　Karl Barth,, *Göttingen Dogmatics: Volume 1* (Grand Rapids, 1991), hereafter *GD*.

[4]　Barth summarizes § 19 "The Word of God for the Church" on pp. 527-37 and succinctly indicates there many of the most important implications of thinking *from* divine action for the doctrine of Scripture.

[5]　Barth, *CD 1.2*, p. 513. See also *GD*, p. 212 for a similar passage. The great sympathy with which he viewed his own hermeneutics with that of the Reformers is indicated in Karl Barth, *The Theology of the Reformed Confessions* (Philadelphia, 2004), pp. 56-62.

[6]　Barth, *CD 1.2*, p. 503.

speak about a divine disposing, action and decision" and is in no way attributable to any human action "but in obedience to a judgment of God already made in the light of the object, and in preparation for one which has again and again to be made in the light of it."[7]

The freedom of the person and the obedient reading of Scripture in that freedom are both carefully proscribed in their relation to this prior divine action. This proscription Frei did faithfully retrieve from Barth, albeit that he located it in a quality of *all texts*, thus formalizing a principle that, for Barth, is a material theological acknowledgment specific to Holy Scripture. Barth had some rather severe judgments about approaching Scripture strictly from the vantage of whatever human agency it contained or enacted. He called this "daemonism and magic" and argued that this

> Daemonism and magic as such constitute a power which is, of course, characteristic of Scripture, but which at bottom it has in common with other writings, and which, therefore, does not basically distinguish this subject from others. To feel this power is still not to recognize the freedom of God's Word. This freedom is not recognized, and the daemonic magic of Holy Scripture is not correctly appraised, until in these evidences of its human and therefore not unique power … the power of the theme, that is of God's revelation in Jesus Christ, is recognized … if we interpret, appreciate and defend the Bible from the standpoint of its immanent human qualities regarded *in abstracto*, we necessarily remain on a level on which the characteristic power of this subject cannot be unequivocally displayed, and on which it can be rivaled if not surpassed by similar powers.[8]

The unique characteristics of the true freedom of the subject in his or her obedient and faithful response to the Word of God, are dependent upon and determined by the action of the God whose gracious power provides and enables that freedom. The proper way to speak of this freedom is with reference to God's action in Christ.

The doctrine of inspiration is also defined in terms of the freedom and priority of divine action.[9] In his historical account of this doctrine Barth locates the problem with modern accounts of inspiration in the reversal of the relationship of human and divine agency. In the period before the reversal Barth suggests that the inspiration of Scripture was thought in terms of "God or the Holy Spirit is its *autor primarius*"[10]. Over the course of time this relationship was no longer assumed, became awkward and eventually dissolved. Then, the humanness of the text became a "problem" to surmount on the way to hearing the divine Word and the search for certainty, likewise, in regard to the authority of Scripture shifted from the divine agency that formerly underwrote it to some unique qualities it possessed in its humanness.

It subsequently became a "paper pope"[11] for Protestants. Moreover, as a result of its divorce from the auspice of the primary divine author, it "was wholly given up into the hands of its interpreters. It was no longer a free and spiritual force, but an

---

[7]   Barth, *CD 1.2*, p. 502. The full exposition of the nature of the authority of the Word of God and its relationship to the relative authority of the Church is in *CD* § 20.

[8]   Barth, *CD 1.2*, p. 675.

[9]   Barth, *CD 1.2*, pp. 514-26. See also Barth *GD*, pp. 222-226 and Barth, *Theology of Reformed Confessions* (Louisville: Westminster John Knox Press, 2002), pp. 56-64.

[10]   Barth, *CD 1.2*, p. 523.

[11]   See also Barth, *GD*, p. 205, 217 and *God Here and Now*, pp. 55-8.

instrument of human power."[12] "Inspiration," which formerly was seen as an action undertaken by God in the work of the Holy Spirit, became an essence or quality of the biblical text perceivable apart from its relationship to God's action. Barth is sympathetic to the doctrine of inspiration as long as it is cast in the former way. This is shown in a contrasting comment he makes comparing his own views with the hermeneutics of Friedrich Schleiermacher; a hermeneutics that consistently relocates inspiration in just these terms. As a result of Schleiermacher's hermeneutics, Barth writes,

> Grammatically and psychologically, then, we are to deal with everything at a purely human level, and here, too, everything must be according to universal rules ... How remarkable that [Schleiermacher] does not seem to have considered the possibility that the thought which I understand in what is said by someone else, whether with or without his system of any other hermeneutics, might be contingently, without any qualitative or quantitative possibilities of misunderstanding, the truth of the Word of God, and that I should then have good reason to treat this address more specifically and more seriously than any other as the bearer of *this* content, a reference to *this* subject ... Why should not God have spoken to man in a way that is necessarily and compellingly understandable? And why should not human speech be necessarily and compellingly understandable as God makes it so? If God is God? But here we come up against the frontier beyond which we do not pass in Schleiermacher or in his tracks.[13]

The prioritization of divine action also has implications for how Barth describes other aspects of his hermeneutics as well as the doctrine of Scripture. For example, concerning the Christian Canon.[14]

An important key to understanding Barth's view of Scripture is related to this notion of Scripture as "witness (*Zeugnis*) to divine revelation."[15] This idea implies both a limitation in its relationship to God's revelation and a positive assertion about the uniqueness that Scripture has in this relationship that other potential witnesses lack.[16] The limitation is seen in that "A witness is not absolutely identical with that to which it witnesses ... In the Bible we meet with human words written in human speech" therefore we have a "witness which as such is not itself revelation, but only—and this is the limitation—the witness to it."[17] Despite this the "Bible is not distinguished from revelation. It is simply revelation as it comes to us, mediating and therefore accommodating itself to us" and "by this means it has become for us an actual presence and event."[18] The power of Scripture as this witness, again, derives solely from its relationship to divine agency: "In the final analysis, therefore,

---

[12]   Barth, *CD 1.2*, p. 525.

[13]   Karl Barth, *The Theology of Schleiermacher* (Grand Rapids, 1982): 182-83.

[14]   Barth, *CD 1.2*, p. 473; and pp. 597-602. Also see Karl Barth, *God Here and Now*, pp. 49-50.

[15]   Barth, *CD 1.2*, § 19, pp. 457 ff. The key discussion of what he means by "witness" begins on 463.

[16]   See Barth, *GD*, p. 202.

[17]   Barth, *CD 1.2*, pp. 463-64.

[18]   Barth, *CD 1.2*, p. 463. Also *The Theology of the Reformed Confessions* (Louisville, 2002): 41-64.

we have to say that Holy Scripture testifies to and for itself by the fact that the Holy Spirit testifies to the resurrection of Christ and therefore that He is the incarnate Son of God."[19]

We see in the examples above how the various facets of Barth's thinking about Scripture are fundamentally oriented from the priority of divine action. This is also the primary feature of type three. We now go on to further clarify his hermeneutics with respect to the corollary issues represented by types one and two.

Barth, when he outlines how Scripture is a "witness", also frequently discusses the accompanying stance required by the reader. Typically, when this question arises, Barth will quickly assert that Scripture's natural reading milieu is the Church:

> The basic statement of this doctrine, the statement that the Bible is the witness of divine revelation, is itself based simply on the fact that the Bible has in fact answered our question about the revelation of God ... Of course, we could not have received this answer, if as members of the Church we had not listened continually to the voice of the Church, i.e., if we had not respected, and as far as possible applied the exposition of the Bible by those who before and with us were and are members of the Church.[20]

Barth, here, indicates the positive and necessary roles for both the synchronic and diachronic influences of the Church. A little later he writes:

> [T]he Church is constituted as the Church by a common hearing and receiving of the Word of God. The common action of hearing and receiving is partly contemporary ... But to a much greater extent it is non-contemporary: it takes place among those who belonged to an earlier and those who belonged to a later age in the Church ... The life of the Church is the life of the members of a body. When there is any attempt to break loose from the community of hearing and receiving necessarily involved, any attempt to hear and receive the Word of God in isolation—even the Word of God in the form of Holy Scripture—there is no Church, and no real hearing and receiving of the Word of God; for the Word of God is not spoken to individuals, but to the Church of God and to individuals only in the Church. The Word of God itself, therefore, demands this community of hearing and receiving. Those who really hear and receive it do so in this community. They would not hear and receive it if they tried to withdraw from this community.[21]

This emphasis in Barth's hermeneutics is stated in somewhat stronger terms in the earlier *Göttingen Dogmatics:*

> In faith the human wording must indeed be heard as God's own Word, as the echo of revelation. If this is so, with what right can we bypass what the Spirit said to spirit before us? With what right can we bypass the series of acts of faith in which those who were before us received the Word? Only if we think we are merely dealing with history, with past events, may we do this. But in these interpretations that also speak and seek to be heard we are dealing with the church, with the church that baptized us and that has set us

---

[19] Barth, *CD 1.2*, p. 486. On the authority of Scripture also see Karl Barth, *God Here and Now*, pp. 45-60.

[20] Barth, *CD 1.2*, p. 462.

[21] Barth, *CD 1.2*, p. 588.

under the Word of promise in a very specific sense. The act of faith[22] that so dramatically precedes me cannot possibly be of indifference to me, is not of indifference to me, even though I may think that I should adopt so directly a historical posture. Here, too, the saying is true that we are blessed if we know what we are doing. We have to realize that we always live by authorities. What we have to see is by what authorities, and with what right.[23]

Barth is surprisingly affirming and sympathetic to the influence that tradition plays in the reading of Scripture. However, whatever positive place that tradition assumes here, it is always framed by and submissive to the prior free divine action of the Word of God. We can, then, further define Barth's location on our typology with respect to the pertinent issues related to the second corner of type two. While being sympathetic to the constructive role that tradition plays in contributing to the stance the reader assumes, it is consistently the case that Barth submits that posture to the Word of God that addresses us in the human witness of the Bible. Therefore we can locate Barth firmly on the left side of the triangle but not as far as Vanhoozer, who we saw was much more reticent about the issues pertaining to the agency of the reading/type two.[24]

---

[22] On how the faithfulness of the Church and the Church tradition absolutely determines the nature of its authority see Barth *CD 1.2*, pp. 574-85.

[23] Barth, *GD*, p. 237. Important qualifications and clarifications of his views on the nature of the authority of the tradition of reading in relation to the authority of Scripture as its "*autopistia*" are on pp. 241-249. Also, "In fact, if Scripture as testimony to Jesus Christ is the Word of God, and it if is therefore neither a book of religion nor of magic, whose contents could be mastered and professed by certain men with a gift for such study, who then can expound Scripture but God Himself? And what can man's exposition of it consist in but once more in an act of service and attentive following after the exposition which Scripture desires to give to itself, which Jesus Christ as Lord of Scripture wishes to give to Himself? But if this is so, then church history, i.e. the history of the church's coming to terms with the theme given her in Scripture, cannot primarily be understood as the history of the human opinions, resolutions and actions which have emerged in the course of her coming to terms with her theme. It cannot primarily be understood as the history of the men, whether pious or impious, intelligent or foolish, good or less good, who in the course of the centuries have sought directly or indirectly to understand Scripture. Church history must rather be understood primarily as the history of the government of the church by the Word of God, the history of the exposition of Scripture accomplished by Scripture, i.e. by Jesus Christ Himself in the church. *Scriptura scripturae interpres*—Scripture is the interpreter of Scripture … And where the speech and action of the church of to-day is concerned—and this is especially important—the human opinions and resolutions which are indispensable here can never be brought up for discussion in the abstract as human opinions and resolutions, but the opinion and the action of the Word of God which governs the church must be brought up for discussion simultaneously—indeed previously when we consider the matter objectively." Karl Barth, *The Knowledge of God and the Service of God According to the Teaching of the Reformation* (New York, 1939): 180-82. On the principle *Scriptura scripturae interpres* also see Barth, *God Here and Now*, pp. 52-3. On the *autopistia* of Scripture in Barth's view and related to the Reformers hermeneutics see Barth, *Theology of the Reformed Confessions*, pp. 62-4.

[24] For a nice summary statement on these issues see Barth, *CD 1.2,* pp. 684-85.

This location is different from the way that many readers interpret Barth. They attribute to him a rigidly actualist hermeneutic. It is suggested, the Word only "becomes" in Barth and never "is." Conservative reactions to this often conclude that, for Barth, the Bible's authority is located strictly in the contemporary reader. This way of reading Barth would put him in an extreme form of type two. There are passages where Barth could be read to be saying this, but a more careful reading of his overall theology and hermeneutics shows otherwise. To read Barth this way also affirms our contention that modern thinkers tend to frame the hermeneutical issues surrounding the reading of the Bible in terms of the single and simplistic tension between "text" and "reader." To those who are inclined this way, Barth's criticism of attributing divine qualities to the human text of Scripture will be automatically read as a move toward giving greater authority to readers. To them there is no third option.

We now consider this accusation: that Barth is consistently an actualist in his hermeneutics and that he denies the possibility of talking about Scripture in essentialist terms. Again, Barth will appear to want to assert this. For example in *Table Talk*, which is a more popular and accessible text for English readers who are interested in Barth's thinking about the Word of God: at one point he responds to a question saying, "For me the Word of God is a *happening*, not a thing. Therefore the Bible must *become* the Word of God, and it does this through the work of the Spirit."[25] Barth, however, anticipated the objections that his view of the Word becomes contingent on the human hearer. He responds:

But there is an obvious doubt whether this really does sufficient justice to the objectivity of the truth that the Bible is the Word of God, whether this description is not at least exposed to the danger and may be taken to imply that our faith makes the Bible into the Word of God, that its inspiration is ultimately a matter of our own estimation or mood or feeling. We must not blind ourselves to this danger. But we must ask ourselves how we are to meet it, how we can in fact do justice to the objectivity of inspiration of the Bible. Yet obviously we can do justice to it only by refraining from even imagining that we can do so. We do justice to it by believing and resting on the fact that the action of God in the founding and maintaining of His Church, with which we have to do in the inspiration of the Bible, is objective enough to emerge victorious from all the inbreaks and outbreaks of man's subjectivity. To believe in the inspiration of the Bible means, because of and in accordance with its witness, to believe in the God whose witness it is. If we do not, how are we helped by even the strongest assurance of the divinity of its witness? And if we do, how can we ask for any special assurance of it? Is it not to believe without believing, if we want to make such an assurance indispensable? ... That the Bible is the Word of God is not left to accident of to the course of history and to our own self-will, but to the God of Abraham, Isaac and Jacob, the triune God as Him whose self-witness alone can and very definitely does see to it that this statement is true, that the biblical witnesses have not spoken in vain and will not be heard in vain.[26]

This quote is as clear and concise a statement on the three issues that animate the three corners of our triangle that we have from Barth and needs no unpacking.

25 Barth, *Table Talk*, p. 27.
26 Barth, *CD 1.2*, 534-35.

We have now discerned the basic features of Barth's hermeneutic as a prototypical example of type three. The rest of this section on Barth will be used to explore three other related issues: first, the ethical implications involved in the bearing we assume when we read Scripture and, second, the question of whether there is a "general hermeneutics" under which we read all texts and third, how these issues pertain to Barth's attitude towards historical critical methods.

On the former, the true reading of Scripture, for Barth, is not limited to simply perceiving the gist of what is said: if so, then the speaker (or writer) will have spoken in vain.[27] Understanding is only achieved when this clarity then achieves an "encounter" of the encounter with the speaker *and* that the subject matter to which the speaker is directing our attention is also known: that all of these aspects of the speech act are successful.[28]

We will see below that Nicholas Wolterstorff's hermeneutic also treats the problems in interpretation only in the context of successful acts of communication. This is in contrast to the hermeneutics of James K. A. Smith who orients his hermeneutics from the emphasis about human communication in its ambiguity, its "undecidability."[29] Another point of favorable comparison between Barth and Wolterstorff appears as Barth continues; discussing the ethical implications inherent in the stance one takes up towards this "encounter" with the author:

> Did he say something to me only to display himself? I should be guilty of a shameless violence against him, if the only result of my encounter with him were that I now knew him or knew him better than before. What lack of love! Did he not say anything to me at all? Did he not therefore desire that I should see him not *in abstracto* but in his specific and concrete relationship to the thing described or intended in his word, that I should see him from the standpoint and in the light of this thing? How much wrong is being continually perpetrated, how much intolerable obstruction of human relationships, how much isolation and impoverishment forced upon individuals has its only basis in the fact that we do not take seriously a claim which in itself is as clear as the day, the claim which arises whenever one person addresses a word to another.[30]

Wolterstorff makes a very similar argument suggesting that the stance we assume with a text is one which should assume the ethical implications involved in an exchange and encounter between persons.[31] These ethical and moral concerns pertaining to biblical hermeneutics were held consistently by Barth as he indicated these as early as when he was composing the preface to the first edition of his Romans commentary.[32] There is, however, an important point of departure between them. Barth insisted that a greater point of distinction, and the *greatest* moral bearing

[27]   Barth, *CD 1.2*, p. 464.

[28]   Barth, *CD 1.2*, p. 465.

[29]   See discussion below.

[30]   Barth, *CD 1.2*, p. 465.

[31]   Nicholas Wolterstorff, "Resuscitating the Author," in *Hermeneutics at the Crossroads* (Bloomington, 2006) pp. 1-2 of his paper.

[32]   Karl Barth, Preface Draft 1 A cited in "Appendix 2: The Preface Drafts to the First Edition of Barth's *Römerbrief*" in Burnett, *Karl Barth's Theological Exegesis*, p. 281. Much of this survived and was included in the final draft.

is implied when we read Scripture insofar as it is not only a human word but is also the witness to God's Word.[33] The quote below succinctly unpacks Barth's thinking on this set of issues:

> We can follow the thoughts of others only when, however slightly, we can think something with our own thoughts as well. "We are with you," we say, and we mean that we are able with our own thoughts to accompany the thoughts of others along a particular path. Scripture, too, comes to me only as there is in my own ideas at least some place or possibility of contact for its ideas, and I am with it only as I can accompany, however modestly, the thoughts that may be seen in these ideas ... These are the unqualified facts which do not differ from the facts in similar spheres. Homer or Goethe could and can come to me in the same way ... But ... scripture comes to us as the Word of God ... [this] obviously means that I have not merely to think the thoughts of Scripture after it, to think with these thoughts, to think them for myself, but that I have also to think them as truth ... What is at issue ... is the acknowledgment of truth. The fact that scripture comes to us as God's Word means that we regard its thoughts as true, that is, that we accept its reference to revelation ... There is no possibility of folding our arms and adopting the stance of onlookers or spectators. The only possibility is that of seriousness, of decision, of being taken captive of faithfulness, of an act of supreme spontaneity.[34]

Barth links the ethical implications of reading the Word to both the question of "general" hermeneutics and to the question of the place and legitimacy of historical critical methods. On the former, in Barth's typical table turning fashion, he argues that the only proper way for us to think about the encounter between human persons is *in the context* of what we learn from our encounter with the Word of God. "It is from the word of man in the Bible that we must learn what has to be learned concerning the word of man in general." [35] There is no "general" category or consideration of humanity (or by extension, a human word), apart from the shape it is given and how it is named in God's Word. This is the crux of the link between Barth's insistence that we think *from* God's prevenient activity and the question of "general" hermeneutics and the study of the "history" of Holy Scripture. He continues:

> This is not generally recognized. It is more usual blindly to apply to the Bible false ideas taken from some other source concerning the significance and function of the human word. But this must not confuse us into thinking that the very opposite way is the right one. There is no such thing as a special biblical hermeneutics. But we have to learn that hermeneutics which is alone and generally valid by means of the Bible as the witness of revelation. We therefore arrive at the suggested rule, not from a general anthropology, but from the Bible, and obviously, as the rule which is alone and generally valid, we must apply it first to the Bible.[36]

This "suggested rule" was alluded to in our discussion above. It is grounded in the fact that Scripture has as its self asserting and self determining content the witness

---

[33] Barth, *CD 1.2*, p. 466.

[34] Barth, *GD*, pp. 253-254.

[35] Barth, *CD 1.2*, p. 466.

[36] Barth, *CD 1.2*, p. 466.

to God's revelation in Jesus Christ, and particularly in the incarnation, the birth and resurrection of Christ. This is the "rule" which stands at the heart of the particular hermeneutics of Scripture. And this is the key: it is *only* from the standpoint of this rule that we understand what it means to be human, and therefore what it means to read a human word:

> That [one] derives this hermeneutic principle from the Bible itself, i.e., that the Bible itself, because of the unusual preponderance of what is said in it over the word as such, enforces this principle upon [us], does not alter the fact that this principle is necessarily the principle of all hermeneutics, and that therefore the principle of the Church's doctrine of Holy Scripture, that the Bible is the witness of divine revelation, is simply the special form of that universally valid hermeneutic principle … It cannot, therefore, be conceded that side by side with this there is another legitimate understanding of the Bible.[37]

This is set in absolute contrast to other attempts to describe a "general" hermeneutics which trade on the "problems" or ambiguities in human speech and communication. We, again, anticipate a point of contrast between Wolterstorff and Smith which we will discuss and describe below. In this Wolterstorff follows Barth while Smith follows Schleiermacher. Barth's denial of such an approach is as follows:

> There will be no question of the assurance of an hermeneutics which is based on the necessity of irrelevance, nor of the meaninglessness to which human words generally would in fact be condemned, were it not that they had with them with all its promise the human word of Holy Scripture, and their own future was revealed by this human word. In view of the future of every human word which is already present in Holy Scripture, we will, of course, read Homer and Goethe and even the newspaper differently than if we did not know the future.[38]

This is how the particular rule at the heart of the particular hermeneutic of the Word becomes the basis for a general hermeneutics of reading all books. We learn what it means to be truly human in the witness of Scripture to Jesus Christ. Therefore it is only in this witness that we can learn how to listen and read other human words with justice and love. This is a point of contrast with much of the earlier work of Kevin Vanhoozer, except that he grounded his "general" hermeneutics in the doctrine of creation whereas Barth locates it in the Christology of the Word. We will see below that Smith suggests a kind of "incarnational" analogy by which to underwrite a phenomenology of all human language. However, Smith's analogy is

---

[37] Barth, *CD 1.2*, p. 468.

[38] Barth, *CD 1.2*, p. 472. See also *GD* p. 213. Also: "Our present concern is to establish that when we have to do with revelation as the content of the biblical word and with the hermeneutics prescribed by this content, we are not dealing with a mysterious thing apart which applies only to the Bible. Biblical hermeneutics must be guarded against the totalitarian claim of a general hermeneutics. It is a special hermeneutics only because hermeneutics generally has been mortally sick for so long that it has not let the special problem of biblical hermeneutics force its attention upon its own problem. For the sake of better general hermeneutics it must therefore dare to be this special hermeneutics." *CD 1.2*, p. 472.

radically different than Barth's "rule" in that Smith's is strictly a formal analogy and underwrites a general hermeneutics of language apart from the particular definition we receive in the person of Jesus Christ, whereas Barth's "rule" is absolutely determined by the material implications of Jesus' birth, death, resurrection, ascension, and heavenly session. Jesus as the Christ is the "New Adam:" Jesus as the Word is the "new hermeneutic."

The ethical implications of reading, along with Barth's view of the singular way that we receive a "general" hermeneutics by way of Christ in the Word results in a significant point of tension with other purported "historical" hermeneutics.[39] In an ironic twist, the very methods that invest so much in human capacity to objectively evaluate and discover the "historical" approach Scripture in such a way that, Barth suggests, is really inhuman and unhistorical. For example, the view of the Canon which results from the historical development of historical critical work on the Bible is one which

> [M]eans succumbing to the temptation to read the Canon differently from what it is intended to be and can be read—which is the same thing. The universal rule of interpretation is that a text can be read and understood and expounded only with reference to and in the light of its theme. But if this is the case, then in the light of the theme—not *a priori*, but from the text itself—the relationship between theme and text must be accepted as essential and indissoluble. The form cannot therefore be separated from the content, and there can be no question of a consideration of the content apart from the form.[40]

Further, Barth levels the playing field between historical critical readings and theological readings arguing fervently that these are all variations of reading with a confession of some sort:

> No one has ever read the Bible only with his own eyes and no one ever should. The only question is what interpreters we allow and in what order we let them speak. It is a pure superstition that the systematizing of a so-called historico-critical theology has as such a greater affinity to Holy Scripture itself and has therefore in some sense to be heard before the Apostles' Creed or the *Heidelberg Catechism* as a more convincing exposition of the biblical witness. What we have [in the historical critical theology] is simply the commentary of a theology, if not a mythology. The only thing is that this commentary has not been affirmed by a Church, that so far the theology or mythology has wisely hesitated to claim the character of a real decision. Obviously we cannot choose between the biblical text and a Church confession. We are definitely pointed and bound to the text, and not to the commentary. Again, we cannot choose between the possibility of using all available commentaries for and understanding of the text, including that of the historico-critical theology—or that of using only a few more convenient ones, including, of course, the Church confession. But we have the possibility of giving first place among all the voices

---

[39] "Under the caption of a truly "historical" understanding of the Bible we cannot allow ourselves to commend an understanding which does not correspond to the rule suggested: a hearing in which attention is paid to the biblical expressions but not to what the words signify, in which what is said is not heard or overheard; an understanding of the biblical words from their immanent linguistic and factual context, instead of from what they say and what we hear them say in this context." Barth, *CD 1.2*, p. 466.

[40] Barth, *CD 1.2*, p. 493. See also *GD*, pp. 215-216.

which have to be heard to that of the Church confession, i.e., to listen to it first on the assumption that it has something particular to say to us as the solemnly gathered deposit of the significant existing experience of the Church with Holy Scripture. We then have to be constantly ready for corrections of its view either by other voices of by our own insight … If we cannot do this, if we have to reject as contrary to Scripture the direction indicated by the confession, we then have to face the difficult problem of an exchange of confessions, that is, an alteration of our ecclesiastical position.[41]

He implies, here, that historical critical methods are not exempt from assuming a theological stance, despite their claims otherwise. Blindly accepting the implicit theological terms of historical critical methods has serious dogmatic and ecclesial implications. Barth argues, instead, that it is not a question of removing ourselves from the influence of other voices (vis-à-vis the stance Kant recommends) but that we carefully and honestly choose which voice is allowed to be heard first and which one will be loudest. Nevertheless, all the voices we heed should still be open to correction by the Word of God in the process of reading. Historical critical methods still offer great assistance in understanding the cultural features and settings in Scripture but "we still have to reject it as an interpretation of the Bible—and on the very ground that it does not take the human word of the Bible as seriously as according to the Bible itself it ought to be taken."[42]

At first blush this seems like an odd claim. However, recalling the ethical point Barth made above, this is the case insofar as historical critical methods investigate Scripture primarily or exclusively as if they are engaged in an act of textual archaeology and insofar as this distracts them from doing full justice to the author and to the subject matter of the text. When given too much pride of place these methods foreclose in advance on the very thing that the Bible *is* as a *witness*.

Barth's ambivalence with other attempts at "general" hermeneutics, including those which underwrite historical critical studies of the Bible, does not, therefore, dictate that his position on the triangle would be necessarily removed far from the bottom left corner of type one. Rather, we saw above, and see further below, that Barth still maintains a strongly Reformed view on the unique authority of Scripture[43] and thus between the two corners of types one and two his sympathies clearly lie with the former. His place in the triangle, then, is in the highest position among those we survey. By virtue of his giving authority to the Bible over tradition or contemporary readerly agency he is also to the left side in the top corner of the triangle, but not as far as Vanhoozer or Watson insofar as his statements on the value of reading in the

---

[41]   Barth, *CD 1.2*, pp. 649-51.

[42]   Barth, *CD 1.2*, p. 467.

[43]   Barth saw his hermeneutic as being very much in sympathy with John Calvin's. Barth's way of describing his own views on Scripture and its reading are, thus, very similar to the way he describes Calvin's hermeneutic. See Karl Barth, *The Theology of John Calvin* (Grand Rapids, 1995), § 17, pp. 386-393. See the similarity between his view and his description of Calvin's view on inspiration on pp. 167-168. Barth's great sympathy for Calvin is also evident in his *The Theology of the Reformed Confessions*, pp. 46-48. On the positive comparison of Barth's hermeneutic in his Romans commentary with Calvin's see Richard E. Burnett *Karl Barth's Theological Exegesis*, (Tübingen, 2001): 250-53.

context of the past and present Church settings is more substantial in his account. The chart below shows his place in relation to Vanhoozer and Watson, who as we saw in Chapter 3, are type ones who have moved on the border or into type three.

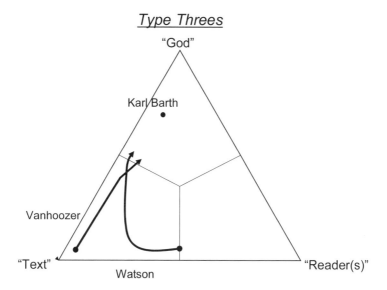

Type Threes

"God"

Karl Barth

Vanhoozer

"Text"   Watson   "Reader(s)"

Fig 5.1   Comparing the Hermeneutical Positioning of Kevin Vanhoozer, Francis Watson and Karl Barth

Nicholas Wolterstorff: Reading for Divine Discourse

Nicholas Wolterstorff's *Divine Discourse* touched off a new and invigorated discussion of a very old and very simple idea; that God speaks. He explores this by way of a rich and creative engagement with speech act theory.[44] We will focus our attention on his notion of "double discourse" and the corresponding "double hermeneutic" that, he suggests, we would do well to assume when we read Scripture.

First, he defines what he calls "authorial discourse interpretation." Succinctly put,

> Authorial-discourse interpretation is interpretation aimed at discerning what the speaker or writer said—that is to say, which illocutionary act he or she performed. Let me say again that our English word 'interpretation' covers a variety of different and legitimate activities; authorial-discourse interpretation is just one of those activities. What I claim for it is not that it is the only *right* mode of interpretation, not that it and it alone is *truly* interpretation. What I claim is only that it's the mode of interpretation that most of us

---

[44] Wolterstorff, "Promise," p. 84. Also see the bibliography for other relevant writings by Wolterstorff.

engage in most of the time, and that we usually assume to be basic to whatever other modes of interpretation we might want to practice.[45]

"Authorial discourse interpretation" is not a grand general theory under which he intends to account for all modes of reading. It is simply what he suggests most of us do, in our everyday lives, most of the time when we listen or read. It is the normative aspect of the larger notion "interpretation." There is a commonsensical rationale for starting here; that the exceptions, complications and problems of interpretation will only be properly construed and examined in relation to the normal, by and large successful, communicative happenstances of human speech and writing.

Authorial discourse interpretation aims at discerning what the speaker or writer did say and not at something else.[46] We see here common ground that he shares with Hans Frei. He does not deny that the search for the intention of the author is not a useful activity, only that it should be neither the foundational nor a comprehensive definition of interpretation.[47]

So: Wolterstorff enters the hermeneutical fray like a breath of fresh air, suggesting that communication is far more straightforward and far less complicated than many theorists and hermeneuticians would have us believe. He explores speech act theory as a way of unpacking this by way of his notion of "double agency discourse":

> What I have in mind is those cases in which one person performs some illocutionary act by way of another person performing either some locutionary or some illocutionary act, and that this assists in understanding how it is that Scripture is the "manifestation of God speaking by way of human beings speaking, and then of interpreting accordingly."[48]

In *Divine Discourse* he describes the "first" and "second" hermeneutics in which we discern what God "was" saying and "is" saying (respectively) by way of human speech acts. The "first hermeneutic" then, is preeminently concerned with the human authorial discourse indicated in the text of Scripture as a means of discerning what God "was" saying.[49]

He then introduces two (of many potential) ways of thinking about how one speech agent may make a speech act by way of another person's speech act. These two, he feels, are particularly helpful in unpacking how we might begin to think about how God does so in the Bible. The first is called "deputation." In it, if "one person is deputized to speak in the name of another, then the deputy's discourse counts as the other person's discourse." In this instance there is a prior arrangement in which the deputy carries with him or her a relationship and assumption that they are speaking on behalf of the deputizer.

---

[45]   Nicholas Wolterstorff, "The Promise of Speech-act Theory for Biblical Interpretation," in *After Pentecost*, p. 82. Hereafter "Promise".

[46]   Nicholas Wolterstorff, "The Importance of Hermeneutics for a Christian Worldview", p. 43-4, in Roger Lundin (ed.), *Disciplining Hermeneutics* (Grand Rapids: Eerdmans, 1997): 25-47.

[47]   Wolterstorff, "Promise," p. 82.

[48]   Wolterstorff, "Promise," p. 83.

[49]   Wolterstorff, *DD*, p. 186, emphasis his.

The other way is what he calls "appropriation." In this the speech act of one person is designated as an expression which another person finds agreeable or compatible with something they wish to communicate. A first speech act is taken up and used by the second speech agent. It is this second model that Wolterstorff finds compelling for the study of "first hermeneutics": of what God said in the speech acts of the authors of Scripture.[50] He also uses this "appropriation model" to discuss the "second hermeneutic" and puts it into relationship with the first hermeneutic in a paper written a few years after *Divine Discourse*:

> [F]irst one interprets these writings so as to discern the human discourse of which they are the trace; then, and only then, does one move on to interpret for what God said by way of this human discourse…It's only when we move to the second hermeneutic that explicit use of the theological conviction that Scripture is God's book comes into play. This is not to say that the first hermeneutic can be practiced in a neutral fashion—whatever that may be. It's only to say that in the first hermeneutic one does not employ that theological conviction.[51]

Mary Hesse responded to this paper and, particularly, to the claim that Wolterstorff was focusing on the immanent human speech action contained in Scripture apart from any informing theological judgments pertaining to divine agency. Her construal of Wolterstorff's hermeneutic assumes that he is advocating something like the Kantian approach we described in Chapter 1 while her response shares a similar concern that underwrites our typology. She responds, arguing that what he admits here about the *second* hermeneutic should apply to *both*. That first and second hermeneutics each require some 'ontology' or criteria for truth and, in this case, assumptions about divine action.[52]

Hesse helpfully directs our attention to this important issue. In the end it can be suggested that, in the course of his preoccupation with defending the notion that God *speaks*, Wolterstorff has neglected to adequately unpack the relationship of divine and human agency in how it is that God *spoke* in his *first* hermeneutic. Expanding on Hesse's suggestion, there is also lacking an overall consideration of the overarching framework of divine agency that links and administers to all these moments of divine discourse. He certainly can be read this way. However, the absence of this in his should not be baldly read as its denial but rather that he was exploring one question in a deceptively simple way; unpacking some rather straightforward but neglected and ignored conclusions about how uncomplicated the idea of God's speaking truly should be.[53]

So: even thought he does not explore it in any length in *Divine Discourse*, he does indicate elsewhere that one's understanding of whether or how one assumes God "spoke" does have an important bearing on how one reads for how God is

---

[50] Wolterstorff, *DD*, p. 186.

[51] Wolterstorff, "Promise," p. 87.

[52] Mary Hesse, "How to Be a Postmodernist and Remain a Christian: A Response to Nicholas Wolterstorff" in *After Pentecost*, op. cit., pp. 94-5, hereafter "Response".

[53] Much of what follows is indebted to personal conversations and correspondence with Wolterstorff. He has given me permission to note this.

presently "speaking." Double agency discourse is advantageous in just this way "for by enabling us to understand how it can be that God speaks by way of Scripture, it opens up to us the possibility of interpreting Scripture for what God said and says thereby—the possibility of interpreting Scripture for divine discourse."[54] We see here, again, that his primary concern is ultimately the present speaking of God.[55]

One of the more obvious ways to redress this unaddressed aspect of double divine discourse is to argue that it is the case that the human authorial discourse is itself necessarily read differently depending on both how one understands God to act in or not act, generally speaking, in time and space, and further, how and whether one believes God was "saying" something then and there constituently with the original human speech action. Thus the positive and negative assumptions one assumes both about divine action *in general* as well as about the *particular* relationship of God's speaking to the human speech action is, then, a kind of "Christian ontology" that one brings to both the first and second hermeneutic in the way Hesse suggests.

Wolterstorff has hinted at the role that this set of *general* beliefs about God's action plays in the varieties of biblical criticism and the quite different conclusions that result. What follows is a lengthy, but highly suggestive, quote from this earlier article.

> If you take the fundamental significance of the Bible to lie in its being a record and report of divine discourse and revelation that are of prime interest to you, and if you believe that on matters of such importance one should never believe writers on their say-so, then obviously you are forced to consider the reliability of these reports. In the course of that consideration you will naturally bring everything you firmly believe into the picture. If you believe that miracles do not occur, then you will find yourself trying to get at the real events that lie behind the miracle stories in the Bible and offer hypotheses as to why the writers would have used miracle stories to describe nonmiraculous events. If you have convictions as to the criteria for a literary text being well composed and you assume that the biblical writers operated with the same criteria, and if you then find that the biblical text at certain junctures violates those criteria, you will speculate that the text was assembled by somewhat absent-minded redactors from previously existing documents that did satisfy those criteria. If you are of the theological conviction that God's economy moves from law to grace, and you find that the Old Testament text as we have it does not exhibit that pattern very well, you will propose a dating and a reorganization that will exhibit it. If you find discrepancies in the biblical narratives, you will try to peer behind the discrepancies to see what really happened and will offer hypotheses as to why there are these discrepancies. I have called this whole cluster of inquiries the "historical-critical method" because that is what it is customarily called. But what impresses me, as someone looking in on the discipline from the outside, is how little there is of the historical, how much of the critical. So far as I can see, discoveries in the sand play a quite subordinate role; the discipline has been shaped almost entirely by theological convictions, by epistemological convictions, by convictions as to what does and does not

---

[54] Wolterstorff, "Promise," pp. 84-5.

[55] It should be noted in Wolterstorff's defense, that this intention of only addressing God's present speaking was not intentional. Further, that he had in mind to write an additional chapter in *Divine Discourse* addressing inspiration which would have expanded the discussion in this direction. That chapter was scrapped due in part to editorial limitations.

happen in history, by assumptions of influence, and by literary and rhetorical convictions as to how reasonable human beings would and would not compose texts.[56]

Wolterstorff, here, is acutely commenting on how assumptions about God's agency, *generally* speaking, necessarily shape all the various modes of historical critical studies of the Bible. He goes on to describe how this tension reveals itself in the very different results that are arrived at by Evangelical and more liberal historical critics:

> The fundamental root of the difference between the evangelical position and that of the typical historical critic is their differing assessment of the evidence for the reliability of the biblical writers. The evangelical interprets the evidence available to us as pointing to inerrancy. And he concludes from this that the Bible came about by inspiration, on the ground that only divine inspiration could account for inerrancy on the sorts of matters we find in the Bible. In turn, what especially leads the evangelical to differ from the historical critic in his assessment of the evidence for reliability is his difference of theological conviction as to how God works in history. The evangelical, unlike the typical historical critic, has no difficulty attributing to God the performance of miracles, nor any difficulty attributing to God the enabling of prophets to foretell the future. Where he does have his serious difficulty, as it turns out, is in dealing with the apparent contradictions within the biblical text.[57]

This illustrates how Wolterstorff sees *general* beliefs about God's agency in the world informing the moment of the first hermeneutic: "How God works in history." We can also extend his thinking and explore what roles *particular* beliefs pertaining to how God "spoke" play in the first hermeneutic. This is accomplished by reconsidering his idea of "deputized" double discourse. We begin by revisiting his "two ways" that one person's discourse can come to count as another's; either by "deputation" or "appropriation." In an admittedly awkward passage in *Divine Discourse*, he begins,

> There can be no doubt, of course, that within the totality of the appropriated discourse which constitutes the Bible, some of it is prophetic, and hence deputation discourse … But it's not at all plausible to think of all of it as that—to think of the Psalms, for example, as prophetic discourse, or the book of Esther, or the Song of Songs.[58]

The notion of deputized double speech action is relevant for the first hermeneutic only for pericopes in which the author or prophet know themselves to be speaking on God's behalf. This still leaves open the nature of particular theological assumptions about particular divine speech agency and their relationship to the rest of the Bible, including the examples he names above.

Additionally, Wolterstorff's notion of "appropriated" speech only accounts for the activity of God *after* the composition of the books of Scripture. He is, nevertheless,

---

[56] Wolterstorff, "Importance of Hermeneutics for a Christian Worldview", in *Disciplining Hermeneutics* (Grand Rapids, 1997).

[57] Wolterstorff, "Importance," p. 36.

[58] Wolterstorff, *DD*, p. 186-187.

fully aware of the problem that arises if one were to view Scripture's relationship to divine agency as one where the Bible is *only subsequently* appropriated by God. Thus the relationship of God's authorial action and the original human authorial speech actions now contained in Scripture but *not* overtly deputized speech remains unaccounted. In the continuation from the quote above, he responds to this potential difficulty, suggesting that

> Of course it would be bizarre to think of God as just finding these books lying about and deciding to appropriate them; the appropriation model calls for supplementation with some doctrine of inspiration. But what's worth noting is that, on this way of thinking of the matter, a doctrine of inspiration really is a supplement.[59]

Considering Wolterstorff's account *to this point* the following two conclusions *could* be made. First, that God's speech agency as concerned with the writing of Scripture only has a bearing on the reader in those passages when the speaker or writer is overtly claiming to be deputized by God. Second, that God's action subsequent to the composition of Scripture is relevant for the reader but only in the second hermeneutic; reading for divine discourse. The ambiguity of whether or how God's contemporaneous speech action is related in a broader comprehensive sense to both the composition of the whole of Scripture, for the discernment of the authorial discourse contained in Scripture and the theological stance of the reader in the first hermeneutic, again, remains. He concludes, indicating this ambiguity as well as his continued preoccupation with discerning God's *present* speaking: "However these books came about, the crucial fact is that God appropriates that discourse in such a way that those speakings *now* mediate God's speaking."[60]

Certainly if we think of double agency discourse in terms of the double discourse of immanent human agents this makes good sense. Wolterstorff would be correct, then, to see the limitations of reading for deputized speech only in those particular books or passages where the deputization is overt or acknowledged. Much of the rest of Scripture as well as most of the writers themselves would not have considered what they were doing as being divinely deputized speech.

However, there may be a way to expand his notion of deputized speech and revise it to address the problem of providing a fuller accounting of God's providential and concurrent speech action in all the varieties of activities that relate to Scripture. The reconsideration will draw on the potential differences between the terms for human deputized speech and divine deputized speech.

In Wolterstorff's examples the deputizer and the deputy are both aware of the deputy-deputizer relationship. Also, the deputy intentionally carries out the speech action according to the known will of the deputizer. Wolterstorff also describes a situation when the deputy and the deputizer are both aware of their relationship; however the deputy acts or speaks on behalf of the deputizer in specific ways of that the deputizer is unaware.

---

[59] Wolterstorff, *DD*, p. 187.
[60] Wolterstorff, *DD*, p. 187. Emphasis mine.

It follows from the above that not only may an ambassador speak in the name of his head of state without the head of state being aware, in detail, of the words used; the head of state may not even know at the time that the speaking-in-the-name-of is taking place—or may never know. And just as deputations vary in the degree to which the verbal detail of the message is specified, so also they vary in the explicitness of the deputation. Thus doubts and controversies can arise both over whether the ambassador really was deputized to speak in the name of his head of state, and, if he was, over whether he really was deputized to say what he did say in the name of his head of state.[61]

It is at this point that Wolterstorff's description of deputized speech breaks off. However, it is also here that the analogy of the relationship between human agents as deputizers and deputies can be reconsidered in light of the differences that arise when one considers how it is that *God* may be a deputizer. Two points can be made.

First, regarding the knowledge of the deputizer, this last scenario might not apply in the same way if God is the deputizer. The theological implications, both positively and negatively, of whether a human being, deputized by God, would speak or act on God's behalf without or apart from God's knowledge would have to be spelled out. This does not mean that everything that deputy would say would be *approved* by God, only that there may be mitigating issues with respect to the limits or limitlessness of God's knowledge to be considered at this point.[62]

Second, and more importantly for our purposes, we reconsider the role of the deputy's knowledge. Wolterstorff has only discussed two situations in this regard. First, when the deputizer and the deputy are *both aware* of their relationship *and both are also aware* of the desired intention of the deputizer for the speech action of the deputy. Second, when *both are aware* of the relationship but the *deputizer* is *not aware* of the undertaken speech action of the deputy. Wolterstorff has not considered a third scenario; if, or how it could be that a human speech action could be deputized by God *without the deputy's knowledge*.

Setting aside for the moment the issue of the differences between God and human deputizing, could it be possible to conceive of a loosely analogous situation where a human deputizer could deputize someone else's speech apart from their knowledge? Say there is a king who has a son. Their relationship is very close. The father king has been consistently involved with the teaching and training of the son. He is intimately familiar with his son's disposition and has accumulated great confidence in his son's ability and intention to continue to foster his own values and beliefs when he eventually takes over the kingdom. A dispute arises between this king and a neighboring king. The first king sees the dispute as one which has great potential to blossom into a violent confrontation but is still in very early and relatively minor stages. The king and his neighboring regent had, until that point, been on very good terms and had regularly visited each other and fostered strong ties between the kingdoms. The neighbor king has a number of attractive and available

---

[61]   Wolterstorff, *DD*, pp. 44-5.

[62]   I am reminded, here, of Aquinas' argument in Question 1, Article 10 of the *Summa Theologiae*: that since God can do with things and events what people do with words, all of the various meanings that we may observe in the layers of the biblical text are expressions of God's literal meaning.

daughters. The first king has watched his son become increasingly interested in the daughter and, in his heart, has no reservations about his son eventually marrying her.

What if, in order to preempt the potential conflict, the first king tells his son that he wants him to go and live in the palace of the second king; that there are special teachers there whom he wants him to study with. This may, on the face of the matter, all be true, while the first king keeps secret his real intentions. That is for his son to represent his values to the other king and to foster a deeper relationship between the kingdoms. The first king hopes that by sending his son that he would hasten the possibility that his son and one of the other king's daughters might fall in love. Thus the son's presence in the house of the neighbor king would produce a relationship between the two kingdoms that would potentially dissipate the potential conflict. Suppose his plan succeeds. In retrospect could the prince's move, his influence on the second king and on the larger conflict be viewed as, in some sense, a deputized speech act? In this case would the son's not being aware that he was deputized in this regard have any decisive bearing on whether his speech actions could, in the end, be considered deputized? Would not the king take great comfort with his advisors over successfully averting potential conflict in this accomplishment?

In this example we considered human agents to illustrate the point. When we turn and consider how this could be more exhaustively considered given the differences between human and divine agents this option would seem to grow more compelling in relevance to our understanding of the relationship of divine and human speech action in Wolterstorff's first hermeneutic. Thus, even if we grant Wolterstorff's insistence that the subsequent appropriating action of God is of primary interest for us in reading for the second, divine, discourse, is there still a sense in which our general and particular views about the providential action of God as indicated in both God's deputizing and appropriating activity reshape our contemporary view of the canon of Scripture in such a way that it does *all* read as if (*de jure* and *de facto*) it is *and was* deputized? Wolterstorff himself seems to anticipate this possibility as he lays out what he sees as the main benefits of his approach: that

> It offers us a way of understanding the unity of Scripture at a deep level, and thereby opens up before us the possibility of interpreting Scripture in the light of that unity … If all of Scripture is God's deputized and/or appropriated discourse, then it's obvious wherein its fundamental unity lies: in its totality Scripture is God's book. It is not God's *collected works*; it is God's *single* work … the most fundamental thing that unites Scripture will be that, in its totality, it is God's book.[63]

If this is so, is it possibly self-defeating, or even impossible, to read parts of Scripture, in either the first or second hermeneutic, *as a Christian*, assuming they are *not* in some sense God's deputized and appropriated speech; as having an informed relationship to God's general and particular unified speech action. We will return to this below to suggest how this might assist in discerning the relationship between Wolterstorff's two hermeneutics and the larger theological framework within which both proceed.

---

[63] Wolterstorff, "Promise," pp. 84-5.

Earlier above he described the situation when the deputy spoke in his or her deputized capacity in a way that was potentially in conflict with the will of the deputizer. There is another issue in biblical studies that we can address and see as analogous to this. This variance or contention arises in the hearer or reader as a result of there being a real or perceived discrepancy between the speech of the deputy and the explicit will and/or knowledge of the deputizer. This discrepancy is grounds for questioning the relationship of the particular speech of the deputy to that of the person he represents. This results in the speech having an ambiguous relationship to the authority of the head of state whose will it does not, then, seem to represent. This raises the possibility of questioning the speech of the deputy. This is analogous to the application of a "hermeneutics of suspicion" with regard to the human authors of Scripture.

This scenario emerges in biblical studies when certain human authors, certain books of the Bible or sections of books are viewed as having a suspect relationship to the traditionally assumed author or to a more reliable or faithful core of the book in question or to Scripture as a whole. Paul's writing about women and about sexual ethics are presently two more prominent examples of this. In one example something like the following argument is made: "If Paul knew what we now know he would not have said such and such." Another example is when Paul's teaching on women is suggested to be a redaction or later addition to his letters which places that portion in a suspect position within the canon; as if it can be safely set aside or ignored. The net result of these kinds of arguments is to see politically unfashionable speech actions in Scripture as having an adverse relationship with God's speech action. This clears a space, and relieves a possible textual tension, and permits the reader to assume a stance towards the issue in question that traditionally would have been perceived as being in conflict with these passages.

The analogy to Wolterstorff's point comes into play in the following way. The degree to which biblical scholars and theologians construe certain passages as relativized, of suspect origin, or even mistaken is the degree to which the writing is also construed to be at variance with, or distant from God's speech action. In other words, it is the *perceived* relationship between the speech of the deputy and the will and/or intention of the person on whose behalf the deputy speaks that has a fundamentally decisive bearing on how that deputized speech is read or received. In the case of reading Scripture this relationship is even more decisive insofar as the deputizer and appropriator is God. However, despite implicit claims otherwise, asserting a questionable status of certain authors, ideas, or passages does not necessarily relieve those passages of their deputized and/or appropriated status as God's speech. This entails a judgment that God *did not*, *could not* or *does not* deputize or appropriate this or that passage regardless of its origin as writings of an apostle or a later redactor. This claim about the relationship of God's appropriating action in this scenario could never be "proven" one way or the other but only asserted.

The necessity of assuming a stance regarding divine action in reading Scripture is also illustrated in Wolterstorff's examples in that the proximal distance between the deputy and his leader as *human* agents are assumed. However, in the case of Scripture, the proximity or distance of the human authors and God can not be assumed in the same manner. Human beings, by their limitations, *can* be assumed to be absent or inactive: God, by nature of His being God, cannot be thus assumed. Thus the "objectivity" we can and do perceive in the distance (and distanciation) between the speech actions of the leader and the deputy we cannot assume in the same, given, way in the relationship between God and the human authors of Scripture. Rather, an assertive stance must be taken up as one reads regarding the manner and mode of God's absence or presence and activity or inactivity in relation to the human authorial discourse of Scripture *regardless* of its ultimate origination. This line of argument compels the point that, regardless of one's position or theological or ecclesial persuasion, one's attitude towards the text of the Canon necessarily contains attitudes towards God's speech action. This stance is inherently "theological" and, in some sense of the word, "dogmatic." The consideration of this requires greater consideration within the proposals of biblical scholars.

In making this argument I am not so much interested at this point in deciding what kind of assertions about divine speech agency one *should* or *should not* take up when one reads Scripture. Nor am I arguing for one position versus another in the debates I alluded to above. I am simply drawing attention to the fact that, using Wolterstorff's example, one always takes up theological judgments pertaining to divine action and its relationship to Scripture when one takes a position on these issues.

Once we recognize the necessity of the relatedness of divine and human action in *both* modes of Wolterstorff's hermeneutic we can read some of his supplemental comments in a different light. For example, when he tells us that

> Where I differ from Gadamer is over what it is that one must bring to interpretation so as to enable it. Gadamer, as an advocate of textual-sense interpretation, holds that we must bring with us pre-judgments concerning meaning. I hold that we must bring with us convictions concerning the author—specifically, convictions as to what he would have wanted to say with these words in the situation in which he ascribed them.[64]

Insofar as we "bring with us pre-judgments concerning the author" this would have to include pre-judgments pertaining to both human and the divine author and their relationship in both hermeneutics. This does not, however, necessarily resign us to the whimsy of human imagination or the potentially violent and repressive side of eisegesis.

> Obviously it's also true that we learn things about authors from texts; we don't just bring things we already know to our interpretation of the text. Things we know about the author enable us to interpret a text. From that interpretation we then typically learn new things about the author and in turn use that new knowledge to interpret the text more closely and also to interpret other texts by the same author.[65]

This, again, is true for our knowledge of both the human and divine Author. So he asks, rhetorically,

---

[64]   Wolterstorff, "Promise," p. 88.
[65]   Wolterstorff, "Promise," p. 88.

Don't we learn everything we know about God *from* Scripture? I think not. Reliable interpretation for divine discourse can only occur in the context of some knowledge of God.[66]

Finally, we suggest that, to "for divine discourse" in the following quote could be added "and human discourse."

Interpreting Scripture for divine discourse is an inherently and unabashedly 'dogmatic' mode of interpretation…in which one employs distinctly theological convictions in one's interpretation.[67]

In closing our consideration of Wolterstorff's hermeneutics we offer a revised way of construing his double hermeneutic. The first hermeneutic is construed as reading for what God *said* by means of the human authorial discourse of Scripture. In this first stage we acknowledge that general and particular beliefs about God's action inform our reading stance. Nevertheless, our primary concern, in this first mode, is reading for the human authorial speech action. The second hermeneutic is reading for what God *is saying*. In this second stage the beliefs about God not only inform our reading but assume a greater directive role, while the net results of the first hermeneutic assume the lesser, informing role. This arrangement alleviates the ambiguity in Wolterstorff's writings and gives the two moments of reading a greater organic unity and mutual accountability.

His preference for using the appropriation image over deputization can also be revisited. We need to continue to be mindful that these are only two of any number of possible ways of talking about double agency speech discourse. If we focus on these two it is noteworthy that deputization tends to link us more directly and intuitively to issues related to the authority of the deputized speech act while appropriation leads us, I think, to issues around the relationship of the appropriated work to other works or speech acts of the appropriator. These two tend to conflate, however, when we shift from talking about a human to a divine deputizer and appropriator. Thus the appropriation of Scripture by God calls to mind the nature of its unity as a Canon as well as its authority as Canon[68] and the divine deputization of the speech acts involved in the composition of the texts of Scripture will, likewise, have implications in both senses.

Wolterstorff is located on our typology in the upper corner of type three. His commitment to a formative role for the human authorial action in the text positions him, within the top corner, towards the left corner. His positioning is not to an extreme in this second regard, however, in that the action of the reader, within the context and influence of both the synchronic and diachronic community keeps him towards the middle of the triangle, within type three, but just on the "text" side of the line between types one and two. There is a sense in which Wolterstorff, in this position, will not

---

[66] Wolterstorff, "Promise," p. 88.

[67] Wolterstorff, "Promise," pp. 85-6.

[68] On this point see Nicholas Wolterstorff, "The Unity Behind the Canon" in Christine Helmer and Christof Landmesser (eds), *One Scripture or Many?: Canon from Biblical, Theological, and Philosophical Perspectives*. (Oxford, 2004)

make any of the more stringent members of any of the three types very happy. The variety of responses he has received from all theological and philosophical quarters bear this out. Theologians want a more comprehensive theological accounting of God's action; biblical scholars and type one hermeneuticians are dissatisfied with what they perceive as his inadequate account of textual determination; finally, functionalist hermeneuticians view his assumptions about God's speech and his commitment to authorial discourse as dogmatic (in the bad sense), antiquated, and even maybe even "evangelical."

For the purposes of our work, and despite the ambiguity we discerned above in his writing, his work is a subtle and determined effort to ask a fundamental question in such a way that it has compelling power and deceptively powerful effects in reconfiguring the basic nature of the conversation. As such, the implications of his writings also offer a good measure of sympathetic currency for the typology as we have proposed it.

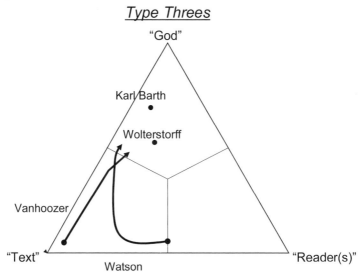

Fig 5.2   Locating Nicholas Wolterstorff on the Triangle

James K. A. Smith: Post-Phenomenological Language of God

Wolterstorff's proposal turns on the normative and largely successful aspects of human communication. The basis for this view is the created capacity and stability of communication when human speech actions are functioning correctly and properly; language in its normative transparency; its general decidability. Wolterstorff begins here and emphasizes this aspect.

James K. A. Smith's approach, at this important point, is an inversion of Wolterstorff's. Smith, like Wolterstorff, centers his hermeneutic on the created status of language. The normativity that Smith emphasizes, however, is language as *undecidable*.

Only a hermeneutic that recognizes the creational nature of faith can truly recognize the all-the-way-downness of undecidability…it is precisely undecidability that requires that we choose, in spite of the fact that our decision of faith is haunted by undecidability.[69]

This gives Smith a very different theological and hermeneutical bearing than Wolterstorff, particularly with respect to divine action. This is summarized neatly in his appeal to Derrida in support of his positive proposal about the role of language as "praise."

It would seem, then, that we can subvert Derrida's thesis regarding praise as predication … I would agree with Derrida that every "saying something about someone" is predicative *in a sense* and therefore constitutes a "determination"—"formally" or "structurally" we might say. However, not every predication or determination is necessarily an "objectification." … Violent" or "objectifying" predication as the halting of reference, the security of a meaning, and the adequation of the concept and object. But praise is characterized by *in*completion, reference without end, and a fundamental *in*adequation. The intentional aim is not halted in praise, but only deflected, without consummation or completion.[70]

This theme originates in Smith's first book: *The Fall of Interpretation: Philosophical Foundations for a Creational Hermeneutic.*[71] We will discuss three characteristics of his hermeneutics in it. The first is the fundamental undecidability of language. He opens with perceptive critical evaluations of Evangelical and Deconstruction approaches to reading Scripture. He develops his own view in dialogue with these: an approach he calls a "creational hermeneutic" or a "creational-pneumatic model."[72] The common denominator between Evangelicals and Deconstructionists is that they both link interpretation to "fallenness."[73] They "ontologize the Fall", whereas we should be careful: *"neither* identifying finitude with fallenness…[Evangelicals] *nor* identifying finitude with violence (contra Heidegger and Derrida)."[74] In this the "undecidability" of language is a fundamental feature of its original and good created capacity.

Smith's creational hermeneutic, in response, draws on a Wesleyan reading of Augustine to produce an "Augustinian philosophic hermeneutic" which emphasizes "the import of the affirmation of finitude for hermeneutics": which is "primordially good and remains such in a postlapsarian world, and therefore it is not to be construed as necessarily violent nor understood as a state of affairs to be 'overcome.'"[75] In this the "undecidability" of language is a fundamental feature of its original and good created capacity.

A second key characteristic in this first book is shown when Smith goes on to describe the hermeneutical moment as informed by "traditionality and intersubjectivity."[76] These are essentially the synchronic and diachronic influences of

---

[69]   James K. A. Smith, *The Fall of Interpretation* (Downer's Grove, 2000), p. 161.

[70]   James K. A. Smith, *Speech and Theology: Language and Logic of Incarnation* (New York, 2002), p. 133.

[71]   James K. A. Smith, *The Fall of Interpretation* (Downer's Grove, 2000).

[72]   Smith, *Fall*, p. 134.

[73]   Smith, *Fall*, p. 134 et al.

[74]   Smith, *Fall*, p. 136.

[75]   Smith, *Fall*, p. 148.

[76]   Smith, *Fall*, p. 152.

other agents on the hermeneutical subject. Smith, in challenging the same modernist tendencies we outlined in Chapter 1, argues that these should not be thought of as necessarily or pervasively violent or sinful.

These first two ideas begin to give us an idea where Smith will initially be located on our triangle. The first indicates a positive gesture toward those aspects emphasized in type two while the second would be a negative gesture toward the type one tendencies to forefront the stable linguistic character of the Bible. This last point is reinforced by the absence of any substantial discussion of the role that Scripture plays in its reading and interpretation: a feature that will continue to be present throughout his work to date, and thus indicates his place along the right edge of the triangle somewhere near the border between types two and three along the right edge.

The third characteristic of his early work relates to a gesture he makes toward the constructive role for divine agency. This relates to the role of "faith" in hermeneutics. We will return to look more closely at what "faith" is for Smith below. For now we simply note that it is more a formal idea; not tied to a particular or defined understanding of God but rather to a general attitude in the knower/reader. An attitude in which there are always "commitments" present which cannot be proved or given justification.[77] In a lengthy quote he sums up this third aspect in the matrix of the other two to give a succinct summary of the first book:

> [R]eason is grounded, structurally, in commitments, trust, pledge. Before knowledge there is acknowledgment; before seeing there is blindness; before questioning there is a commitment; before knowing there is faith ... Given this primordial trust, as the correlate of the goodness of creation, space is made for a plurality of interpretations, a multiplicity of tongues, which is also a very pneumatic-Pentecostal notion ... Given the phenomenological constraint of the world (that which is interpreted) and the pneumatological criterion in the fundamental guidance of the Spirit as rooted in a primordial trust ... The heart of a creational-pneumatic hermeneutic is a space, a field of multiplicitous meeting in the wild spaces of love (James Olthuis) where there is room for a plurality of God's creatures to speak, sing and dance in a multivalent chorus of tongues.[78]

In his next book, *Speech and Theology: Language and the Logic of Incarnation*,[79] Smith offers an account of hermeneutics that further develops these themes. In it Smith also moves beyond the former work in exploring new concepts. The one that will animate most of his discussion here is the Incarnation as an analogy for understanding the appearance of transcendence. He does this by way of a brilliant[80] exposition and analysis of some the seminal phenomenological thinkers who presently

---

[77]   In a way not unlike the analysis Michael Polanyi gives to science in *Personal Knowledge* (Chicago, 1962).

[78]   Smith, *Fall*, pp. 183-184. See also the discussion on pp. 158-159.

[79]   James K. A. Smith, *Speech and Theology* (London, 2002).

[80]   Smith truly has a rare gift for accurately, critically and accessibly presenting the thought of opaque and difficult writers. This is a consistent feature of his work of which should also be noted the recently published *Introducing Radical Orthodoxy* (Grand Rapids, 2005) and *Jacques Derrida: Live Theory* (Harrisburg, 2005).

exert great influence in philosophy and hermeneutics, including Edmund Husserl, Martin Heidegger, Emmanuel Levinas, Jean-Luc Marion and Jacques Derrida.

Smith identifies the chief problem he sees in the immanent reduction of Husserl that "God…has no right to appear in Husserl's phenomenology."[81] Smith's discussion of this point in relation to the phenomenological tradition is in deep sympathy with our own of Kant in Chapter 1. Smith and I are both pointing to the problem of the reduction to immanence within the modern philosophical project as a symptom of what may be an inherent anti-religious (and even more so anti-Christian) bias. In contrast he calls for a reconsideration of the question of the appropriate use of "concepts" in order to stage his own proposal:

> Could there be a kind of concept, and therefore a kind of theory, which does not treat objects as present-at-hand, but rather both honors the transcendence and answers the call for reflection? That is, could the violence of the (traditional) theoretical concept signal the development of a new kind of concept and set of conceptual categories, precipitated by a fundamental redirection of philosophy to pretheoretical experience? … The construction (or recovery) of just such a third way is precisely the task of this book: to provide an alternative interpretation of concepts which do not claim to grasp their object, but rather signal the phenomenon in such a way that respects its transcendence or incommensurability rather than collapsing the difference and denying otherness.[82]

He links the possibility of these concepts to the work of Derrida: in "formalizing the problem of negative theology, in order to open up new a dialogue with phenomenology… to provide an account of how phenomenology can recognize religious experience and the appearance of transcendence."[83] Smith also appeals to the work of Jean-Luc Marion who also indicts Kant as a co-conspirator in the reduction to immanence.[84] As appreciative as Smith is of Marion, he is also severely critical in that:

> Marion's "religious phenomena" is collapsed into a *theological* phenomenon; correlatively, his (albeit impossible) phenomenology of religion slides toward a very possible, and very particular, theology. The result is both a *reduction* of religion to theology, and also a *particularization* of religion as Catholic or at least Christian—which, of course is also a kind of reduction, a reduction which reduces the size of the kingdom and bars the entrance to any who are different. Part of my project will be to locate the *ethical* issues behind these apparently benign discussions of method, suggesting that behind Marion's understanding of the phenomenology of religion lies a certain kind of *injustice*.[85]

Smith sees Marion's Christian particularization as an ethical injustice. We will see Smith have an apparent change of heart on this when we look at his most recent writings on this subject below. For now we see that the "kingdom" for Smith, should be open to members of all religions. Smith is, then, not only critical of any particular,

---

[81] Smith, *Speech*, p. 33.
[82] Smith, *Speech*, p. 6.
[83] Smith, *Speech*, pp. 3-4.
[84] Smith, *Speech*, pp. 33-4.
[85] Smith, *Speech*, p. 95.

exclusive religious claims in Marion (or others) but also of what he sees as his reduction of religion to "theology." With respect to these he writes,

> But what if we were to delineate religious phenomena *differently*, in the plural? My goal is to argue that just such a space for difference is opened in the work of the young Heidegger ... [in which he] wants to recover or liberate (*relever?*) religion, as a pretheoretical mode of existence, *from* its theoretical sedimentation as a "science of God" in theology. The phenomenology of religion, as a *Religionswissenschaft* distinct from theology, brackets committed participation in a faith community and analyzes the intentions or meanings of a religious community or tradition. As such, it stands in contrast to theology, which investigates religious existence *from within* the commitments of the community; but it also stands in contrast to a traditional philosophy of religion (if there is one) which generally becomes linked to a particular theism. Heidegger's phenomenology of religion does not consider its "field" to be God but rather the experience and constructions of meaning within religious communities, opening space for a more pluralist field with space for difference. Thus Heidegger's attention to the distinctions between phenomenology and theology in fact opens the space for a distinct science of religion of "religious studies" (*Religionswissenschaft*)—which would be precisely a phenomenology of religion distinct from both phenomenology (as ontology) and theology. This is a space for the study of religion for which Marion provides no account. Further, and perhaps more importantly, this distinction between theology and religion opens the space for an understanding of religion or religious experience as a pretheoretical mode of being-in-the-world, rather than a "theologized" body of dogma. In other words, religion is a matter of the heart, whereas theology is a matter of cognition. While this does not exclude the latter, we ought not reduce religion to a theology.[86]

The advantages of the early work of Heidegger with respect to these issues are ones which Smith sees as important and helpful for his own argument. Smith advocates the study of religion which discerns the nature of religious life as a "pretheoretical mode of existence." This comports with his stated desire at the outset, above, to develop a "new set of concepts" which simply discern and describe "pretheoretical experience" of religion.[87] The former, violent ways that Smith seeks to "bracket" in relation to this pretheoretical religious phenomenon are "theology" as well as the role that the "committed participation in a faith community" plays in the phenomenological study of religion. This also reflects his prior commitment to the undecidability of language we saw in *Fall*. The table of theology is best set, according to Smith, by thoroughly clearing and scouring it clean beforehand.

The posture toward "pretheoretical religious phenomena" that Smith advocates here is confusing in light of some of his other comments. We will see below that he adamantly claims that he is not recommending some kind of neutral sphere vis-à-vis modernity, from which to view the religious landscape. Yet the bracketing of committed participation in a faith community seems to envision such a space; at least a space that transcends the particularities of faith communities that gather and receive their identity through creeds and confessions. Also, one of his stated

---

[86]   Smith, *Speech*, pp. 95-6.

[87]   This, apparently, is a related or revised version of his commitment to "empirical transcendentals" in *Fall*, pp. 169 ff.

goals at the beginning of the book is to account for the "possibility" of theology. Theology is, largely, only counted a villain in Smith's account. It is the apparent abuses of theology that Smith is concerned with throughout and not its usefulness or "possibility" in the normal sense that we would understand the word. No: here the possibility of theology is really an attempt to restrict theology to only a perpetual possibility: actualized theology is inherently violent.

The synergy of these two ideas combine to reinforce our location of Smith as being very near type two and to the far right side of the triangle. The priority of transcendent action that he proscribes is (like *Dasein* in early Heidegger) an anonymous transcendent agency. This accounts for why his attention turns so frequently to the agency of the person in the act of construal. It is ultimately here that the responsibility lies for the religious and theological action. Here Smith's account bears a strong similarity to Jeanrond's. The one feature that distinguishes them, and their respective location in the typology, is Smith's desire to maintain some kind of priority for the appearance of transcendence, whereas Jeanrond's focus is nearly exclusively on the activity of reader(s).

Smith, like Jeanrond, also argues strongly that any kind of exclusive view of divine action in the Christian faith is a violent restriction. We suggested then, as now, that to state the opposite, as they do, remains its own kind of restriction with respect to divine agency in that it disallows God the possibility of acting particularly and exclusively. Nowhere will this limitation be more compelling in Smith's account than in his use of the incarnation as a "principle" or "paradigm."[88] This is developed in *Speech* as he continues to develop his criticism of Marion, linking him to Aquinas as well. Here he offers even harsher criticisms of the exclusive claims of Christianity:

> Thus for Marion, as for Aquinas, the phenomenology of religion remains tied to the God of Abraham, Isaac, and Jacob as its horizon … The result of this rather insidious movement is two-fold: first, this conception of a phenomenology of religion *reduces* religion to theology; that is, it effects a leveling of the plurivocity of (global) religious experience and forces it into a rather theisitic, or at least theophanic, mold. Religion, for Marion, turns out to be very narrowly defined and, in a sense, reduced to its theological sedimentation. Second, and as a result of this, Marion *particularizes* religion and the religious phenomenon as quite Christian—at best, monotheistic, and at worst, downright Catholic. (After all, once one pushes beyond the limits of phenomenology, the saturated phenomena will be *recognized* as the God of Abraham, Isaac, and Jacob—even God on the cross.) This *particularization* is yet another kind of *reduction*: a reduction which reduces the size of the kingdom, which keeps the walls close to Rome and makes it impossible for any who are different to enter. First, one has to make it past the bishop, "the theologian par excellence."[89]

Although he does not discuss it, it would be natural to assume that the exclusive claims of *any* religion would be just as suspect and "insidious" to Phenomenology as the "preamble to revealed theology."[90] Again, Smith's criticism of Marion being

---

[88]   Smith, *Speech*, p. 156.
[89]   Smith, *Speech*, p. 98.
[90]   Smith, *Speech*, p. 98.

insidiously "downright Catholic" will be difficult to square with his most recent work which we will look at below. Smith continues his attack here:

> [F]or Marion, though the phenomenology of religion is without faith, it nevertheless remains tethered to the God of faith; the "God of phenomenology" is, of course, behind the veil, the God of Abraham, Isaac, Jacob, and Pope John Paul II. Marion's reduction, then, is also a particularization which reduces the size of the field and restricts both entry and appearance ... The result is that religion itself is reduced and particularized—or, more aptly, colonized in the name of a Christian imperialism.[91]... Marion's *piety* leaves no room for difference and will not permit any other gods to appear; indeed, one may be concerned that this pious phenomenology of religion is not beyond crusading to eliminate such paganism.[92]

Marion is too restrictive in not allowing for "other gods" to appear. Smith appeals to the early work of Heidegger to begin to make the necessary corrections to Marion at this point, "[L]iberating religion from such colonization ... and providing space for plurality and alterity—though I would also suggest that his mission fell short of a radical liberation of religion from theology, since he retains a focus on Christian religion."[93] Heidegger's rescue of "religion" from the oppression of "theology" was not as exacting as Smith now suggests it needs to be.

The key to his constructive response to these problems rests in his proposal on behalf of an "incarnational paradigm" which is "both the paradigm and condition of possibility for the proper understanding of language in general and theological language in particular."[94] The incarnational paradigm is the "concept" of which he asks his reader to reconsider, which we discussed above. He gives the following succinct definition:

> My goal ... is to outline an understanding of philosophical (and theological) "concepts" as "incarnational" (following Augustine) "formal indications" (following Heidegger). By this, I mean to suggest that such revised "concepts" are able to indicate that of which they speak without claiming to make them objectively present ... I mean to show that the transcendent phenomenon is not reduced to the sphere of ownness; rather ... we see an appearing which is at the same time a withholding, such that the Other is both present and absent. I will describe this as "incarnational" insofar as it bears analogy to the appearance of God within humanity, such that the Other appears within the sphere of immanence without giving up its transcendence.[95]

This "concept" underwrites all language and even all "appearances" of transcendence, potentially in any and all human religious experiences. The ambiguity that permeates the book in this regard is whether what he describes as Incarnation, "the appearance of God within humanity" is simply a formal category. So, again:

91 On Marion's "Christian imperialism" also see Smith, *Speech*, p. 98.
92 Smith, *Speech*, p. 101.
93 Smith, *Speech*, p. 102.
94 Smith, *Speech*, p. 154.
95 Smith, *Speech*, p. 10.

God's incarnational appearance is precisely a condescension to the conditions of finite, created perceivers. How could he appear otherwise? The Incarnation signals a connection with transcendence which does not violate or reduce such transcendence, but neither does it leave it in a realm of utter alterity without appearance.[96]

The principle of incarnation that Smith describes is, strictly speaking, limited to the possibility and necessity of transcendence "appearing" in immanence.[97] This may be indicated by something as minimal as a sign, a gesture, or more, as God's appearing in the form of a burning bush, a person, or some other effect on the senses of a person, such as speech, or wind. God's appearance, as Smith describes it, could, in some cases, also be God's revelation, depending on what one determines revelation to be and whether that event qualifies. But the point is that the specificity of God's *becoming* a human being, while having several points of comparison with all of the above things, has as its most defining feature a singular point of discontinuity. God does not just appear within immanence but *becomes immanent* and does so uniquely in a particular person. God does not *become* immanent in language.[98] To begin to talk this way employs a rather Hegelian heavy-handedness with the relationship of God's life and the unfolding expressions of creation and creatures in time and space. There are a host of resultant theological problems that result here that may indicate the need for a substantial terminological adjustment.

It is at this point that the absolute deferrals and denials that his appeal to a logic or "principle of Incarnation" finds its own limitation in relationship to its analogous origination. The particularity of the Incarnation of God in Jesus Christ surpasses Smith's purely formal and perpetually deferred logic at the very point of its adequation *and* finality.[99] There is a radical identity in God becoming *a* human, becoming *this* man Jesus Christ and not just "appearing" or "becoming immanent" or even simply "becoming human." There is a finality of identity of God and man, and of all humanity in the Messiah, in Jesus Christ. By nature of its finality and adequacy (full-filment) it cannot serve as a general analogy of a general and forever deferred possibility (for all language) but is the particular embodiment of the particular person who was (and is) the embodied expression of both God and man. Further; that the very terms he sets up by which to invoke it precludes its possible consideration as being this final particular complete and singular embodied act of God.

---

[96] Smith, *Speech*, p. 126.

[97] Smith, *Speech*, p. 156, 164, 176

[98] Elsewhere Smith sees his use of incarnation as a simple extension of Barth's "incarnational analogy": "Barth recognizes that the condescending movement of an incarnational analogy is the condition of possibility of theology, that is, talk about God. Our further claim is that such is the condition of possibility of language in general." Smith, *Speech*, p. 168. See our discussion of Barth above for the important qualification in Barth that theology is, at its best, a following of the gesture of the *witness* to the incarnate Word, and does not, properly speaking, extend or enact the incarnation.

[99] For another criticism of the kind of formalistic and universalist (as opposed to material and particularist) language that Smith employs here see the brilliant analysis in David Bentley Hart's *The Beauty of the Infinite: The Aesthetics of Christian Truth* (Grand Rapids: Eerdmans, 2003).

Very early on in the book, he acknowledges the inescapability of employing theology in this use of an "incarnational principle":

> I will concede that my employment of the notion of "incarnation" draws on a theological understanding, rather than a merely philosophical notion of "embodiment" ... By describing my account as "incarnational," I mean to invoke the analogy of the Incarnation, of the appearance of God within humanity in the person of the God-man, Jesus of Nazareth ... This is an instance of the transcendent appearing within the immanent, without sacrificing transcendence. In the Incarnation, the Infinite shows up within the finite, nevertheless without loss. My task, however, in no way involves the defense of a Christology, though it perhaps presupposes one. I invoke the Incarnation as a metaphor, bracketing strictly christological questions, but nevertheless pursuing a question about the philosophical possibility of theology itself.[100]

"Presupposes" a Christology? There is an ambiguity that emerges again here. This relates to the analogy Smith sees between the incarnation, which he admits is a particular theological notion, and with what he offers as an analogous metaphorical concept of transcendence appearing within immanence. This idea of setting up a general account for all language prefaced on a (at least formally, in Smith's case) theological notion is one we see he shares with the early work of Kevin Vanhoozer in that the claims made about God's action are defined as universal and general categories. But, as we saw in Frei's criticism of his own early work that we noted in Chapter 4, this way of setting things up creates the possibility of the compromise of the particular as well as the general aspect it is intended to underwrite. Thus, using Frei's metaphor, in the end, despite the claim that the "principles" cart is self-propelled, the theological horses are simply hiding, pushing from behind. In anticipation to this kind of objection that his project is theologically invested Smith writes,

> I do not, however, consider my project part of a classical "natural theology" which presupposes a neutral, objective "rationality"; nor am I attempting to clear the space for theology by means of a "secular" philosophy ... In fact, I am arguing that a *Christian* theology can only be possible on the basis of a *Christian* philosophy, a radically *incarnational* philosophy. Even more radically, I am suggesting that it is the Christian confession and understanding of the Incarnation which ought to undergird a general philosophy of language.[101]

He could be read, here, and in the quote above, to have reclaimed for himself all that he took away from Marion. However, he believes this not to be the case. These two notions, the "Christian confession and understanding of the Incarnation" as well as "faith" are not intended to be overt material theological notions as one would normally read them, but as formal, "pretheoretical concepts" as he indicated at the outset. We saw above that, for "incarnation" this means nothing more than the formal idea of the possibility and/or necessity of the appearance of transcendence in immanence.

---

[100]　Smith, *Speech*, p. 10.
[101]　Smith, *Speech*, p. 155.

Smith helpfully elaborates his definition of "faith" in an earlier article, "The Art of Christian Atheism: Faith and Philosophy in Early Heidegger"[102]. He identifies two types of "Christian a-theism": one is represented by Heidegger, the other by the "death of God" theologians. He writes,

> Heidegger's Christian atheism is different than the death of God theologians: His Christian atheist is a philosopher, one who has a knack for being both a philosopher and a Christian, which means being both an atheist and yet religious. Heidegger was not concerned about the idea of a theistic philosophy ... [that second] form of Christian *a-theism* is marked by the refusal to equate the God of Abraham and the God of metaphysics, the Christian *atheism* of Heidegger is concerned with excluding faith from philosophy, keeping philosophy pure from such contaminations.[103]

He goes on to locate his own bearing in the midst of these two:

> Now, while I would confess that I am a Christian a-theist, I would at the same time confess that I am a Christian philosopher. And so here I am ... between South Bend and Freiburg, and a-theist Christian philosopher, soliciting the ire of both theists and atheists.[104]

On the one hand, with the "a-theists" he refuses to identify the Christian God with the God of metaphysics yet, on the other, still understands his posture as a philosopher to be informed by some formal notion of "faith." Later he concludes, discussing a comment by Derrida, giving us an even clearer picture of what he means by "faith"; that

> Here we are directed to an "originary allegiance" or "commitment" which precedes every questioning, before any distinction between yes and no; that is, one begins by *trusting* a promise, a commitment before the word...And this pledge...this 'already,' is essential because it reaches back to a moment of already-having-trusted, an older event, part of a past which never returns, and never 'was.' This analysis strikes at the very heart of the Heideggerian notion of methodological atheism by positing a commitment before the question ... Deconstructively, I have argued that Heidegger's insistence of faith free philosophy is impossible ... faith and philosophy are inextricably linked, opening the door for the development of a Christian philosophy ... And it is precisely in the context of postmodern and deconstructionist discourse that an avenue is opened for such work, because it is in this context that the role of commitment in all theory is recognized ... Of course, I will continue to insist that Christian philosophy remain atheistic; not in the sense of being without faith, but in the sense of rejecting the idol of theism.[105]

On "faith" Smith also, with one caveat, affirmingly quotes from his former mentor John Caputo in his earlier book *The Fall of Interpretation*,

---

[102]   James K. A. Smith, "The Art of Christian Atheism: Faith and Philosophy in Early Heidegger" *Faith and Philosophy*, v. 14 no. 1, January 1997, pp. 71-81.

[103]   Smith, "The Art of Christian Atheism," pp. 71-2.

[104]   Smith, "The Art of Christian Atheism," p. 72.

[105]   Smith, "The Art of Christian Atheism," pp. 78-9.

Faith is a matter of a radical hermeneutic, an art of construing shadows, in the midst of what is happening. Faith is neither magic nor an infused knowledge that lifts one above the flux or above the limits of mortality. Faith, on my view, is above all the *hermeneia* that Someone looks back at us from the abyss, that the spell of anonymity is broken by a Someone who stands with those who suffer, which is why the Exodus and the Crucifixion are central religious symbols. Faith, does not, however, extinguish the abyss but constitutes a certain reading of the abyss, a hermeneutics of the abyss.[106]

The one qualification that Smith makes is that Caputo's reading of the world is "already a construal"; that it sees the world as "cold" and frigid.[107] This stacks the creational deck too much in the favor of Nietzsche. Smith insists that the primordial state of affairs in creation is inherently good. Violence is the interloper. "Faith" is "primordial trust, as the correlate of the goodness of creation" and given this

[S]pace is made of a plurality of interpretations, a multiplicity of tongues, which is also a very pneumatic-Pentecostal notion. When we recognize both the situationality of human be-ing and the fundamental trust of human be-ing, then…a hermeneutical space is opened that invites our creation, that beckons us to heed the call and accept the gift and risk of human be-ing in its creatureliness, refusing both the metaphysical dream of immediacy and the differential narrative of violence.[108]

Smith's most recent writings indicate both continuity and discontinuity with these ideas. First, his preoccupation with using the incarnation as a generic idea continues and is expanded in *Who's Afraid of Postmodernism?* In it he refers to his approach to writing in the book as an "incarnational strategy" which he defines as "attempting to accommodate thought to language that is accessible to an audience"[109]; film, as well as both the eucharist and the "arts in general" are all "incarnational medium"[110]; worship is "incarnational"[111]; "A more persistently postmodern church must be radically incarnational"[112]; we should also resist the "modern aversion to the logic of incarnation"[113]; and that the affirmation of the particularity of God's incarnation in the person of Jesus Christ is "extended in and by the body of Christ, which is the church."[114]

Also, summarizing his proposal in *Who's Afraid of Postmodernism?*: suggesting

[T]hat a more persistent postmodernism, articulated by Radical Orthodoxy, begins from a primary affirmation of the incarnation … I argued that if our theology and practice are going to be fundamentally incarnational, then they should be the catalysts for a reaffirmations of the particularities of Christian dogma, confession, and ecclesial practice

---

[106] John D. Caputo, *Against Ethics* (Bloomington, 1993), p. 245, quoted in Smith, *Fall,* p. 160.
[107] Smith, *Fall*, pp. 160-61.
[108] Smith, *Fall*, p. 183-4
[109] Smith, *Who's Afraid*, p. 21.
[110] Smith, *Who's Afraid*, p. 24, 77-8.
[111] Smith, *Who's Afraid*, p. 78.
[112] Smith, *Who's Afraid*, p. 135.
[113] Smith, *Who's Afraid*, p. 129.
[114] Smith, *Who's Afraid*, p. 122.

... the incarnation should entail a deep affirmation of time and history, which should translate into church practice that is catholic and traditional (though in a postmodern mode).[115]

In an apparent change from his earlier writing he makes the case here and elsewhere that "the most persistent postmodernism should issue in a thickly confessional church that draws on the very particular (yet catholic) and ancient practices of the church's worship and discipleship."[116] Another signal of stronger points of difference between his present thinking and those with which he attempted to mine for resources in the past is indicated when he suggests that

[A] more properly postmodern theology will reject the very terms of [Derrida and Caputo's religion without religion] critique and, in fact, be much more hospitable to both dogmatic theology and the institutional church.[117]

Likewise, he also has shifted his thinking on the "contact point" issue which he was very critical of Karl Barth in *Speech and Theology*. There he insisted that "contact between the divine and human does happen on the basis of conditions which characterize finitude."[118] He now says that "in order to come to know the truth, the learner (disciple) must receive from the Teacher (God) not only the content of the truth but also the very condition for receiving it. The dispensation of the condition is an act of grace by the work of the Holy Spirit."[119] In light of these one wonder whether the criticisms of Barth, and even Marion, would now be tempered.

We also see in *Who's Afraid of Postmodernism?*, for the first time in his major writings, an overt claim pertaining to the role of Scripture in the way that Christians perceive the world.

If all the world is a text to be interpreted, then for the church the narrative of the Scriptures is what should govern our very perception of the world. We should see the world through the Word. In this sense, then, Derrida's claim could be resonant with the Reformers claim of *sola scriptura*, which simply emphasizes the priority of God's special revelation for our understanding of the world and making our way in it.[120]

He, nevertheless, also continues to emphasize that the ubiquity of interpretation, as a feature of created creaturely epistemological limitations, is both good, and is inherently pluralistic and diverse.[121] Thus the correlate to the role for Scripture is the importance Smith sees in the role of the reading community. By way of an excellent and succinct summary of some of the key features of Derrida's thought Smith discusses this for the interpretation of Scripture. Concluding his analysis he suggests:

---

[115]   Smith, *Who's Afraid*, p. 127.
[116]   Smith, *Who's Afraid*, p. 25.
[117]   Smith, *Who's Afraid*, p. 120.
[118]   Smith, *Speech*, p. 168.
[119]   Smith, *Who's Afraid*, p. 27 fn. 19.
[120]   Smith, *Who's Afraid*, p. 55, also pp. 76-7.
[121]   Smith, *Who's Afraid*, pp. 50-51.

Communities fix contexts, and contexts determine meanings. The role of community will become central as we think about what it means to interpret the Scriptures.[122]

And a few pages later,

[T]o interpret the Scriptures, and interpret them *well*, I cannot shut myself off from the community that is the church; rather, I need to be formed and informed by the breadth of this community, both geographically (the global church) and temporally (history of the church's witness).[123]

In addition to those noted above, this theme is an important shift from his thinking in *Speech and Theology*. There, not unlike Jeanrond, he advocated the use of pre-theoretical categories that would be derived from a universal human experience or capacity, phenomenologically limited to the immediacy of the present. In other words, taking stock of the present manifestations of the transcendence in all human experience. Here he emphasizes the role of the particular community, within a historic confessional bearing. This way of talking by Smith sounds very similar to Frei's later work.

These developments in Smith are substantial. They illuminate a limitation of our triangle typology, however, in that they will not result in much change with regard to his location. For example: the shift from categories of universal human experience to particular and confessional influences of readerly communities and tradition and the accompanying shift from synchronic to diachronic themes in Smith's hermeneutic cannot be mapped. We alluded to this in passing at the beginning of Chapter 4. The thing that remains consistent in all these is the investment in some aspect of readerly agency. Insofar as all varieties of investment in human readers are measured in relation to one corner of the triangle as we have set it up; Smith's location remains the same. This has, however, an unintended advantage when it comes to the particular instance of Smith's writing.

Our survey of Smith's work reveals what appears to be significant ebbing and flowing on certain points. There are two ways, I would suggest, we can account for this. One possibility is that there is a largely heretofore unarticulated way that Smith sees he can hang all these variations and themes together; an explanatory scheme or principle of pragmatism that permits the robing of his thinking in any variety of sets of terms, functionally defining them as he goes. The other is that we are witnessing a fertile and substantial process of development in Smith: an intense *fides quaerens intellectum* in which there is, in fact, a substantial changing of his mind. These qualifications are necessary at this point, in that, of the authors we surveyed, discerning a stable position on the immediately relevant questions for our typology was most opaque with Smith. Thus the limitation in our triangle is an unexpected benefit insofar as his position is more confidently noted regardless of which of these is the case and to which brand of human readerly agency he is most loyal. We do show a slight shift below to indicate his recent gestures towards the role of Scripture in the Christians perception of the world. This particular aspect of Smith's thinking

---

[122]   Smith, *Who's Afraid*, p. 53.
[123]   Smith, *Who's Afraid*, p. 56.

has not been fully discussed in his work. He is not a theologian, however, and so we may not expect one. Nevertheless, it is possible to extrapolate certain propensities toward the issues in our typology and we have done so in the figure below.

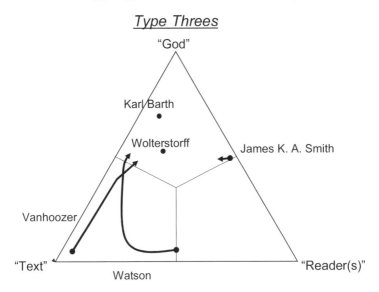

Fig 5.3 Mapping James K.A. Smith in the Typology

The Implications of Type Three: Benefits and Detriments

We close, once more, with a brief consideration of some of the results of assuming this type of approach. The methodological benefit of type three is related to the methodological benefit of type two. Type two approaches, we recall, assist us in recognizing the necessary limitations and locatedness that characterizes our stance as readers. Type twos tend to cast these limitations from within the immanent epistemological limitations as set forth by the Enlightenment. So, then, they proscribe the defining agency of the act of reading Scripture in terms of the limitations and orientations of the human reader or reading community. Type threes expand and correct this by defining those same features in broader terms; within the prior context of the transcendent actions of God. This strength of type threes also, then, provides an accountability to the theological weakness of type two which is to grant human agency the primary or exclusive responsibility for the construal of meaning in reading Scripture.

Related to this, the theological benefit of type three is an expansion and clarification of the theological benefit of type one. Type one's theological strength is the persistent acknowledgement of the priority of "the text" as determining its own meaning. We suggested in Chapter 1 that this way of talking is really shorthand for a host of assertions pertaining to God's character and actions. Thus type threes locate more adequately the self-determining agency in Scripture to the self-determining agency of God. Just as above, this also provides a counter balance for the tendencies in type one to attribute characteristics to the text of Scripture which only, properly speaking, belong to God. In both of these ways, then, type threes focus on the priority of divine action and agency supplement the strengths and counter balance certain strengths and weaknesses of types one and two. Conversely, the strengths of types one and two provide accountability to the potential problems of type three.

The detriments of type three can be seen from this standpoint, as in the other two types, as the abstraction of its strengths from the balance and accountability of the issues which the other two types represent to it. For example, the methodological detriment of extreme type three approaches relates to the well known problems of eisegesis in biblical studies. Thus type three shares the potential problem of type two in their possible abstraction from the accountability provided by the text. In both cases our theological frameworks become heavy handed and over determined in relation to the text in the reading. This is not to assert the opposite; that we should not bring our assumptions about divine agency and human agency to the reading, as we saw before this is a necessary part of our immanent bearing as creatures. However, the beliefs we bring to the text in the reading should always be made available to the correcting action of God in, with and under the reading.

Similarly, the theological detriment is that which type three shares with type one in its natural relationship with type two. Thus just as the potential theological detriment of type one is that it proceed in the reading of Scripture as if the context in which it does so and the pertinent issues that shape that context can be set aside. This translates into a similar potential problem in type three approaches insofar as a reader reads Scripture as if it is a direct link to God, giving that person specific individual information that has little or no relevance to that person's location in the various communities she lives. Thus the contextual concerns of type two present this abstracting tendency in both types one and three with accountability. This reminds both that God's speech action is first and foremost that of God towards His elect people; in saving, correcting, encouraging, and shaping those people to His will and glory. Thus the reading of Scripture will always have a fundamental collective cast and will always be relevant with respect to its communal *telos*.

The temptation of type three is to allow one's view of divine or transcendent agency to have an over-determining role in the reading. The common concern about eisegesis as expressed in biblical studies in the modern construal of the careful and distinct relationship to systematic theology is an example. This is a tricky issue insofar as we necessarily bring these beliefs to Scripture. Therefore it may be preferable to actively discern what beliefs one has and does bring rather than ignoring or attempting to remove ourselves from these beliefs.

Chapter 6

Implications of the Triangle Typology: A Modest Proposal for A Divine-Rhetorical Hermeneutics

Wading through the expansive pool of literature on biblical hermeneutics from the last half century one quickly discerns that one of the greatest areas of consensus is negative; that it is in transition or some sort of "crisis."[1] Many who reflect on this state of affairs assume that the problems incipient to these shifts are original or recent. However, many of them are constituent of Christianity from its inception. Proposed solutions that vest tradition, the community, reason, or the "text in itself," with the mantle of resolving them are not original either. Rather, the forms of the crises and the thematic variations that have played themselves out as responses carry an all too familiar melody when compared to other periods and controversies surrounding the reading and role of Scripture.

For example, the crisis as it expressed itself between Evangelicals and their interlocutors in the United States in the 20th century is similar in respects to that which arose in the Dutch Republic in the late 16th and early 17th centuries which set the stage for Baruch Spinoza's *Theologico-Political Treatise* (1670).[2] One focal point for the tensions in both was sorting out the implications of the competition between developments in fields of study indirectly related to the study of Scripture and the negotiation of the claims of that work with those of traditional religion. For Christianity this tension came to bear weight most severely on the authority of Scripture in the face of emerging scientific advancements. One of the hallmarks of the debates in Spinoza's time was the increasing commitment to "objectivity" to relieve the tension. So Cartesian deduction, Baconian induction, or some mix of the two, was advanced as producing the ideal form of knowledge for all areas of life and

---

[1]   Brevard Childs, *Biblical Theology in Crisis* (Philadelphia, 1972) is frequently cited as a definitive text for the "crisis" in its most recent form. Bernard Anderson, "The New Crisis in Biblical Theology", *The Drew Gateway*, 45 (1975) is a good succinct introduction to the scholarship that led up to Childs's book. Also see Mark Brett, *Biblical Criticism in Crisis?* (Cambridge, 1991). For a more recent succinct discussion of how the disarray in biblical studies continues see Joel B. Green, "Practicing the Gospel in a Post-Critical World: The Promise of Theological Exegesis," *Journal of the Evangelical Theological Society*, 47/3 (September 2004): 387-97.

[2]   See the important studies by J. Samuel Preus, *Spinoza and the Irrelevance of Biblical Authority* (Cambridge, 2001), and *Explaining Religion: Criticism and Theory from Bodin to Freud* (New Haven, 1987). Preus's discussion of Spinoza can be read as a supplement and corrective to Harrisville & Sundberg, *The Bible in Modern Culture* (Grand Rapids, 2002).

culture, *including religious knowledge.* The bearing of these issues on the reading of Scripture was a consequence and one of the detrimental features of this effect has been the preoccupation of this book.

These terms account for the similarities that persist over how to read Scripture from Spinoza's time to our own with the result that the shape of the debates constantly return to familiar patterns like a determined canine pursuing its tail. One has to wonder, in light of this, whether "crisis" is the best descriptor and whether "ongoing disarray" might be more appropriate.[3]

There may, however, be an important difference in the most recent embodiment of the crises. The postmodern criticism of Enlightenment objectivity, which seeped its way into the main lines of the debates, has contributed in providing us with a greater epistemological awareness that the idea of pure detached reason as the sole legislator for the terms of religious inquiry is highly dubious. The preceding analysis stands indebted to the so-called postmodern tradition, insofar as it also is critical of standard modernist conjectures of objectivity.[4] I would, however, add several caveats.

For one, I believe the criticisms of postmodernity are, in large effect, the critical mass of modern critical epistemological expectations turning on themselves[5]; thus there is something inherently parasitic about most of what calls itself "postmodern" to that which is "modern." This dependency needs to be more clearly observed than is often the case. So: postmodernism's service should be historically conscribed to the particular criticism of what Lyotard has famously named modern "metanarratives."[6] In this respect postmodernism is thoroughly and inherently a negative moment linked to a distinct kind of epistemological truth claim. When it seeks to extend its critical purchase in any broader sense, historically or epistemologically, or claim to present a positive, constructive epistemological alternative moving forward, it surpasses its purview and tends to repeat the very errors it redresses.

Secondarily, the service that postmodernism provides is a kind of leveling of the epistemological playing field where the possibility of making truth claims is not foreclosed in advance, but, rather acknowledged as, *prima facie* both possible and necessary. The sorting out of the inevitable conflict between the truth claims of regions, groups, or "language games" is not done in advance nor subsequently resolved (via "metanarratives"), but is revealed and understood in the *ad hoc* encounter (and struggle) between them ("resolution" or "ultimate agreement" are now acknowledged as myths).

Thirdly, this has immediate implications for theological hermeneutics and dogmatic theology and their relationship to other sciences. Even as a non-

---

[3] "Monographs, commentaries and articles accumulate, but the proliferation of positions and the constant deferment of the hoped-for consensus may be indicative not of progress but of circularity." Francis Watson, *Text, Church and World* (Grand Rapids, 1994) p. 47.

[4] I have discussed this issue further in my article "Objectivity" in *The Dictionary for Theological Interpretation of the Bible* (Grand Rapids, 2005).

[5] See Linda Hutcheon, *A Poetics of Postmodernism* (New York, 1988) for one of the most reasonable assessments of this issue of which I am aware.

[6] The best accessible discussion of what Lyotard was really after in this, to my knowledge, is found in James K. A. Smith's *Who's Afraid of Postmodernism?* (Grand Rapids, 2006).

negotiable difference between theological science and "hard" science is recognized, acknowledging this does not result in the banishment of one or the other to the hinterlands of "truth." Spelling out those differences is fundamental for the proper understanding of the act of reading the Bible: yet, finding scholars who actually do so, in this day and age, is a very rare thing.[7] In modernity (and in most of what has passed for postmodernity in public universities) banishment continues to be the fate for any activity that bears the stamp of particular Christian claims.[8] Properly speaking, however, the primary gesture of postmodernity is (in theory) welcoming; equally any and all traditionally located knowledge.

With the benefit of postmodern hindsight one issue is beginning to come to some resolve among biblical scholars. It is now *de rigueur* to acknowledge that the reader is incapable of fully escaping his or her assumptions or orientations in the engaging moment of reading Scripture. Subsequently it is also widely accepted that there must be, *at some point*, a necessary break in the modern casting of the analogous methodological relationships between "hard" sciences and theology, and even more so with historical investigation as *Historie*[9] in relation to the interpretation of Scripture.[10]

But what do we do now? What do we do with these indictments of pure reason? And what do we do with these assumptions we inevitably bring to the interpretive task? Are they to be considered a useless annoyance, like reminders of the pigeons on the statue of King George in Queen's Park? Alternately are they the only thing that the interpretive task is "really" about? Is reading Scripture simply an exercise that seeks out our own reflections, that learns about ourselves, and attentively listens to our own voices? In these responses many so-called "postmodern" reactions to the concreteness of our hermeneutical locatedness have tended toward minimalist and maximalist versions of arguments which are still dependent on the traditions of Enlightenment epistemology.

The minimalist version recognizes that we bring an orientation to the task of reading but proceeds under the assumption that, as far as one is able, one is to

---

[7]   I suspect this is not entirely attributable to willingness, but ability. The modern schema for seminary and graduate theological education systematically excludes the kind of interdisciplinary skills and imagination required. A major overhaul of the philosophy of theological education is necessary if the deficiencies indicated in this work are to be sufficiently redressed.

[8]   One of the clearest remnants of modern epistemological imperialism in Western Universities is the indefensible bias of religious departments which presently encourage and embrace scholars and perspectives that speak from particularist and exclusivist religious traditions bar one: the Christian.

[9]   There is debate on the exact nature of the difference between *Historie* and *Geschichte*. I use the term following Karl Barth's helpful definition in *Karl Barth's Table Talk* (Richmond, 1962): "*Historie* is something that can be proved by natural science, whereas *Geschichte* is something that really takes place in space and time, but may or may not be proved.", p.45.

[10]   One helpful recent account of the relationship of historical criticism and biblical theology is found in A.K.M. Adam, *Making Sense of New Testament Theology* (Macon, 1995). Adam effectively challenges the hegemony of history (in its modernist form) as the exclusive entry point to doing New Testament Theology.

strictly minimize any constructive role for them in the actual process. Theological judgments are still seen as properly only a *byproduct* of the reading. The maximalist reaction sees the reading of any text, including Scripture, to be hopelessly entombed in politically invested frameworks. All interpretations, by this view, are efforts at manipulation and are, by necessity, inherently oppressive and violent.[11] In the former, a vestige of modern valuation of objectivity continues in a chastised form; in the latter, it is as though we have all passed the sign to Dante's hell—"abandon hope all ye who enter here"—and interpretation of texts becomes little more than a Nietzschean/Darwinian battle of survival of the fittest.

Both minimalist and maximalist reactions seek to maintain control in the midst of the vying interests that comprise the reading of Scripture. Further, both the maximalist and minimalist responses still tend to account for these influences primarily or exclusively within the purview of immanent human activity. The minimalist version banks on some form of human reason to control and tame the interloping effects of imagination and opinion. The maximalist version simply turns the tables, declaring reason impotent against the overpowering force of human imagination and political will. Insofar as this characterization is true both remain committed to the dominant tradition of Enlightenment epistemology which created the disarray in Biblical studies in the first place and are impotent in moving beyond them.

Actually, blindness is a better metaphor than impotence. This is an important point: what one *perceives* to be the range of possible avenues to address the question of "antecedent judgments" is an important key to how one responds to their persistent operation in human knowing and reading. It is here that the hindering influence of Enlightenment restrictions on epistemology is restricting the contemporary theological imagination. A fuller and more exacting exposition of the nature of these epistemological themes and the extent of their continuing influence on the perception of the role and place of presuppositions in the act of doing theology and reading Scripture is needed. If for no other reason, this investigation is warranted because our hermeneutical assumptions are constituent in our created perspectives as immanent creatures, and the *constructive and appropriate* role they play when we, as Christians, read and interpret Scripture is a neglected question which falls in between the cracks of the minimalist and maximalist accounts.

This book enters at exactly this point. This project is designed to illuminate the fundamental nature of the (theological) assumptions we live with as creatures and as Christians as we read Scripture.; theological assumptions pertaining to divine agency which are present in, with, and under theological activities as timed and placed beings. Any discomfort we continue to harbor in relation to these limitations, and the constricting role they play in our hermeneutic situatedness, is derivative of a misguided *overvaluation* of modern objectivity. This is accompanied by a corresponding *devaluation* of the role of theological judgments that we bring to the investigative task. The resulting exaltation of this kind of detached objectivity stands in direct conflict with the biblical and confessional account of our nature as creatures that are utterly dependent on God. Yet, it is these same limited conditions which are

---

[11]   See the accessible and highly illuminative discussion of Foucault in James K. A. Smith's *Who's Afraid of Postmodernism?*, (Grand Rapids: Baker Academic, 2006).

features inherent to our created natures that God sees at the end of the sixth day of creation and calls "very good."

In the construction and description of the triangle typology we have pursued a line of thinking which acknowledges the inherent limits of language as an essential aspect of our created condition, yet attempts to negotiate a more theologically congruent picture of the place that it occupies at the heart of the tensions over the nature of the crisis in biblical theology. The triangle is designed to assist thinkers from various fields and hermeneutical orientations to negotiate the various facets of our hermeneutical stance which vie for our attention and loyalty in the act of reading and interpreting the Bible. This, we hope, then, will be a useful map by which to navigate the pertinent issues that arise in considering our created hermeneutical stance and how these issues bear on any and all readings and interpretations of Scripture. The net result is that this investigation allows us to begin to see a more promising path out of the forest and thickets of the crises in biblical studies.

The rest of the space in this book, generously given but strictly defined by editorial pronouncement, will shift gears and do two things: firstly it will briefly discuss the implications of this work for the use of "principles" in reading Scripture, and secondly it will offer a cursory sketch of a new proposal for reading Scripture that has great potential in redressing the weaknesses that still persist in biblical hermeneutics as indicated in the analysis of the triangle typology. This sketch also serves as the broader outline of what will, God willing, be the next book of this author on the subject.

Before, Beside or Beyond the Bible: The Role of 'Principles' in Theological Interpretation of Scripture

We will now abandon the abstract language of "antecedent judgments" and "epistemological limitations" and assume a more mundane vernacular. We will begin by briefly discussing role and place for "principles" in reading the Bible, particularly in light of the growing interest in "theological hermeneutics" and "theological interpretation." We begin by interrogating three myths about principles that attained prominence in the modern era and, to various degrees, still perdure. We will then identify a single issue that explains a common denominator in the problematic nature of these myths and illustrate this problem by way of a brief re-engagement with the hermeneutical thought of Hans Frei. Finally, then, we will offer a modest gesture towards a new model by which to properly frame our understanding of the act of reading the Bible and correct the deficiencies that have been the result of this problem; deficiencies that have been prevalent for centuries and remain remarkably insular to criticism.

Before I begin I need to make one qualifying comment. This section will be preoccupied with the way that principles are employed in reading the Bible. Ultimately, the most appropriate way to frame this activity is by way of locating it within the larger economy of divine agency that encompasses and informs all human agencies. This is, properly speaking, a dogmatic description and would account for the milieu of God's action in the total fullness of all of its Trinitarian and salvific manifestations.[12] Further, that the community of believers is, in kind, the proper context to describe the event of that reading. These require theological and dogmatic descriptions that I will not even attempt to do anything remotely like justice to here. This modest sketch is, in this important respect, an abstraction.

So then: unless you have been living on a remote island you will likely be well aware of the burgeoning field of theological hermeneutics. A substantial tide of books has appeared in recent years, accompanied by an explosion of interest in the subject at theological and religious conferences. We add to this the arrival of an important reference work: *The Dictionary for the Theological Interpretation of the Bible*.[13] Also, commentary series are starting to be produced that explicitly look to do "theological interpretation" and explore the value of pre-Enlightenment interpretations of Scripture.[14]

Those who contract to do these (as well as any of the rest of us who wish to do theological interpretation moving forward) are confronted by pressing questions: "What is theological interpretation?" "How does one do it?" "What are the rules or principles which one follows?" "Are there manuals that outline what is and is not the right way?" Let's consider what sorts of things "principles" for interpretation are and give some examples as we move toward the constructive sketch of a new model for a divine-rhetorical hermeneutic.

Mundanely speaking, two types of principles can be employed to read Scripture: formal principles and material principles. A formal principle is the sort which guides the reader in a general manner in their handling of a text and has potential utility in relation to any text. In other words, formal rules are not text specific, that is, they are not materially related to the content of any particular book but, in theory, could be applied to any book.

Some examples of this type of principle are:

- the rule that there is a "single meaning";
- the "fourfold levels of meaning" (which was dominant in the Medieval period) fits here as it was often used, for example, to interpret Dante's *Divine Comedy;*
- "typology";
- "allegory";
- "*sensus plenior*";
- "historical-grammatical";
- "historical-critical";
- the priority of the "literal" meaning.

This list is familiar. Modern debates over the interpretation of Scripture tend to focus exclusively on formal principles. So, in one manifestation of the way things proceed under a formal principle, the activity of the responsible reader of a book is

---

[12] See John Webster, "The Dogmatic Location of the Canon", *Neue Zeitschrift Für Systematische Theologie* 43 (2001): 17-43.

[13] *The Dictionary for the Theological Interpretation of the Bible*, edited by Kevin Vanhoozer, N.T. Wright, Craig Bartholomew and Dan Treier, (Grand Rapids, 2005).

[14] Even as I type this I have received word of another series, this one devoted to the interpretation of Scripture by Reformed theologians to be published by InterVarsity Press.

framed by the question whether there is a "single" meaning for this book or passage or text, and what is or are the means by which one determines what is that meaning.

The other type is "material" principles. These are rules which share a distinct relationship to the content of a specific text. Some examples of this type are:

- Augustine: in De Doctrina Christiana in which the overarching rule for reading the Bible is so that "love of God and love of neighbor" is the outcome;
- Luther: interpreting Scripture so that the work of Jesus Christ can be manifest in the heart of the believer giving rise to faith;
- Calvin: Reading for the "true knowledge of God and true knowledge of ourselves" (and all that this implies holistically, i.e. NOT simply some sort of cognitive assent);
- the pre-critical practice of reading by the "rule of faith";
- feminist hermeneutics: reading explicitly by way of biblical themes that resonate with "womanist interests" and "experience";
- liberationist hermeneutics: reading with a post-colonial political lens via themes present in Scripture, often by asserting the primacy of the "exodus narrative".

The discerning reader will, rightly, question the division of formal and material principles at this point, recalling, for example, that Augustine and Calvin also discuss the priority of literal or "plain" meanings in reading Scripture, which are more nearly formal principles. This qualification is correct and important. Nevertheless, we should not take the additional step, as many do, and assert that if Augustine or Calvin knew what we know now, they would have elevated the formal principle, cleansing it of its eisegetical dirt and mud and from the subjective violence of material principles.[15]

To the contrary, a key to understanding the true nature of "principles" for all good and true readings of the Bible is recognizing that persons who the Christian tradition sees as exemplary readers will normally advocate a pattern of principles which include *both* material and formal variety. It is at *this* point that the distinction between formal and material principles begins to break down: not, then, in the interest of their separation and cleansing, but in that the two share an integrated and ingredient coexistence in the interpretive gestures of faithful interpreters.

Redefined in this light: patterns of material principles mutually reinforce and resonate with patterns of formal principality. In other words material and formal principles ebb and flow together: there is no sense in which we can identify any moment of reading which is not accompanied by both formal and material principles. Some compelling examples of this interdependence include:

- Augustine: particularly in books two and three of *De Doctrina Christiana*, where the originary horizon guiding the reading is the *ethos* of the rule of faith, directed towards the *pathos* of "love of God and love of neighbour" while he recommends that this indicates a preferential attitude towards the "plain" meaning.
- Aquinas: Question 1, Article 10 of the *Summa Theologiae*. Here he makes a compelling connection between formal and material principality. His argument runs thus: that since God can do with things and events what people can do with words, all of the various

---

[15] Something like this typically occurs in historical treatments of biblical hermeneutics. See, for example, the otherwise helpful and astute account in Manlio Simonetti's *Biblical Interpretation in the Early Church* (Edinburgh, 1994).

meanings that we may observe in the layers of the biblical text are all expressions of God's literal meaning.

- Calvin: in his biblical commentaries he adjudicates between various interpretive options and opinions by unhesitatingly moving back and forth between so-called formal and material arguments.

The proper way to understand formal and material principality in reading the Bible is that there is an organic fittingness, a resonance that exemplary interpreters of the Bible recognize between formal and material principles. In light of this we can identify and banish three myths about "principles" for reading the Bible.

Interrogating Three Modern Myths of Reading and Interpreting the Bible:

1. Myth of Independence

This myth is the idea that formal and material principles properly enjoy some measure of independence. This is the natural outcome of the embrace of modern versions of "objectivity" that suggest that the unbiased attitude of scientists is also the recommended attitude of readers of Scripture.

To the contrary: formal and material principles are both necessary and interdependent in the proper understanding of the theological interpretation of the Bible. Indeed, if there is a constructive lesson to be learned from the postmodern movement it is this: that the situation cannot be otherwise; that there is no purely formal space, nor is there any purely formal moment within which one can take up any text, and read it. This is *even more true* for the Bible than it is for other books.

2. Myth of Priority

This is the idea that formal principles somehow operate "prior to" material principality or that formal principles serve a kind of privileged watchdog function in the hermeneutical process: guarding against the trespassing of human projection and imagination.

The notion that formal principality enjoys some priority or privilege is ultimately an illusion. An adequate awareness of the subjective elements of human knowing leads us down the dead end of a chicken and egg debate. Even the otherwise helpful image of the "hermeneutical spiral" or "circle" can be misleading on this point if one asserts that there is some moment in the spiral which is purely formal or that the formal aspect serves a more salutary function than the material.

This observation does not negate the need to make decisions regarding levels or degrees of authority regarding the "sources" of theology. So, the proper place for the authority of Scripture or the need for good exegesis is not in any way diminished. Rather, as we will see below, a fuller account of the authoritative role of the Christian Canon can be better explicated by locating that work at a critical and crucial juncture in the midst of the reading instead of operating prior to or "above" the reading.

3. Myth of the Ideal Method

This is the sought after Holy Grail for modern readers of the Bible. The sense is that, with enough work, we could somehow develop a flow chart or time line in which the proper arrangement of formal rules is set. This would result in something like an assembly line that could receive any biblical passages and spit out the proper meaning at the other end. This myth comes in two variations. The first envisions what comes out at the end as the finished product, an end to itself, like an automobile out the door at a General Motors plant. The other model sees the product as a "raw material" or "raw data" which, now purified and refined, can be delivered to theologians who go on to build things with it.

Both of these models are inadequate. Just as there is no single rule or principle, either material or formal, that even begins to adequately account for the reading of the Bible, there is no single ideal "method" by which to interpret Scripture. There are no ideal methods or ideal interpretations, only ideal (but sinful) interpreters.

In contrast to these myths a model of principality emerges that acknowledges the interdependence of formal and material principality and the *ad hoc* application of rules by the gifted, skilled, wise and faithful interpreter. Further, that this web of material and formal principles that accompany the reading of the Bible arises from the recognition of its utter uniqueness as it resides within the larger providential and gracious guidance of God's oversight and co-activity. This distinctiveness can be described, albeit with limitations, as *both* a textual quality *and* as the inimitability of the act of its reading: so, both essentialist and actualist accounts of, for example, the authority of Scripture, are truthful but not exhaustive in their descriptions.

On the former, essentialist view, this implies a set of principles related to the ontology of the Bible (as canon). Taking up *this* book and not another, in its unique arrangement, implies a host of material claims related to the work of God in the history of his dealings with His people, and particularly in the divine Trinitarian economy which administers and supervises the production, canonization and reading of the Christian Scriptures. This resonates with certain ways of reading this book which can, in turn, be described in principles that are more formal in nature. Thus the way that we understand God to work in and through time and history is both affirmed in reading this collection of texts, and implies a certain "benefit of the doubt", and even preference for reading those events *in* this text where we see God at work in a straightforward, plain, or "literal" sense.

On the latter, that there are formal and material principles that resonate and emerge from and with the practice of the intratextual reading of the canon. So: just as there is a resonance between the *external* event of canonization that is implied by taking up *this* set of texts and a textual ontology, there is also a resonance that emerges *within* that canon in the act of its reading. As the reader acquires an intimacy with the macro-canonical patterns as material principles, certain arrangements of formal principles will resonate with them. The material principles that guide our reading, in this, are, again, founded on claims related directly to the divine Trinitarian economy which presents itself in the overall shape of divine self-attesting activity witnessed to in, with and under the text.

In light of this it is imperative that we recognize that reading the Bible is a *sui generis* event: that it is fundamentally different and unique from reading any other book and that uniqueness, in both its essence and activity, in the ingredience of its formal and material principality, originates in its being a creaturely device which is given its very nature by being caught up in the divine economy, the *viva vox Dei*: the living and gracious self-giving and self-revealing of God's presence and action in the self proclaiming work of the risen Christ.

The Heart of the Problem: Interrogating Hans Frei

Earlier I challenged some contemporary myths related to the arrangement of material and formal principles. There is a typical response to this that many may be pondering at this moment. It can be expressed in certain types of questions, like: "What does this all mean for the authority of the text?" "Does this put us on the slippery slope towards giving the reader too much of a role in imposing things on the Bible?" Fears naturally emerge here on both sides of the modern hermeneutical divide between those committed to the preference of "texts" and their natural combatants, those committed to the priority of "readers." This, it would seem, then, brings us back to the familiar text versus reader debate. However, it is the modern tendency to assume this way of framing the hermeneutical problem which lies behind the myths we name above and the point at which a major correction needs to be made. We will offer one illustration by way of Hans Frei as a negative example.

Hans Frei mounts a powerful and influential argument in *The Eclipse of Biblical Narrative* in favor of the idea that precritical interpreters find the principles meaning to reside exclusively within the text. Calvin is the exemplary interpretive model for Frei. In his discussion of Calvin's hermeneutics he discusses the importance of the unity of literal (or "realistic") and figural interpretations in a way that helpfully illuminates our discussion.

He begins by suggesting that, for Calvin, (and, arguably, for Frei as well) the entire canon of Scripture possesses a "single cumulative and complex pattern of meaning."[16] This pattern is "ingredient" in the unity of the entire canon as one story. The rendering of the meaning of this one story depends on this unity of literal and figurative readings. Literal readings illuminate the meaning at the micro level, in particular sections of the Bible, while figural reading works at a macro level. Frei describes this as:

> [A] grasp of a common pattern of occurrence and meaning together, the pattern being dependent on the reality of the unitary temporal sequence which allows all the single narrations within it to become parts of a single narration.[17]

Frei's analysis here tends to focus on formal principles and issues. This is a characteristic of much postliberal theology. He presents examples of literal and figurative interpretation as if the proper evaluation of them would be to reduce them

---

[16]   Frei, *The Eclipse of Biblical Narrative*, p. 33

[17]   Ibid., p. 34.

to formal principles. However, upon closer inspection his apt description of figural interpretation reveals itself to necessarily have material principles ingredient to it as well. This is shown in posing the question to Frei: How is it that the single stories in the Bible become a "single narration." Does not a single narration imply a single narrator. Who is this narrator?

Frei continues his discussion, giving *Calvin's* answer:

> Calvin ... speaks about the internal testimony of the Spirit in enlightening the heart and mind to see what the text says in any case.

But then moves immediately moves on to what he sees as the real heart of the issue:

> [This] does not add a new dimension to the text itself. The meaning, pattern, or theme, whether upon literal or figurative reading or, most likely, upon a combination of both, emerges solely as a function of the narrative itself. It is not imprinted on the text by the interpreter or by a multifarious interpretive and religious "tradition."[18]

This is telling. Frei puts his finger on the key thing for Calvin, which involves the relationship of divine agency to the act of reading the Bible. He does not seem to be distracted even for a moment, however, from pursuing the question in those more familiar terms of "text versus reader" as if the hermeneutical problem can best be sorted out in those terms. Frei is not unique in this. Few contemporary readers of Frei are given to any sort of pause here.

This tendency is also reflected in the ubiquitous use of terms such as "what the text says" in the literature and discussions as if this way of talking properly accounts for the matrix of speech agencies involved in reading. Texts don't "say" anything. Speakers say things; agents make speech acts; texts are mediums. Calvin is well aware of the way that God's agency permeates all hermeneutical aspects of reading the Bible. Frei, like most of his modern contemporaries, is somewhat oblivious to the importance of this distinction. For him the battle is between the qualities of a text (any text) as a byproduct of human authorial agency, in competition with human readerly agency. But where did God go? Is God involved in any way? Thus there emerges a significant level of opacity in the modern era that continues today with respect to carefully considering the makeup and nature of the complexity of divine and human agency which animates the reading of the Bible.

In exhibiting these tendencies most contemporary accounts of biblical hermeneutics are deistic *de jure* if not *de facto*. The only action required by God is creation: setting up normative conditions for human communication and maintaining the stability and clarity of the created conditions for language. Meaning is discerned by giving an account of the formal principles, like natural laws, which structure the production of human language. This contributes directly to the modern myths of principality.

The point which we saw Frei moving past all too quickly in his treatment of Calvin is more aptly summarized by Thomas Torrance: his comment is also serviceable as

---

[18] Ibid.,, p. 34-5.

an indication of the direction advocated here toward the proper understanding of the place of principles in reading the Bible. He writes:

> Calvin was deeply aware that the interpretation of the Holy Scriptures, in which knowledge of God is mediated to us, cannot be sealed off from the epistemological and theological questions that are raised by the *fact* of the knowledge of God, for as we cannot know God except in accordance with the way in which he has revealed himself to us, so we cannot interpret the means which he has provided as the medium of that revelation except *in the light of its actual content in the knowledge of God.* Interpretation and understanding go hand in hand together.[19]

In light of this contemporary frameworks for understanding the act of reading Scripture need a thorough revision. A model that comports with the above analysis and which we suggest offers great potential corrective power is proffered by way of the ancient study of rhetoric. Thus the act of reading will be initially framed by the acknowledgment that the primary author of this text, God, is present and "speaking"; as "divine rhetoric." It compels us to not lose track of the priority of God's agency as we consider all the other various aspects of reading that follow.

Reading the Bible as Divine-Rhetorical Hermeneutics

Contemporary hermeneutics, including biblical hermeneutics, are held hostage to the myths of principles and to a "text versus reader" framework. This is reinforced by lingering investments in distinctly modern notions of objectivity that emerge from and are dependent upon an essentially deistic worldview. The perceived gap between us and the source of meaning, the human author, is besieged by the complications of the practice of historical investigation and the gnawing sense of "distanciation" is its companion. As long as these are the terms by which we enter into our understanding of reading the Bible there is no way out except by way of valiant efforts to uncover, protect and preserve the immanent historical lifelines between human authorial speech agency and human readerly actions: hermeneutical archaeology.

However, there is a better way to approach the reading of Scripture. This is achieved if we make a simple choice at the outset. This choice is not to begin by framing the act of reading the Bible as an investigation into the written speech act of a dead human author but rather as the encounter with the living Christ who is confronting us in his Word. The terms are thereby set under the boundless and limitless activity of the eternal Trinity, in the absolute and simple freedom that God possesses beyond, beneath, in, with and under time and space. Freedom that manifests itself in the gracious reaching out to creatures. In this the basic terms for understanding the reading of the Bible emerge from the testament to the givenness of Jesus Christ's ubiquity and clarity as the fulfillment of God's *opera ad extra*. In this model the reading of the Bible begins less as an act of isolated and desperate textual archaeologists but more as spiritually hungry and thirsty creatures who are

---

[19]   T.F. Torrance, *The Hermeneutics of John Calvin* (Edinburgh: T. & T. Clark, 1988) p. 61. Emphasis mine.

confronted with the abundant and bountiful gospel in the living speech of the very embodiment of life and truth Himself. Thus, for biblical hermeneutics, there is a great divergence between its hermeneutics and those of all other books. The ancient study of rhetoric as the encounter with a living and breathing speaker affords us a great advantage in framing the hermeneutical encounter with God in the Bible in this fashion. Ancient rhetorical theory was concerned with perceiving and describing the terms under which speakers engage and move hearers in just such intimate encounters.

Aristotle at the beginning of *Ars Rhetorica* locates rhetoric within the universal sphere of human communication, insofar as all people communicate by means of constructing coherent arguments (Dialectic) and both promote and defend their arguments (Rhetoric). He defines three "species" in rhetoric which encompass all the varieties of things which speakers themselves provide or influence in the process of making their speech. These three are *ethos, logos,* and *pathos. Ethos* is the character of the speaker as embodied in the act of speaking. *Logos* is the shape of the speech itself. *Pathos* is the response produced in the hearers. For Aristotle all three of these are considered to be (more or less) under the control of the speaker. George Kennedy offers a helpful clarifying remark at this point when he suggest that

> *Ethos* in Aristotle means "character," esp. "moral character," and … is regarded as an attribute of a person, not of a speech, … *pathos* [likewise] is an attribute of persons, not of a speech.[20]

Kennedy's point is that Aristotle sees *Ethos* as well as *Pathos* as being a genuine reflection of a person's character and not, as the Sophists (and most modern studies of rhetoric) are prone to argue, simply an aspect of the speech which has relative independence of the speaker or hearer. Aristotle has a good case to be made on this point; one that has additional bearing on the relevance of our typology and attention to divine action in reading Scripture. We all read or hear things differently depending on the perceived character of who is saying or writing them. If a speaker has a certain reputation, demonstrates a capacity to speak, shows that he or she is informed and trustworthy and can present the message clearly then the message itself (*logos)* is both received and appropriated (*pathos)* in a way that is different than if the speaker is perceived or known to be shady, incapable, or muddleheaded.[21]

Aristotle goes so far as to argue that "character is almost, so to speak, the controlling factor in persuasion."[22] This insight brings us back to our typology and strongly underscores the point. If the character of the speaker is *the* determinate, or even in any way *a* determinate factor in the appropriation of the message, and, if God is in any way an agent that "speaks" in, with, and under the reading of the text of Scripture, then there must be a fuller consideration of the location and function of the shaping role of the character of the divine speaker/author in any and all accounts

---

[20] Aristotle, *Rhetoric*, n. 40, p. 37-8.

[21] A simple example would be if one were watching television and a person appeared behind a desk announcing "And now, the evening news." One hears what comes next completely differently if the person behind the desk is either Tom Brokaw or John Cleese.

[22] Aristotle, *Rhetoric*, p. 38.

of reading Scripture. This observation quickly expands immensely in scope when we consider the implications of moving from the role that the character of human speakers plays in the rhetorical speech-moment, to that which God as divine speaker plays in the disclosure of the divine Word.

So: in distinction from Aristotle's discussion, which is only concerned with the nature of *human* communication, we need to recognize that there is an important point of departure in our typology insofar as we are considering *divine* communication and speech action. This is the origin of the utter uniqueness of the act of reading Scripture as compared to the listening to other persons or the reading of other writings. It is also in the purview of divine action that the distinctly modern proposal for reading Scripture "as any other book" is challenged. The uniqueness of reading Scripture is, from this point of departure, defined in two ways. First, the reading of Scripture is different from reading other books and thus will bear a stronger affinity with the rhetorical moment in that the speaker (God) is an "authorial" agent who is presently speaking in, with and under the reading. Human authors can also be present in rare situations and can then personally assist us in clarifying what they intend in their written communication. However theories of reading tend to not give this situation attention and for good reason: human authors leave after speaking; human authors sleep and forget; human authors die.

Not only is the reading of Scripture unique because the speaking agent (God) is active and present, but also because it is *God* who is present. To the degree that God is different in nature and action from humans are to the same degree that God's speech action will transcend attempts at building or drawing from human analogies. These two points of differentiation underscore the present need to develop a typological instrument which better accounts for God's action as it shapes the perception of the act of reading Scripture.

We noted above that a limitation of our comparison to rhetoric is that Aristotle's discussion only has the human speech act in mind. If his work still has value and relevance in indicating for us fundamental aspects of the way rhetorical human speech interactions proceeds, it bears asking what this implies about the hearing and appropriating of God's speech *by* human creatures. Thus the consideration of the necessary and orienting role that *ethos* plays in the reading and interpretation of Scripture is raised. In other words, if we understand the reader and interpreter of Scripture to be responding to the *viva vox Dei,* then the question of how hearers receive and appropriate the rhetorical action of human discourse becomes a relevant and informing field of inquiry for also perceiving how creatures listen and respond to the speech of God. Further, if God's *ethos* plays a directive role, following Aristotle's suggestion, in how the human reader(s) construe the message (*logos*) and appropriate it in their own actions (*pathos*) then there arises a necessary reconsideration of the shape of confessions and doctrines as indications of the stance we bring as creatures to the reading of Scripture.

It will be illuminative at this point to overtly link our discussion of Aristotle's view of rhetoric with the triangle typology. There is a sense in which the three facets—*ethos-logos-pathos*—can be linked with the three aspects of the triangle: The top corner (type three) as the divine *ethos* of theological hermeneutics; the bottom left corner (type one) as the *logos*; and the bottom right corner (type two) as the *pathos*.

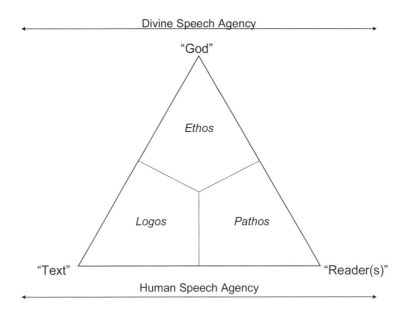

Fig 6.1 Theological Rhetorical Hermeneutics: Redefinining the Triangle

We can then begin to reframe the analysis in the development of the typology in previous chapters and construct a methodological proposal for theological hermeneutics as divine rhetoric. Type ones, for example, tend to locate the decisive sphere for meaning in the *logos* which is the message itself and subordinates and often neglects the roles of *pathos* and *ethos*. The second type, conversely, locates the decisive sphere in *pathos* which is the appropriation and response of the hearers to the message downplaying or ignoring the roles of *logos* and *ethos*. The third type is the group which would be most in keeping analogously with Aristotle's view of rhetoric, attributing the production of meaning primarily to the realm of *ethos*.

This image is helpful in showing the relationship between the three aspects of the triangle in relation with the three facets of rhetoric. However, this way of illustrating them undermines one of the goals of this work; to push towards a more dynamic understanding of divine agency as the proper horizon for theological hermeneutics. Therefore, having made this important link to the typology, we will now briefly comment on the new proposal presented here by refashioning the rhetorical schema as follows:

Flow of Theological-Rhetorical Hermeneutics

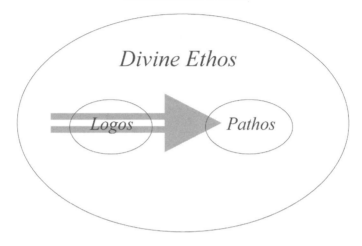

Fig 6.2   The Flow of Theological Rhetorical Hermeneutics

This way of representing the event of theological hermeneutics encourages us to do fuller justice to the fundamental character of divine agency in our thinking about theological hermeneutics. It presents us with the ubiquity of divine agency that permeates all aspects of biblical hermeneutics; the infinite and universal dimension of the trinitarian self-announcement to which Holy Scripture serves. We will briefly comment on each aspect.

Ethos

We recall that, for Aristotle, the *ethos* of the speaker was a primary determinate factor in the speech event. The character of the speaker, their reputation in the community, the knowledge, authority and linguistic skill they indicate in the speech itself; all these things play a determinate role in the shape of the speech itself (*logos*) as well as the way that the speech is received and appropriated in the response of the hearer (*pathos*).

Reading Scripture involves the unique feature of the dual divine-human agency question which translates into a dual speakership. The more fundamental *ethos* between the two is the divine. In fact, the divine *ethos* gives Holy Scripture its very nature: all aspects of its production, acknowledgment by the Church as Canon, preservation and present reading, are unified by their common origin in the gracious self-announcement of the Triune God. Therefore the determinative *ethos* of the theological interpretation of the Bible is the divine *ethos*. It encompasses and precedes all human agencies that were elected and caught up in its salvific and sanctifying wake.

How does this correspond to the preparation and execution of the human creature who intends to read Scripture? To begin, this requires not the jettison of one's confession and catechesis: to the contrary, to prepare to listen to the living word of God begins with learning all one can about this God and this Word. So: the study of Church history, of dogmatics, of traditions of reading and so on, is prerequisite. The pre-modern model of formation in which one graduated from one's theological work to the status of reader of Scripture approximates this.

Further, the preparation for reading Scripture as it is related to its divine *ethos* is as much a macro oriented task as it is micro. The better one understands the broad sweep of the history of God's dealing with creation and humanity, the geographical and architectural features in the theological landscape in which Scripture originates—the better one is equipped to read intertextually and intratextually, recognizing the divine movement in its self declaration.

Logos

This aspect includes those facets of studying the text that have been prevalent in biblical studies for several centuries. It is the study of the text as a "natural" entity. Included are historical-critical, cultural, linguistic studies, etc., and, interestingly enough, the study of the *human* authorial activity related to Scripture which explores that activity in its rhetorical dimension. All these are included in this aspect of theological-rhetorical hermeneutics. There remains, then, an important and necessary place for the activities involved in the investigation of this human book. In light of this the arrangement of this aspect within the schema of theological-rhetorical hermeneutics begs two questions.

First, the conscription and relocation of the array of activities that have tended to be viewed as having primacy of place in recent centuries is disorienting to many and concerning to more. We cannot begin to exhaustively pursue that question here. Suffice to say that in what follows here and broadly speaking in new work on theological interpretation it is clear that neither the value of post-Enlightenment biblical studies nor the authority of Scripture need necessarily be jettisoned as a result of recasting the task of reading Scripture.

Second, the arrangement promoted above overtly acknowledges what many biblical scholars have been saying for decades: that there is some confessional or theological dimension that all readers, including academic readers, both bring to their reading and employ in making judgments regarding its features. This way of framing the interpretive act of reading the Bible acknowledges this as both inescapable, appropriate, and even as necessary. The foundation of these beliefs originates in the horizon of divine activity that encompasses them. It is a maximalist attitude toward bringing all that we are as a people shaped by God's gracious acts into the ongoing encounter with God in his living Word.

There is a simple sense in which it becomes absurd to continue to promote any alternative; as if there is some advantage or preference in "setting aside" our theological hermeneutical orientation as creatures (given the rather large assumption that "setting aside" is even possible). To the contrary, there are two significant reasons to pursue a maximalist theological approach to reading Scripture.

First, there is something odd about coming to listen to God's living speech under some impression that it would be better to do so setting aside some aspect of our confession or beliefs. What kind of condition would this produce? In what "place" would this occur? Pursuing this line of questioning it quickly becomes absurd to advocate the removal or abstraction of our prior relationship to the divine Word as if there were some advantage in then returning to it. Can we eschew the effects of our conversion? Of our salvation, justification and sanctification? Even if we could, why would we? What possible advantage could be obtained?

Second, in order to be transformed in the encounter with the divine Word, something must be presented to *be* transformed. In order for Scripture to serve its authoritative role in reforming creatures it best performs that work when creatures wholly and completely submit everything under its penetrating purview. In fact, the proper authoritative function of Holy Scripture may, in the end, require a maximalist approach with regard to bringing the meager things, the modest offerings of the interpretive loaves and fishes of our humanity, so that they may be transformed and reformed and multiplied.[23]

Either of these points is compelling on its own terms: together doubly so. Thus suggesting that the divine *ethos* is the fundamental hermeneutical horizon for reading Scripture and relativizing modern biblical studies related to the *logos* as the byproduct of human speech agency does not necessarily undermine the authority of Scripture in the Church and in theological reasoning but may very well serve to promote it.

Pathos

The *pathos* of theological interpretation originates from and is given both its form and impetus in the divine *ethos*. This directly parallels the claim that the mission of the Church is an echo of the *missio dei*. This final aspect of theological-rhetorical hermeneutics completes the schema laid out above. It offers us two important qualifications in how we view the act of reading the Bible.

One, that neither of the first two aspects arrives at the *telos* of the reading: that its end is the manifestation or outworking of the reading in the appropriating response of hearers/readers. If we see the divine *ethos* as that which gives theological hermeneutics its bearing and impetus, then the *pathos* is the consummation of those directions and actions. As such it receives its bearings from God's missional activity in all its forms *by means of* the *logos*. Thus all the various activities that proceed in the pursuit of the understanding of the text of Scripture are, on the one hand, not permitted an independence that envisions those activities as ends to themselves apart from the practical outworking of the purposes of the divine *ethos* in the church and in the *kosmos*. On the other hand, that same work and future work can be evaluated for its relevance to the missional *ethos* of Scripture based on its proximity and ability to foster its *pathos*.

Two, following this, that there is a corresponding relationship between the divine *ethos* and the *pathos* of reading Scripture. There is a kind of symmetry between the shape of the divine mission and the form that the response readers should assume as they hear and respond. The various forms that the church's mission assumes, then,

---

[23]   This image was inspired by a remarkable wedding homily by Rev. Dr. Merv Mercer.

reflect and are caught in the wake of God's mission: missional acts that we grow in our understanding as we continue to engage God's Word. A great deal of work assisting us in understanding this facet of biblical hermeneutics is emerging under the rubric "missional hermeneutics." We cannot pursue this all important aspect any further here but this should not be read in any sense as an underestimation or valuation of this valuable new field of work. Again, we hope to return to this in more detail in a future work.

Conclusion

In linking this proposal for a theological-rhetorical hermeneutic of Scripture to the general study of rhetoric there is also issued challenge the pejorative sense the term typically carries in modern times. The term can be rehabilitated in a manner like the simple definition that Paul Ricoeur has given:

> The function of rhetoric ... is persuasion, i.e., influencing people by means of discourse which is neither the means of proof nor of violence, but rather the means of rendering the probable more acceptable.[24]

With respect to the reading and interpretation of Scripture, the potential value and use of various methodologies and hermeneutics is determined by the degree to which it is perceived as aiding in the promotion of the "acceptance" of divine "probabilities." Methods should, then, not be seen primarily as instruments of "proof" but as aids of conviction; implements in the persuasion of the living speech of the divine speaker though the work of faithful interpreters.[25] This does not eliminate a more substantial apologetic purpose for methods but properly locates that activity as secondary and *ad hoc*.

If, on the other hand, in the deployment of methods in the reading of Scripture we continue to be influenced by the Enlightenment's expulsion of God as an appropriately influencing and speaking agent; if we continue to perceive the act of reading Scripture as an activity that we pursue as lone human agents, in the company of other independent agents; if we see the reading of Scripture as solely a dialogue with ourselves and each other, as efforts to control and manipulate each other; then Kant's moral fears are fully warranted and his limitations are necessary and "rhetoric" is nothing more than manipulation.

However, if we believe that God is present and active, in, with and under our frail attempts to hear and respond to His Word, then we can have confidence that we are not trapped in a closed hermeneutic circle but that the God who creates and sustains

---

[24]   Paul Ricoeur, "Biblical Hermeneutics," *Semeia*, Volume 4, (Missoula: Scholar's Press, 1975) p. 76.

[25]   "Persuasion" here should be read in a thinking and holistic sense and not simply in terms of some form of mental assent.

our circles also breaks into them, speaking: both confirming in us that which is true and pleasing and good and correcting that which is violent and oppressive.[26]

Redefining hermeneutical debates over methods, norms and sources in this way— as divine theological-rhetorical hermeneutics—produces two effects. Both of these effects have limiting and freeing sides. The first effect is that we recognize that all readings of Scripture are theologically invested, including our own. All readings thus share rhetorical functions with respect to this investment. By this acknowledgment we are freed to consider broader varieties of ways of reading. We would, then, be *initially* less inclined to see different views which are derived from foreign methods as alien and threatening and more apt to see them as simply different. This is a better response to the modern tendency that equates methodological commitments with confessional ones.

If, further, we see our own theological expressions, as well as that of others, as residing within the limitations of its present rhetorical function, we would also have a greater freedom to consider the theological articulations of others.[27] Thus we would limit and restrict the investment we may have in our pet methodologies and allow ourselves to listen to readings which employ other methods.

The second effect is that the real points of disagreement between different ways of reading the Bible become clearer.[28] The true nature of the tensions between various hermeneutics becomes more accessible as we examine them in light of the direction they receive from the divine *ethos*. This results, on the one hand, in freeing our own methodological articulations from the great weight of needing to be the final word on any one matter. We would recognize our expressions to be that of a theological pilgrimage; on the way to wisdom and greater understanding.

This second effect also produces a restriction. Approaching the issues in this manner brings greater awareness of the nature of the tensions between the different confessional aspects which underwrite the articulated theologies and methodologies. As the confessional aspects of these views are acknowledged and uncovered, the real point of disagreement, with all the investment of the historical debates over orthodoxy, and the implications for agreement or disagreement, are also brought to bear on the debates.[29]

---

[26] See Kathy Eden, *Hermeneutics and the Rhetorical Tradition* (New Haven: Yale University Press, 1997)

[27] James J. Buckley models this hermeneutical virtue suggesting "In any case, the second part of our deadlock is that we disagree over the nature and ordering of the diverse functions of scripture. Whether we wish to say that 'the ultimate test is pragmatic and functional' or (as I prefer) that one test is pragmatic and functional." "Beyond the Hermeneutical Deadlock", in John Webster and George Schner (eds), *Theology After Liberalism* (Oxford: Blackwell, 2000), p.193.

[28] Buckley, *Deadlock*, p.189.

[29] Buckley supplies us with a negative example of the problem in his discussion of Terence Tilley's criticisms of George Lindbeck in Terrence Tilley, "Incommensurability, Intratextuality, and Fideism", *Modern Theology* 5 (1989), pp. 87-111. He summarizes saying "I do not know if Tilley is criticizing Lindbeck for not holding authentic Christian teaching about Scripture--or for not being consistently cultural-linguistic; the former is heresy, the latter mere bad anthropology. I suspect that Tilley would say the latter." Buckley, *Deadlock*,

The synergy of these two effects and their freeing and limiting sides would shift the location for our hermeneutical discussions. It would encourage us to begin to speak once again regarding our common and uncommon confessions and reflect more deeply (in a way not unlike the *resourcement* movements) on our theological heritage. For many Enlightenment figures the vagueness with which they associated or articulated their confessional commitments in relation to their theological and philosophical arguments was something of an innovation and viewed with suspicion. We now stand in the opposite position where vagueness and caution in articulating what we believe in public and academic settings is, in many corners, still considered a virtue while overt confessional stances are tolerated but suspect. If we acknowledge the degree to which our confessions accompany our methodological choices we will be pressed to once again speak about the self involving[30] nature of our confessions,[31] about the necessary diachronic and synchronic role for the faith community in forming these beliefs,[32] and thereby to regain a necessary willingness to "talk about God"[33] as the one who creates, forms, sustains and redeems the *kosmos* and calls and forms a community to render the gracious benefits of the *viva vox Christi* to the world and all peoples. It is only then that we will relearn the art of theological interpretation; of prayerfully attending to Christ's self-publication as we are swept up in His mission.

---

pp. 195-196. Buckley is left to speculate about the true nature of the disagreement. It is a rather serious problem if we do not know whether our theology is being questioned as heresy. This example is indicative of the problem which can begin to be resolved if we view the conversation in the terms I have argued for in this paper.

[30] I use this term keeping in mind Donald Evans' *The Logic of Self-Involvement: A Philosophical Study of Everyday Language with Special Reference to the Christian Use of Language about God as Creator* (New York, 1969). See also Briggs, *Words in Action.*

[31] See Briggs, *Words in Action,* chapter 5. This also accords with, but expands upon, Francis Watson's call to "take seriously, from the start, the expectations that accord with the genre of the biblical texts as the holy scripture of a worshipping community." *Text, Church and World*, p. 229.

[32] This is what Nicholas Wolterstorff is getting at when he talks about the possibility of our theology "recovering from Kant." Nicholas Wolterstorff, "Is It Possible and Desirable for Theologians to Recover From Kant?" *Modern Theology* 14/1, January, 1998, pp. 1-18. He suggests that "Though many theologians and philosophers have found Kant's problem, along with the philosophical framework generating that problem, compelling, few have found his solution compelling."

[33] Karl Barth's theological method is the most significant modern example of an attempt in this direction. Joe Mangina suggests that for Barth "Rather than seeking to justify talk about God he talks about God, rightly finding God a more interesting topic than his own post-Enlightenment skepticism. The amazing thing about Barth in the landscape of modern Christian thought is that he *gets started*, thereby offending against the endless deferrals that characterize a timid age." Mangina, *Karl Barth's Sixteen Answers*, p.13. John Webster makes a similar point about Barth, indicating a quality that postliberal theologians like Frei and Lindbeck did not maintain in their appropriation of other aspects of his work. John Webster, "Hermeneutics in Modern Theology: Some Doctrinal Reflections" in *Word and Church*. Also see Stanley Hauerwas on his own realization of this problem in his own work in *Sanctify Them in the Truth* (Edinburgh: T & T Clark, 1998) Chapter 2: "The Truth About God: The Decalogue as Condition for Truthful Speech." pp. 37-59.

Bibliography

Abraham, William, *The Divine Inspiration of Holy Scripture* (New York: Oxford University Press, 1981).

_____, *Divine Revelation and the Limits of Historical Criticism* (Oxford: Oxford University Press, 1982).

_____, *Canon and Criterion in Christian Theology* (Oxford: Oxford University Press, 1998).

Adam, A.K.M., *Making Sense of New Testament Theology* (Macon: Mercer University Press, 1995).

Aichele, George, *Sign, Text and Scripture* (Sheffield: Sheffield Academic Press, 1997).

Anderson, Bernhard, "The New Crisis in Biblical Theology", *The Drew Gateway*, 45 (1975): 159-74.

Augustine, *Teaching Christianity: De Doctrina Christiana* (New York: New City Press, 1996).

Auld, A. Graeme (ed.), *Understanding Poets and Prophets: Essays in Honour of George Wishart Anderson* (Sheffield: JSOT, 1993).

Austin, J. L., *How to Do Things With Words* (Oxford: Oxford University Press, 1975).

Barth, Karl, *The Knowledge of God and the Service of God According to the Teaching of the Reformation* (New York: Charles Scribner's Sons, 1939).

_____, "No!", In *Natural Theology* (London: Geoffrey Bles, 1946).

_____, *Church Dogmatics* (14 volumes, Edinburgh: T and T Clark, 1956-1975).

_____, *Karl Barth's Table Talk* (Richmond: John Knox Press, 1962).

_____, *God Here and Now* (New York: Harper & Row, 1964).

_____, *The Theology of Schleiermacher* (Grand Rapids: Eerdmans, 1982).

_____, "Philosophy and Theology", in *The Way of Theology in Karl Barth* (Allison Park: Pickwick Press, 1986): 79-95.

_____, *The Göttingen Dogmatics: Volume 1* (Grand Rapids: Eerdmans, 1991).

_____, *The Theology of John Calvin* (Grand Rapids: Eerdmans, 1995).

_____, *The Epistle to the Philippians* (Louisville: Westminster Press, 2002).

_____, *The Theology of the Reformed Confessions* (Louisville: Westminster John Knox Press, 2002).

Bartholomew, Craig, *Reading Ecclesiastes: Old Testament Exegesis and Hermeneutical Theory*, Analecta Biblica, vol. 139 (Rome: Pontificio Istituto Biblico, 1998).

_____, "Uncharted Waters: Philosophy, Theology and the Crisis in Biblical Interpretation", in Craig Bartholomew (ed.), *Renewing Biblical Interpretation* (Grand Rapids: Zondervan, 2000): 1-34.

_____, "Before Babel and After Pentecost: Language, Literature and Biblical Interpretation", in Craig Bartholomew (ed.), *After Babel* (Grand Rapids:

Zondervan, 2001): 131-70.

_____, "Warranted Biblical Interpretation: Alvin Plantinga's 'Two (or More) Types of Scripture Scholarship'", in Craig Bartholomew (ed.), *History and Biblical Interpretation* (Grand Rapids: Zondervan, 2003): 5-22.

Bartholomew, Craig, Colin Greene and Karl Moller, (eds.), *After Pentecost: Language and Biblical Interpretation* (Grand Rapids: Zondervan, 2001).

_____, *Renewing Biblical Interpretation* (Grand Rapids: Zondervan, 2000).

_____, *History and Biblical Interpretation* (Grand Rapids: Zondervan, 2003).

Barton, John (ed.), *The Cambridge Companion to Biblical Interpretation* (New York: Cambridge University Press, 1998).

Berkouwer, G. C., *Holy Scripture* (Grand Rapids: Eerdmans, 1975).

Bloesch, Donald, *Holy Scripture* (Downer's Grove: IVP, 1994).

Blumenberg, Hans, *The Legitimacy of the Modern Age* (Cambridge: MIT Press, 1983).

Braaten, Carl and Robert Jenson (eds.), *Reclaiming the Bible for the Church* (Grand Rapids: Eerdmans, 1995).

Brett, Mark G, "Four or Five Things to Do With Texts: A Taxonomy of Interpretive Interests", in Stephen Fowl and Stanley Porter David J. A. Clines (eds), *The Bible in Three Dimensions* (Sheffield: Sheffield University Press, 1990): 357-77.

_____, *Biblical Criticism in Crisis?* (Cambridge: Cambridge University Press, 1991).

Briggs, Richard S., *Words in Action: Speech Act Theory and Biblical Interpretation* (Edinburgh: Continuum T & T Clark, 2001).

Brueggemann, Walter, *Texts under Negotiation* (Minneapolis: Fortress Press, 1993).

Buckley, James J., *Seeking the Humanity of God: Practices, Doctrines, and Catholic Theology* (Collegeville: The Liturgical Press, 1992).

_____, "Beyond the Hermeneutical Deadlock", in John Webster and George Schner (eds), *Theology After Liberalism* (Oxford: Blackwell, 2000): 187-203.

Buckley, Michael, *At the Origins of Modern Atheism* (New Haven: Yale University Press, 1987).

Burnett, Richard E., *Karl Barth's Theological Exegesis* (Grand Rapids: Eerdmans, 2004).

Campbell, Charles, *Preaching Jesus* (Grand Rapids: Eerdmans, 1997).

Caputo, John D., *Radical Hermeneutics* (Bloomington: Indiana University Press, 1987).

_____, *Against Ethics* (Bloomington: Indiana University Press, 1993).

Carson, D. A. and John Woodbridge (eds), *God and Culture* (Grand Rapids: Eerdmans, 1993).

_____, *Hermeneutics, Authority and Canon* (Grand Rapids: Zondervan, 1986).

_____, *Scripture and Truth* (Grand Rapids: Zondervan, 1983).

Cashdollar, C. D., *The Transformation of Theology: Positivism and Protestant Thought in Britain and America* (Princeton: Princeton University Press, 1989).

Castelli, Elizabeth A. Stephen D. Moore, et al. (eds), *The Postmodern Bible* (New Haven: Yale University Press, 1995).

Charry, Ellen T., "Cure of Body and Soul: Interpretation as Art and Science", in Roger Lundin (ed.), *Disciplining Hermeneutics* (Grand Rapids: Eerdmans, 1997): 85-97.

_____, *"By the Renewing of Your Minds": The Salutarity of Christian Doctrine* (New York: Oxford, 1997).

Childs, Brevard, *Biblical Theology in Crisis* (Philadelphia: Westminster Press, 1970).

_____, *Introduction to the Old Testament as Scripture* (Philadelphia: Fortress, 1979).

_____, *Biblical Theology of the Old and New Testaments* (Minneapolis: Fortress Press, 1993).

_____, "On Reclaiming the Bible for Christian Theology", in Carl Braaten and Robert Jenson (eds), *Reclaiming the Bible for the Church* (Grand Rapids: Eerdmans, 1995): 1-17.

_____, "Jesus Christ the Lord and the Scriptures of the Church", in Ephraim Radner and George Sumner (eds), *The Rule of Faith* (Harrisburg: Morehouse, 1998): 1-12.

_____, "The Nature of the Christian Bible", in Ephraim Radner and George Sumner (eds), *The Rule of Faith* (Harrisburg: Morehouse, 1998): 115-25.

_____, "The One Gospel in Four Witnesses", in Ephraim Radner and George Sumner (eds), *The Rule of Faith* (Harrisburg: Morehouse, 1998): 51-62.

Clayton, Philip, *The Problem of God in Modern Thought* (Grand Rapids: Eerdmans, 2000).

Clouser, Roy A., *The Myth of Religious Neutrality: An Essay on the Hidden Role of Religious Belief in Theories* (South Bend: University of Notre Dame Press, 1991).

Comstock, Gary, "Truth or Meaning: Ricoeur versus Frei on Biblical Narrative", *Journal of Religion* 66 (1986): 117-40.

_____, "Two Types of Narrative Theology", *The Journal of the American Academy of Religion* 55 (1987): 687-717.

Croatto, J. Severino, *Biblical Hermeneutics* (Maryknoll: Orbis Press, 1987).

Cunningham, Mary Kathleen, *What is Theological Exegesis?* (Valley Forge: Trinity Press International, 1995).

Dalferth, Ingolf, *Theology and Philosophy* (Cambridge: Blackwell, 1988).

de Lubac, Henri, *Medieval Exegesis Volume 1: The Four Senses of Scripture* (Grand Rapids: Eerdmans, 1998).

Demson, David, *Hans Frei & Karl Barth: Different Ways of Reading Scripture* (Grand Rapids: Eerdmans, 1997).

Dodd, Brian and R. P. Martin (eds), *Where Christology Began* (Louisville: Westminster John Knox Press, 1998).

Dorner, Isaak, *History of Protestant Theology Particularly in Germany Viewed According to Its Fundamental Movement and in Connection with the Religious, Moral and Intellectual Life* (Edinburgh: T & T Clark, 1871).

Dupre, Louis, *Metaphysics and Culture* (Milwaukee: Marquette University Press, 1994).

Eden, Kathy, *Hermeneutics and the Rhetorical Tradition* (New Haven: Yale University Press, 1997).

Fiorenza, Francis Schüssler, "The Crisis of Scriptural Authority: Interpretation and Reception", in Everett J. Tarbox jr. (ed.), *Theology at the End of Modernity* (Philadelphia: Trinity Press, 1991): 353-68.

Fish, Stanley, *Is There a Text in This Class?* (Cambridge: Harvard University Press, 1980).

Ford, David F., "Barth's Interpretation of the Bible" in S. W. Sykes (ed.), *Karl Barth: Studies of His Theological Method* (Oxford: Clarendon Press, 1979): 55-87.

_____, "Review of 'Text, Church and World'", *The Journal of Theological Studies,* 49/ 1 (April 1998): 500-504.

Fowl, Stephen E., "The Canonical Approach of Brevard Childs", *The Expository Times,* 96/6 (March 1985): 173-76.

_____, "The Ethics of Interpretation; or What's Left Over After the Elimination of Meaning", in S. E. Fowl D.J.A. Clines, and S. E. Porter (eds), *The Bible in Three Dimensions* (Sheffield: Sheffield Academic Press, 1990): 379-98.

_____, "Making Stealing Possible: Criminal Reflections on Building an Ecclesial Common Life", *Perspectives* (September, 1993): 14-17.

_____, "Who Can Read Abraham's Story?", *Journal for the Study of the New Testament*, 55 (1994): 77-95.

_____, "How to Read the Spirit and How the Spirit Reads." In J. Rogerson et al. (eds), *The Bible and Ethics* (Sheffield: Sheffield Academic Press, 1995): 348-365.

_____, "Texts Don't Have Ideologies" *Biblical Interpretation*, 3/1 (1995): 1-34.

_____, "Christology and Ethics in Phil. 2: 5-11" In B. Dodd and R. P. Martin (eds) *Where Christology Began* (Louisville: Westminster John Knox Press, 1998): 140-153.

_____, *Engaging Scripture* (Oxford: Blackwell, 1998).

_____, "Learning to Narrate Our Lives in Christ" In Christopher Seitz and Kathryn Greene-McCreight (eds) *Theological Exegesis: Essays in Honor of Brevard S. Childs* (Grand Rapids: Eerdmans, 1999): 339-54.

_____ (ed.), *The Theological Interpretation of Scripture: Classic and Contemporary Readings* (Oxford: Blackwell, 1997).

Fowl, Stephen E. and L. Gregory Jones., *Reading in Communion* (Grand Rapids: Eerdmans, 1991).

Fowl, Stephen E., D. J. A. Clines, and S. E. Porter (eds) *The Bible in Three Dimensions* (Sheffield: Sheffield Academic Press, 1990).

Fowler, Robert M., *Let the Reader Understand* (Minneapolis: Fortress Press, 1991).

Frei, Hans W., "Letter to William Placher", New Haven, Yale University Library, Divinity Library Special Collections, Record Group No. 76, Box 4, Folder 78.

_____, "The Doctrine of Revelation in the Thought of Karl Barth, 1909-1922", (Ann Arbor: University of Michigan Microfilms, 1956).

_____, "Niebuhr's Theological Background", in Paul Ramsay (ed.), *Faith And Ethics; The Theology of H. Richard Niebuhr* (New York: Harper & Row, 1957): 9-64.

_____, "The Theology of H. Richard Niebuhr", in Paul Ramsay (ed.), *Faith And Ethics; The Theology of H. Richard Niebuhr* (New York: Harper & Row, 1957): 65-116.

_____, "Theological Reflections on the Accounts of Jesus' Death and Resurrection", *Christian Scholar*, 49 (1966): 263-306.

_____, *The Eclipse of Biblical Narrative* (New Haven: Yale University Press, 1974).

_____, "Scripture as Realistic Narrative: Karl Barth as Critic of Historical Criticism", 2nd Barth Colloquium. Toronto, Emmanuel College, Summer, 1974.

_____, *The Identity of Jesus Christ: The Hermeneutical Bases of Dogmatic Theology* (Philadelphia: Fortress Press, 1975). Originally published as "The Mystery of the Presence of Jesus Christ", *Crossroads Magazine*, January, February, March, 1967.

_____, "An Afterword: Eberhard Busch's Biography of Karl Barth", in H.-Martin Rumscheidt (ed.), *Karl Barth in Review: Posthumous Works Reviewed and Assessed* (Pittsburgh: The Pickwick Press, 1981): 95-116.

_____, "The "Literal Reading" of Biblical Narrative in the Christian Tradition: Does It Stretch or Will It Break?", in Frank McConnell (ed.), *The Bible and the Narrative Tradition* (Oxford: Oxford University Press, 1986): 36-77.

_____, "Response to 'Narrative Theology: An Evangelical Appraisal'", *Trinity*, 8 (1987): 21-24.

_____, "Epilogue; George Lindbeck and the Nature of Doctrine", in Bruce D. Marshall ed.), *Theology and Dialogue; Essays In Conversation with George Lindbeck* (Notre Dame: University of Notre Dame Press, 1990): 275-82.

_____, "Narrative in Christian and Modern Reading", in Bruce Marshall (ed.), *Theology and Dialogue* (Notre Dame: University of Notre Dame Press, 1990): 149-63.

_____, *Types of Christian Theology* (New Haven: Yale University Press, 1992).

_____, "Conflicts in Interpretation", *Theology Today*, 49 (1993): 344-56.

_____, *Theology and Narrative* (New York: Oxford University Press, 1993).

Freyne, Sean and Anton Weiler (eds), *The Bible and Its Readers* (London: SCM Press, 1991).

Fulkerson, Mary McClintock, "Is There a (Non-Sexist) Bible in the Church? A Feminist Case for the Priority of Interpretive Communities", in L. Gregory Jones and James J. Buckley (eds), *Theology and Scriptural Imagination* (Oxford: Blackwell, 1998): 63-80.

Geffré, Claude, *The Risk of Interpretation* (New York: Paulist Press, 1987).

Goldingay, John, *Models for Scripture* (Grand Rapids: Eerdmans, 1994).

_____, *Models for Interpretation of Scripture* (Grand Rapids: Eerdmans, 1995).

Grant, Robert M. and David Tracy, *A Short History of the Interpretation of the Bible* (Philadelphia: Fortress, 1984).

Green, Joel (ed.), *Hearing the New Testament: Strategies for Interpretation* (Grand Rapids: Eerdmans, 1995).

_____, "Practicing the Gospel in a Post-Critical World: The Promise of Theological Exegesis", *Journal of the Evangelical Theological Society*, 47/3 (September 2004): 387-397.

Greene-McCreight, Kathryn, "'We Are Companions of the Patriarchs' or Scripture Absorbs Calvin's World'", in L. Gregory Jones and James J. Buckley (eds), *Theology and Scriptural Imagination* (Oxford: Blackwell, 1998): 51-62.

Griffioen, S. and B. M. Balk (eds), *Christian Philosophy at the End of the 20th Century* (Kampen: Kok, 1995).

Grondin, Jean, *Introduction to Philosophical Hermeneutics* (New Haven: Yale University Press, 1991).

_____, *Sources of Hermeneutics* (Albany: State University of New York Press, 1995).

Gunton, Colin E. (ed.), *The Cambridge Companion to Christian Doctrine* (Cambridge: Cambridge University Press, 1997).

Guyer, Paul (ed.), *The Cambridge Companion to Kant* (Cambridge: Cambridge University Press, 1992).

Harrison, Peter, *The Bible, Protestantism and the Rise of the Natural Sciences* (Cambridge: Cambridge University Press, 1998).

Harrisville, Roy A., and Walter Sundberg, *The Bible in Modern Culture* (Grand Rapids: Eerdmans, 2002).

Hart, David Bentley, *The Beauty of the Infinite: The Aesthetics of Christian Truth* (Grand Rapids: Eerdmans, 2003).

Harvey, Van, *The Historian and the Believer* (Philadelphia: Westminster Press, 1966).

Hauerwas, Stanley and Gregory L. Jones (eds), *Why Narrative? Readings in Narrative Theology* (Eugene: Wipf & Stock, 1997).

Heidegger, Martin, *Being and Time* (Albany: SUNY Press, 1996).

Helder, Christine and Christof Landmesser (eds), *One Scripture or Many? Canon from Biblical, Theological, and Philosophical Perspectives* (Oxford: Oxford University Press, 2004).

Henry, Carl F.H., "Narrative Theology: An Evangelical Appraisal", *Trinity Journal*, 8 (1987): 3-19.

Hesse, Mary, "How to Be Postmodern Without Being a Feminist", *The Monist* 77, no. 4 (1994): 445-61.

_____, "How to Be a Postmodernist and Remain a Christian: A Response to Nicholas Wolterstorff", in Craig Bartholomew (ed.), *After Babel* (Grand Rapids: Zondervan, 2001): 91-96.

Higton, Mike, "Frei's Christology and Lindbeck's Cultural-Linguistic Theory", *Scottish Journal of Theology*, 50 no. 1 (1997): 83-95.

Hunsinger, George, *How to Read Karl Barth* (Oxford: Oxford University Press, 1991).

_____, "Afterword", in George Hunsinger and William Placher (eds), *Theology and Narrative* (New Haven: Yale University Press, 1993).

_____, "Truth as Self-Involving: Barth and Lindbeck on the Cognitive and Performative Aspects of Truth in Theological Discourse", *Journal of the American Academy of Religion*, 61 (1993): 41-56.

Hutcheon, Linda, *A Poetics of Postmodernism* (New York: Routledge, 1988).

_____, *The Politics of Postmodernism* (New York: Routledge, 1989).

Hütter, Reinhard, *Suffering Divine Things* (Grand Rapids: Eerdmans, 2000).

Ingraffia, Brian D., *Postmodern Theory and Biblical Theology* (Cambridge: Cambridge University Press, 1995).

_____, "Deconstructing the Tower of Babel: Ontotheology and the Postmodern

Bible", in Craig Bartholomew (ed.), *Renewing Biblical Interpretation* (Grand Rapids: Zondervan, 2000): 284-306.

Jeanrond, Werner, *Text and Interpretation and Categories of Theological Thinking* (Dublin: Gill and Macmillan, 1988).

_____, *Theological Hermeneutics* (New York: Crossroad, 1991).

Jobling, David, Tina Pippin and Ronald Schleifer (eds), *The Postmodern Bible Reader* (Oxford: Blackwell, 2001).

Jodock, Darrell, *The Church's Bible* (Minneapolis: Fortress Press, 1989).

_____, "The Reciprocity between Scripture and Theology: The Role of Scripture in Contemporary Theological Reflection", *Interpretation*, 44 (October 1990): 369-82.

Johnson, Luke Timothy, *Scripture and Discernment* (Nashville: Abingdon Press, 1996).

_____, "Imagining the World Scripture Imagines", in L. Gregory Jones and James J. Buckley (eds), *Theology and Scriptural Imagination* (Oxford: Blackwell, 1998): 3-18.

Jones, L. Gregory and James Buckley (eds), *Theology and Scriptural Imagination* (Oxford: Blackwell, 1998).

Kant, Immanuel, "The Conflict of the Faculties", in Allen Wood and George Di Giovanni (eds), *Religion and Rational Theology* (Cambridge: Cambridge University Press, 1996).

_____, "Religion Within the Limits of Mere Reason", in Allen Wood and George Di Giovanni (eds), *Religion and Rational Theology* (Cambridge: Cambridge University Press, 1996).

_____, "What Does It Mean to Orient Oneself in Thinking?", in Allen Wood and George Di Giovanni (eds), *Religion and Rational Theology* (Cambridge: Cambridge University Press, 1996).

_____, *Prolegomena to Any Future Metaphysics* (Cambridge: Cambridge University Press, 1997).

_____, *Religion and Rational Theology*, Allen W. Wood and George di Giovanni (eds), The Cambridge Edition of the Works of Immanuel Kant (Cambridge: Cambridge University Press, 1996).

_____, "Groundwork of the Metaphysics of Morals", in Mary J. Gregor (ed.), *Practical Philosophy* (Cambridge: Cambridge University Press, 1996): 37-108.

_____, *Practical Philosophy*, Mary J. Gregor (ed.), The Cambridge Edition of the Works of Immanuel Kant (Cambridge: Cambridge University Press, 1996).

_____, *Critique of Pure Reason*, Paul Guyer and Allen W. Wood (eds), The Cambridge Edition of the Works of Immanuel Kant (Cambridge: Cambridge University Press, 1997).

Kelsey, David, *The Uses of Scripture in Recent Theology* (Philadelphia: Westminster Press, 1975).

_____, "The Bible and Christian Theology", *The Journal of the American Academy of Religion* 48, no. 3 (September 1980): 385-402.

Kolb, David, *The Critique of Pure Modernity* (Chicago: University of Chicago Press, 1986).

Kort, Wesley A., *Story, Text and Scripture: Literary Interests in Biblical Narrative*

(University Park: The Pennsylvania State University Press, 1988).

_____, *"Take, Read": Scripture, Textuality and Cultural Practice* (University Park: The Pennsylvania State University Press, 1996).

Köstenberger, Andreas J., "Aesthetic Theology-Blessing or Curse? An Assessment of Narrative Theology", *Faith & Mission* 15, no. 2 (Spring 1998): 27-44.

Kraus, Hans-Joachim, *Die Biblische Theologie: Ihre Geschichte und Problematik* (Neukirchen-Vluyn: Neukirchener Verlag, 1970).

Kümmel, Werner Georg, *The New Testament: The History of the Investigation of Its Problems* (Nashville: Abingdon Press, 1972).

Lindbeck, George, "The Bible as Realistic Narrative", in Leonard Swidler (ed.), *Consensus in Theology?* (Philadelphia: Westminster Press, 1980): 81-85.

_____, *The Church in a Postliberal Age* (Grand Rapids: Eerdmans, 2002).

_____, "Forward to the German Edition of *The Nature of Doctrine*", in *The Church in a Postliberal Age*: 196-200.

_____, *The Nature of Doctrine* (Philadelphia: Westminster, 1984).

_____, "Toward a Postliberal Theology", in Peter Ochs (ed.), *The Return of Scripture in Judaism and Christianity* (New York: Paulist Press, 1993): 83-103.

_____, "The Story-Shaped Church: Critical Exegesis and Theological Interpretation", in Stephen Fowl (ed.), *The Theological Interpretation of Scripture* (Oxford: Blackwell, 1997): 39-52.

_____, "Postcritical Canonical Interpretation: Three Modes of Retrieval", in Christopher Seitz and Kathryn Greene-McCreight (eds), *Theological Exegesis: Essays in Honor of Brevard S. Childs* (Grand Rapids: Eerdmans, 1999): 26-51.

_____, "Response to Avery Cardinal Dulles", *First Things*, January, 2002: 13-15.

Loughlin, Gerard, "Following to the Letter: The Literal Use of Scripture", *Literature and Theology* 9, no. 4 (December 1995): 370-82.

Lundin, Roger, "Our Hermeneutical Inheritance", in Roger Lundin (ed.), *The Responsibility of Hermeneutics* (Grand Rapids: Eerdmans, 1985): 1-30.

_____, *The Culture of Interpretation* (Grand Rapids: Eerdmans, 1993).

_____, "Interpreting Orphans: Hermeneutics in the Cartesian Tradition", in Roger Lundin (ed.), *The Promise of Hermeneutics* (Grand Rapids: Eerdmans, 1999): 1-64.

_____ (ed.), *Disciplining Hermeneutics* (Grand Rapids: Eerdmans, 1997).

_____ (ed.), *The Promise of Hermeneutics* (Grand Rapids: Eerdmans, 1999).

Lyon, David, *Postmodernity* (Buckingham: Open UP, 1994).

_____, "Sliding in All Directions? Social Hermeneutics from Suspicion to Retrieval", in Roger Lundin (ed.), *Disciplining Hermeneutics: Interpretation in Christian Perspective* (Grand Rapids: Eerdmans, 1997): 99-115.

MacDonald, Neil B., *Karl Barth and the Strange New World of the Bible* (London: Paternoster Press, 2000).

Marion, Jean-Luc, *God Without Being* (Chicago: University of Chicago Press, 1991).

_____, "The Saturated Phenomenon", *Philosophy Today* 40 (1996): 103-125.

_____, *Reduction and Givenness* (Evanston: Northwestern University Press, 1998).

_____, *Cartesian Questions* (Chicago: University of Chicago Press, 1999).

Marshall, Bruce D., (ed.), *Theology and Dialogue: Essays in Conversation with George Lindbeck* (South Bend: University of Notre Dame Press, 1990).

Marshall, I. Howard, ""To Find Out What God Is Saying": Reflections on the Authorizing of Scripture", in Roger Lundin (ed.), *Disciplining Hermeneutics* (Grand Rapids: Eerdmans, 1997): 49-55.

_____, *Beyond the Bible* (Grand Rapids, Baker Academic, 2005).

McConnell, Frank, (ed.), *The Bible and the Narrative Tradition* (New York: Oxford University Press, 1986).

McCormack, Bruce L., "The Significance of Karl Barth's Theological Exegesis of Philippians", in *Karl Barth's Epistle to the Philippians* (Louisville: Westminster John Knox Press, 2002): 1-34.

McGrath, Alister, "An Evangelical Evaluation of Postliberalism", in Timothy R. Philips and Dennis L. Okholm (eds), *The Nature of Confession* (Downer's Grove: Intervarsity Press, 1996): 22-44.

_____, *A Passion for Truth* (Downer's Grove: Intervarsity Press, 1996).

McKim, Donald (ed.), *A Guide to Contemporary Hermeneutics* (Grand Rapids: Eerdmans, 1986).

McKnight, Edgar, *Post-Modern Use of the Bible* (Nashville: Abingdon, 1988).

Michalson jr., Gordon E., *Kant and the Problem of God* (Oxford: Blackwell, 1999).

Milbank, John, *Theology and Social Theory* (Oxford: Basil Blackwell, 1990).

_____, *The Word Made Strange* (Oxford: Blackwell, 1997).

Minear, Paul S., "Barth's Commentary in the Romans, 1922-1972, or Karl Barth vs. the Exegetes", in Martin Rumscheidt (ed.), *Footnotes to a Theology: The Karl Barth Colloquium of 1972* (Canada: The Corporation for the Publication of Academic Studies in Religion in Canada, 1974): 8-30.

Moberly, R. W. L., "Literary Theory and the Bible: A Review of 'Is There a Meaning in This Text?'", *The Expository Times* 110, no. 5 (February 1999).

Moore, Stephen D., *Literary Criticism and the Gospels* (New Haven: Yale University Press, 1989).

_____, *Mark and Luke in Poststructuralist Perspectives* (New Haven: Yale University Press, 1992).

_____, *Poststructuralism and the New Testament* (Minneapolis: Fortress Press, 1994).

Mudge, Lewis, *Rethinking the Beloved Community: Ecclesiology, Hermeneutics, Social Theory* (New York: University Press of America, 2001).

Murphy, Nancey, *Beyond Liberalism & Fundamentalism* (Valley Forge: Trinity Press International, 1996).

Niebuhr, H. Richard, *The Meaning of Revelation* (New York: Macmillan, 1941).

_____, *Christ and Culture* (New York: Harper, 1951).

Norris, Christopher, *Spinoza and the Origins of Modern Critical Theory* (Oxford: Basil Blackwell, 1991).

Olthuis, James H. (ed.), *Knowing Other-Wise* (Bronx: Fordham University Press, 1997).

Osborne, Grant R., *The Hermeneutical Spiral* (Downer's Grove: Inter Varsity Press, 1991).

Rendering the Word in Theological Hermeneutics

Peukert, Helmut, *Science, Action and Fundamental Theology* (Cambridge: MIT press, 1984).

Philips, Timothy R. and Dennis L. Okholm (eds), *The Nature of Confession: Evangelicals and Postliberals in Conversation* (Downer's Grove: Intervarsity Press, 1996).

Pinnock, Clark, *The Scripture Principle* (New York: Harper and Row, 1984).

Placher, William, "Scripture as Realistic Narrative", *Perspectives in Religious Studies* 5 (Spring 1978): 32-41.

_____, "Revisionist and Postliberal Theology and the Public Character of Theology", *The Thomist* 49 (1985): 392-416.

_____, "Paul Ricoeur and Postliberal Theology: A Conflict of Interpretations?", *Modern Theology* 4, no. 1 (January 1987): 35-52.

_____, "Hans Frei and the Meaning of Biblical Narrative", *Christian Century,* 106 (1989): 556-59.

_____, *Unapologetic Theology* (Louisville: Westminster John Knox, 1989).

_____, *The Domestication of Transcendence: How Modern Thinking About God Went Wrong* (Louisville: Westminster John Knox, 1996).

Plantinga, Alvin, "Advice to Christian Philosophers", *Faith and Philosophy* 1, no. 3 (1984): 253-71.

_____, "Christian Philosophy at the End of the 20th Century", in S. Griffion and B. M. Balk (eds), *Christian Philosophy at the End of the 20th Century* (Kampen: Kok, 1995): 29-53.

_____, "Two (or More) Kinds of Scripture Scholarship", in L. Gregory Jones and James J. Buckley (eds), *Theology and Scriptural Imagination* (Oxford: Blackwell, 1998): 81-116.

Preus, J. Samuel, *Explaining Religion* (New Haven: Yale University Press, 1987).

_____, *Spinoza and the Irrelevance of Biblical Theology* (Cambridge: Cambridge University Press, 2001).

Privette, Jeffrey, "Must Theology Re-Kant?", *Heythrop Journal* XL (1989): 166-83.

Radner, Ephraim and George Sumner (eds), *The Rule of Faith: Scripture, Canon, and Creed in a Critical Age* (Harrisburg: Morehouse, 1998).

Ramsay, Paul (ed.), *Faith and Ethics: The Theology of H. Richard Niebuhr* (New York: Harper & Row, 1957).

Reventlow, Henning Graf, *The Authority of the Bible and the Rise of the Modern World* (Philadelphia: Fortress Press, 1985).

Ricoeur, Paul, "Biblical Hermeneutics", *Semeia* 4 (1975): 27-148.

Rogers jr., Eugene F., "How the Virtues of an Interpreter Presuppose and Perfect Hermeneutics: The Case of Thomas Aquinas", *Journal of Religion,* 76 (1996).

Rogers, Jack B, and Donald K. McKim, *The Authority and Interpretation of the Bible* (New York: Harper and Row, 1979).

Rogerson, John W., *W. M. L. de Wette: Founder of Modern Biblical Criticism* (Sheffield: Sheffield Academic Press, 1992).

_____ (ed.), *The Bible and Ethics* (Sheffield: Sheffield Academic Press, 1995).

Schleiermacher, Friedrich, *Christmas Eve: Dialogue on the Incarnation* (Richmond:

John Knox Press, 1967).

Schneiders, Sandra M., *The Revelatory Text* (Collegeville: The Liturgical Press, 1999).

Schner, George S. J., "The Eclipse of Biblical Narrative: Analysis and Critique," *Modern Theology*, 8/2: 149-172.

_____, "Metaphors for Theology", in John Webster and George P. Schner S. J. (eds), *Theology After Liberalism* (Oxford: Blackwell, 2000): 3-51.

_____, "Waiting for Godot: Scripture, Tradition and Church at Century's End." *Toronto Journal of Theology* 17, no. 1 (Summer 2001): 33-54.

Scholder, Klaus, *The Birth of Modern Critical Theology* (London: SCM Press, 1990).

Seitz, Christopher R., "Creed, Scripture and "Historical Jesus" ("in Accordance with the Scriptures")", in Ephraim Radner and George Sumner (eds), *The Rule of Faith* (Harrisburg: Morehouse, 1998): 126-35.

_____, *Word without End* (Grand Rapids: Eerdmans, 1998).

_____, "Scripture Becomes Religion(s): The Theological Crisis of Serious Biblical Interpretation in the Twentieth Century", in Craig Bartholomew (ed.), *Renewing Biblical Interpretation* (Grand Rapids: Zondervan, 2000): 40-65.

_____, *Figured Out* (Louisville: Westminster John Knox Press, 2001).

Seitz, Christopher and Kathryn Greene-McCreight (eds), *Theological Exegesis: Essays in Honor of Brevard Childs* (Grand Rapids: Eerdmans, 1999).

Simonetti, Manlio, *Biblical Interpretation in the Early Church* (Edinburgh: T & T Clark, 1994).

Smalley, Beryl, *The Study of the Bible in the Middle Ages* (Oxford: Blackwell, 1952).

Smith, James K. A., "Originary Violence: The Fallenness of Interpretation in Derrida", *Concept* 19 (1996): 27-41.

_____, "The Art of Christian Atheism: Faith and Philosophy in Early Heidegger", *Faith and Philosophy* 14, no. 1 (January 1997): 71-81.

_____, "How to Avoid Not Speaking Attestations", in James H. Olthuis (ed.), *Knowing Other-Wise* (Bronx: Fordham University Press, 1997): 217-34.

_____, "Respect and Donation: A Critique of Marion's Critique of Husserl", *American Catholic Philosophical Quarterly* 71 (1997): 523-38.

_____, "The Time of Language: The Fall to Interpretation in Early Augustine", *American Catholic Philosophical Quarterly* 72 (1998): 185-99.

_____, "Liberating Religion From Theology: Marion and Heidegger on the Possibility of a Phenomenology of Religion", *International Journal for Philosophy of Religion* 46 (1999): 17-33.

_____, "Between Predication and Silence: Augustine in How (Not) to Speak of God", *Heythrop Journal* 41 (2000): 66-86.

_____, *The Fall of Interpretation: Philosophical Foundations for a Creational Hermeneutic* (Downer's Grove: Inter Varsity Press, 2000).

_____, "How (Not) to Tell a Secret: Interiority and the Strategy of 'Confession' in Augustine", *American Catholic Philosophical Quarterly* 74 (2000): 135-51.

_____, "Taking Husserl at His Word: Towards a New Phenomenology with the Young Heidegger", *Symposium* 4 (2000): 89-115.

_____, *Speech and Theology: Language and the Logic of Incarnation* (New York: Routledge, 2002).

Soskice, Janet Martin, *Metaphor and Religious Language*. (Oxford: Oxford Clarendon Press, 1985).

Spinoza, Baruch, *A Theological-Political Treatise* (New York: Dover, 1951).

Stassen, Glen (ed.), *Authentic Transformation* (Nashville: Abingdon Press, 1996).

Steiner, George, *Real Presences* (Chicago: University of Chicago Press, 1989).

Stout, Jeffrey, *The Flight From Authority* (South Bend: The University of Notre Dame Press, 1981).

Stühlmacher, Peter, *Historical Criticism and Theological Interpretation of Scripture* (Philadelphia: Fortress Press, 1977).

Swidler, Leonard (ed.), *Consensus in Theology?* (Philadelphia: Westminster Press, 1980).

Sykes, Stephen W. (ed.), *Karl Barth: Studies of His Theological Method*. (Oxford: Clarendon Press, 1979).

Tanner, Kathryn, "Scripture as Popular Text", in L. Gregory Jones and James J. Buckley (eds), *Theology and Scriptural Imagination* (Oxford: Blackwell, 1998): 117-36.

Tarbox, Everett J. jr. (ed.), *Theology at the End of Modernity* (Philadelphia: Trinity Press, 1991).

Taylor, Charles. *Philosophical Arguments* (Cambridge: Harvard University Press, 1995).

_____, *Sources of the Self: The Making of the Modern Identity* (Cambridge: Harvard University Press, 1989).

_____, *Human Agency and Language: Philosophical Papers I* (Cambridge: Cambridge University Press, 1985).

_____, *A Catholic Modernity?* (New York: Oxford University Press, 1999).

Thiselton, Anthony, *The Two Horizons* (Grand Rapids: Eerdmans, 1980).

_____, "Reader-Response Hermeneutics, Actions, Models, and the Parables of Jesus", in Roger Lundin (ed.), *The Responsibility of Hermeneutics* (Grand Rapids: Eerdmans, 1985): 79-114.

_____, *New Horizons in Hermeneutics* (Grand Rapids: Zondervan, 1992).

_____, "Biblical Studies and Theoretical Hermeneutics", in John Barton (ed.), *The Cambridge Companion to Biblical Interpretation* (Cambridge: Cambridge University Press, 1998): 95-113.

_____, "Communicative Action and Promise in Interdisciplinary, Biblical, and Theological Hermeneutics", in Roger Lundin (ed.), *The Promise of Hermeneutics* (Grand Rapids: Eerdmans, 1999): 133-239.

_____, "'Behind' and 'In Front Of' the Text: Language, Reference and Indeterminacy", in Craig Bartholomew (ed.), *After Babel* (Grand Rapids: Zondervan, 2001): 97-120.

Torrance, Thomas F., *Divine Meaning* (Edinburgh: T & T Clark, 1995).

Tracy, David, *Blessed Rage for Order* (Minneapolis: Winston Seabury, 1975).

_____, "Project "X": Retrospect and Prospect", *Concilium* 170 (1983): 30-36.

_____, *Plurality and Ambiguity* (San Francisco: Harper and Row, 1987).

Vanhoozer, Kevin J., "The Semantics of Biblical Literature: Truth and Scripture's

Diverse Literary Forms", In D. A. Carson and John Woodbridge (eds), *Hermeneutics, Authority and Canon* (Grand Rapids: Zondervan, 1986): 49-104.

_____, *Biblical Narrative in the Philosophy of Paul Ricoeur* (Cambridge: Cambridge University Press, 1990).

_____, "Christ and Concept: Doing Theology and the "Ministry" of Theology", in John Woodbridge and Thomas Edward McComiskey (eds), *Doing Theology in Today's World* (Grand Rapids: Zondervan, 1991): 99-145.

_____, "The Hermeneutics of I-Witness Testimony: John 21:20-24", in A. Graeme Auld (ed.), *Understanding Poets and Prophets* (Sheffield: JSOT, 1993): 366-87.

_____, "The World Well Staged? Theology, Culture & Hermeneutics", in D. A. Carson and John Woodbridge (eds), *God and Culture* (Grand Rapids: Eerdmans, 1993): 1-30.

_____, "God's Mighty Speech Acts: The Doctrine of Scripture Today", in David F. Wright (ed.), *A Pathway into Holy Scripture* (Grand Rapids: Eerdmans, 1994): 143-81.

_____, "The Reader in New Testament Interpretation", in Joel Green (ed.), *Hearing the New Testament* (Grand Rapids: Eerdmans, 1995): 301-28.

_____, "Does the Trinity Belong in a Theology of Religions?: On Angling in the Rubicon & the "Identity of God", in Kevin Vanhoozer (ed.), *The Trinity in a Pluralistic Age* (Grand Rapids: Eerdmans, 1997): 41-71.

_____, "The Spirit of Understanding: Special Revelation and General Hermeneutics", in Roger Lundin (ed.), *Disciplining Hermeneutics: Interpretation in Christian Perspective* (Grand Rapids: Eerdmans, 1997): 131-65.

_____, "Effectual Call or Causal Effect? Summons, Sovereignty & Supervenient Grace", *The Tyndale Bulletin* 48 (1998): 213-51.

_____, *Is There a Meaning in This Text?* (Grand Rapids: Zondervan, 1998).

_____, "The Trails of Truth: Mission, Martyrdom & the Epistemology of the Cross", in Kevin Vanhoozer and Andrew Kirk (eds), *To Stake a Claim: Mission and the Western Crisis of Knowledge* (Maryknoll: Orbis, 1999): 120-56.

_____, "Body Piercing, the Natural Sense & the Task of Theological Interpretation: A Hermeneutical Homily on John 19:34", *Ex Auditu* 16 (2000): 1-29.

_____, "From Speech Acts to Scripture Acts: The Covenant of Discourse and the Discourse of Covenant", in Craig Bartholoomew, (ed.), *After Babel* (Grand Rapids: Zondervan, 2001): 1-49.

_____, "The Love of God: Its Place, Meaning & Function in Systematic Theology", in Kevin Vanhoozer (ed.), *Nothing Greater, Nothing Better: Theological Essays on the Love of God* (Grand Rapids: Eerdmans, 2001): 1-29.

_____, "Comments on "Developing a Biblical Hermeneutic for a Developing Theology"", in *Beyond the Bible* (Grand Rapids, Baker Academic, 2005).

_____, *First Theology* (Downer's Grove: IVP, 2002).

_____(ed.), *Nothing Greater, Nothing Better: Theological Essays on the Love of God* (Grand Rapids: Eerdmans, 2001).

_____(ed.), *The Trinity in a Pluralistic Age: Theological Essays on Church and Culture* (Grand Rapids: Eerdmans, 1997).

Vanhoozer, Kevin and Andrew Kirk (eds), *To Stake a Claim: Mission and the Western*

Crisis of Knowledge (Maryknoll: Orbis, 1999).

Vanhoozer, Kevin, James K. A. Smith and Bruce Benson (eds), *Hermeneutics at the Crossroads* (Bloomington: Indiana University Press, 2006).

Walhout, Clarence, "Narrative Hermeneutics", in Roger Lundin (ed.), *The Promise of Hermeneutics* (Grand Rapids: Eerdmans, 1999): 65-131.

Ward, Timothy, *Word and Supplement: Speech Acts, Biblical Texts, and the Sufficiency of Scripture* (Oxford: Oxford University Press, 2002).

Watson, Francis, "Strategies of Recovery and Resistance: Hermeneutical Reflections on Gen. 1-3 and Its Pauline Reception", *Journal for the Study of the New Testament* 45 (1992):79-103.

_____, *Text, Church and World* (Grand Rapids: Eerdmans, 1994).

_____, "The Scope of Hermeneutics", in Colin Gunton (ed.), *The Cambridge Companion to Christian Doctrine* (Cambridge: Cambridge University Press, 1997): 65-80.

_____, *Text and Truth* (Edinburgh: T & T Clark, 1997).

_____ (ed.), *The Open Text* (London: SCM Press, 1993).

Webster, John, "Hermeneutics in Modern Theology: Some Doctrinal Reflections", *Scottish Journal of Theology* 51 (1998): 307-41.

_____, "Theology After Liberalism?", in John Webster and George P. Schner S. J. (eds), *Theology After Liberalism* (Oxford: Blackwell, 2000): 52-63.

_____, "The Dogmatic Location of the Canon", *Neue Zeitschrift Für Systematische Theologie* 43 (2001): 17-43.

_____, *Holy Scripture: A Dogmatic Sketch*. (Cambridge: Cambridge University Press, 2003).

_____, *Word and Church: Essays in Christian Dogmatics* (Edinburgh: T & T Clark, 2002).

Webster, John and George Schner (eds), *Theology After Liberalism* (Oxford: Blackwell, 2000).

Westphal, Merold, "Post-Kantian Reflections on the Importance of Hermeneutics", in Roger Lundin (ed.), *Disciplining Hermeneutics: Interpretation in Christian Perspective* (Grand Rapids: Eerdmans, 1997): 57-66.

Wharton, James A., "Karl Barth as Exegete and His Influence on Biblical Interpretation", *Union Seminary Quarterly Review* 28, no. 1 (Fall 1972): 5-13.

Wolterstorff, Nicholas, *Art in Action* (Grand Rapids: Eerdmans, 1980).

_____, *Reason Within the Bounds of Religion* (Grand Rapids: Eerdmans, 1984).

_____, "Evidence, Entitled Belief, and the Gospels", *Faith and Philosophy* 6 (October 1989): 429-59.

_____, *Divine Discourse: Philosophical Reflections on the Claim That God Speaks* (Cambridge: Cambridge University Press, 1995).

_____, "Will Narrativity Work as a Lynchpin? Reflections on the Hermeneutic of Hans Frei", in C. Lewis (ed.), *Relativism and Religion* (Basingstoke: Macmillan Press 1995): 71-107

_____, "The Importance of Hermeneutics for a Christian Worldview", in Roger Lundin (ed.), *Disciplining Hermeneutics* (Grand Rapids: Eerdmans, 1997): 25-47.

_____, "Is It Possible and Desirable for Theologians to Recover From Kant?",

Modern Theology 14, no. 1 (January 1998): 1-18.

_____, "A Response to Trevor Hart", in Craig Bartholomew (ed.), *Renewing Biblical Interpretation* (Grand Rapids: Zondervan, 2000): 335-41.

_____, "The Promise of Speech-Act Theory for Biblical Interpretation", in Craig Bartholomew (ed.), *After Babel* (Grand Rapids: Zondervan, 2001): 73-90.

_____, "Resuscitating the Author", in Kevin Vanhoozer et al (eds), *Hermeneutics at the Crossroads* (Bloomington: Indian University Press, 2006).

_____, "The Unity Behind the Canon", in Christine Helmer and Christof Landmesser (eds), *One Scripture of Many? Canon from Biblical, Theological, and Philosphical Perspectives* (Oxford: Oxford University Press, 2004).

Wood, Allen W., *Kant's Moral Religion* (Ithaca: Cornell University Press, 1970).

_____, *Kant's Rational Theology* (Ithaca: Cornell University Press, 1978).

_____, "Rational Theology, Moral Faith, and Religion", in Paul Guyer (ed.), *The Cambridge Companion to Kant* (Cambridge: Cambridge University Press, 1992): 394-416.

Woodbridge, John T. and Thomas Edward McComisky (eds), *Doing Theology in Today's World* (Grand Rapids: Zondervan, 1991).

Work, Telford, *Living and Active: Scripture in the Economy of Salvation* (Grand Rapids: Eerdmans, 2002).

Wright, David F. (ed.), *A Pathway into Holy Scripture* (Grand Rapids: Eerdmans, 1994).

Yeago, David, "The New Testament and the Nicene Dogma: A Contribution to the Recovery of Theological Exegesis", in Stephen Fowl (ed.), *The Theological Interpretation of Scripture* (Oxford: Blackwell, 1997): 87-101.

Yoder, John Howard, "How H. Richard Niebuhr Reasoned: A Critique of Christ and Culture", in Glen Stassen (ed.), *Authentic Transformation* (Nashville: Abingdon Press, 1996): 31-90.

_____, *To Hear the Word* (Eugene: Wipf and Stock, 2001).

Young, Frances, *The Art of Performance: Towards a Theology of Holy Scripture* (London: Dartman, Longman and Todd, 1993).

_____, *Biblical Exegesis and the Formation of Christian Culture* (Cambridge: Cambridge University Press, 1997).

Index